China and WTO

China and WTO

ISSUES AND CHALLENGES IN TEXTILES AND TELECOMMUNICATIONS

Anil K. Kanungo

SHIPRA

Rs. 750; US$ 37.50

ISBN: 978-81-7541-794-6

First Published in India in 2015

China and WTO: Issues and Challenges in Textiles and Telecommunications

Published by:
SHIPRA PUBLICATIONS
LG 18-19, Pankaj Central Market, I.P. Ext.
Patparganj, Delhi-110092
Tel: 91-11-2223 5152, 2223 6152
E-mail: info@shiprapublication.com
www.shiprapublication.com

Preface

Knowing China has become a cliché. Understanding China is still a mystery. Whatever may be the reason, China is at the centre of an academic debate whose importance is adequately felt in economic, political and strategic spheres. The significance of China grew once it joined the World Trade Organization (WTO). Its post-entry phase, global positioning in world economy and political and strategic relations with the world community at large drew much more attention of academicians, scholars, diplomats and policy makers. Many are currently engaged in such pursuits. It is largely the economic interest which led to conceive the idea of writing this book. Though the book has an emphasis on economic and trade dimension, yet it's broadly a political economy covering a wide canvas of economy, trade and geopolitics.

I am thankful to a few individuals who helped me at various stages in finishing this study. Prominent among them are Dr. D. Varaprasad Sekhar, Associate Professor, Centre for East Asian Studies, SIS, JNU, Dr. Biswajit Dhar, former Director-General, RIS, New Delhi and currently Professor, Centre for Economic Studies and Planning, SSS, JNU, New Delhi and Dr. Patha Pratim Pal, Associate Professor, Department of Economics, Indian Institute of Management, Kolkata, India. Their scholarly advice and constant encouragement helped me to complete this study.

I thank Professors Erik Baark, Lok Sang Ho and Leonard K. Cheng at Hong Kong, Professors Yin Xiangshuo, Wang Guoxing and Xue Lei at Shanghai and Professors Andong Zhu, Wang Yong, Song Hong, Ma Tao and Ma Jiali at Beijing for their insightful inputs and suggestions. Last but not the least, I would like to thank, Srikant, a Ph.D scholar at Peking University, Beijing for helping me to get familiar with the Library and topography of the city, Beijing, where the first timer can be at odds and where English is still not a popular medium of communication.

Finally, I remain fully responsible for any shortcomings.

Anil K. Kanungo

Contents

Abbreviations

AAFA	American Apparel & Footwear Association
AGOA	African Growth and Opportunity Act
APEC	Asia Pacific Economic Cooperation
ASEAN	Association of South East Asian Nations
ATC	Agreement on Textiles & Clothing
CAFTA	China–ASEAN Free Trade Area
CAGR	Compound Annual Growth Rate
CBTPA	Caribbean Basin Trade Partnership Act
CJV	Contractual Joint Venture
CNTAC	China National Textile & Apparel Council
CPC	Catching-Up Product Cycle
DFQF	Duty-Free, Quota-Free
DGP	Directorate General of Posts
DGT	Directorate General of Telecommunications
EEC	European Economic Community
EJV	Equity Joint Venture
EU	European Union
FBOCs	Foreign Business Oriented Corporations
FIEs	Foreign-Invested Enterprises
FTAs	Free Trade Agreements
FTCs	Foreign Trade Corporations
GATT	General Agreement on Tariffs and Trade
GDP	Gross Domestic Product
GEP	Global Economic Prospect
IIT	Intra-Industry Trade
ILO	International Labour Organization
IPRs	Intellectual Property Rights
ITeS	Information Technology enabled Services
ITU	International Telecommunication Union
JETRO	Japan External Trade Organization
JVEs	Joint Venture Enterprises
LDCs	Least Developed Countries
MDGs	Millennium Development Goals
MEI	Ministry of Electronics Industries
MFA	Multi-Fibre Agreement
MFN	Most Favoured Nation
MII	Ministry of Information Industry
MIIT	Ministry of Industry and Information Technology
MNEs	Multinational Enterprises

MOFCOM	Ministry of Commerce
MOFTEC	Ministry of Foreign Trade and Economic Cooperation
MPT	Ministry of Posts and Telecommunications
NAFTA	North American Free Trade Agreement
NAMA	Non-Agricultural Market Access
NCTO	National Council of Textile Organization
NPC	National People's Congress
NIEs	Newly Industrializing Economies
NTBs	Non-Tariff Barriers
NTR	Normal Trade Relation
OECD	Organization for Economic Cooperation and Development
OEM	Original Equipment Manufacturing
PECC	Pacific Economic Cooperation Council
PNTR	Permanent Normal Trade Relations
PRD	Pearl River Delta
PTAs	Postal and Telecommunications Administrations
PTEs	Post and Telegraph Enterprises
RAMs	Recently Acceded Members
RCA	Revealed Comparative Advantage
RMB	Renminbi
ROC	Republic of China
RTAs	Regional Trade Agreements
SASAC	State-owned Assests Supervision and Administration Commission
SDRC	State Development and Reform Commission
SEZs	Special Economic Zones
SETC	State Economic and Trade Commission
SFC	State Planning Commission
SIIA	Swedish Institute of International Affairs
SIIA	Software& Information Industry Association
SITC	Standard International Trade Classification
SMEs	Small and Medium Enterprises
SOEs	State-Owned Enterprises
SPS	Sanitary and Phytosanitary Measures
T&C	Textiles & Clothing
TNCs	Transnational Corporations
TRIMs	Trade-Related Investment Measures
TRQs	Tariff-Rate Quotas
TVEs	Township and Village Enterprise
UNCTAD	United Nations Conference on Trade and Development
UNFCCC	United Nations Framework Convention on Climate Change
USITC	United States International Trade Commission
VERs	Voluntary Export Restraints
WOFEs	Wholly Owned Foreign Enterprises
WIR	World Investment Report
WTO	World Trade Organization
YRD	Yangtze River Delta
ZTE	Zhong Xing Telecommunication Equipment

1

Introduction

China's entry into the World Trade Organization (WTO) in 2001 is a defining moment not only for China but also for the rest of the world, as it facilitated the formal integration of the Chinese economy with the world economy. Being fully aware of the advantages that would accrue from a multilateral trading system governed under the WTO, China had officially applied for the GATT (the precursor to the WTO) membership in 1986. Fifteen years of intense negotiations with developed countries like the United States (US) and the EU (European Union) and other developing countries eventually resulted in its entry into the WTO. Since its entry, China has actively participated in the world economy and in various WTO Ministerial meetings like Cancun, Hong Kong, Geneva and Bali in 2003, 2005, 2009 and 2013. It has raised several concerns of the developing countries in these multilateral fora and took active interest in forming a developing country coalition, namely G-20 to carry forward the core developmental issues by influencing the WTO negotiations.

Though the formal integration occurred in 2001, an informal integration between the Chinese economy and the global economy began in the year 1978 heralding a new phase in the evolution of modern China. As part of this process, it initiated a set of economic reforms coupled with open door policy to modernize its economy. Gradual approach to reforms, optimal utilization of foreign direct investment (FDI), emphasis on export-led growth, and adapting to new challenges especially after opening up the economy, helped China to post consistently high economic growth and expand its foreign trade. As a result, by the late 1980s and early 1990s China had emerged as one of the major economic powers in the world. Having a miniscule share of global trade at the time of reform and opening up in 1978, it has been able to garner more than 10.45 per cent (WTO Statistics Database, WTO March 2014)[1] share of world trade today.

China's entry into the WTO has provided enormous opportunities and challenges. It has gone through an eventful period to join the WTO. Series of negotiations based on political, economic, and trade objectives have been the mainstay of such activities. The task has never been easy throughout this period. China had to succumb to much pressure from the developed countries to agree to difficult terms of agreement as the US and the EU wanted China to join under 'developed country' status. China had argued it is a 'developing country' and still passing through different stages of development, and hence it should enter the WTO under 'developing country' status, so as to fulfill fewer commitments. However finally, it joined the WTO with commitments, which were more stringent than the other developing countries.

Some of these adjustments were in the areas of trade in goods, market access of trade in services, implementation of trade related measures and major institutional commitments such as creation of new ministries and legal system. Accession commitments relating to trade in services included implementation of the General Agreement on Trade in Services (GATS); liberalization of location restrictions; foreign ownership share; and business scope and provision of broadest coverage to developing members. Foreign investment commitments included eliminating performance requirements on foreign companies. Finally, institutional commitments involved trade and investment facilitation, issue of transparency and consistent trade and investment related laws, rules, and policies.

Various scholars have analyzed that China's economy has benefited from the global trading regime particularly in manufacturing and services. These are the two dynamic sectors of the Chinese economy which have expanded during the current phase of globalization. Sub-sectors like textiles and telecommunications from the two major sectors of the economy, namely manufacturing and services have been selected for a detailed study. The book explores the following issues: whether China has benefited from the global trading regime by joining the WTO; how China has progressed through its accession process; the roles that textiles and telecommunications have played in integrating China's economy with the world; the role that FDI has played in creating a robust manufacturing base for China and helped it to promote its exports all over the world.

The book is concerned with two central questions—the first, a theoretical one, relates to China joining the WTO; and the second, an empirical one, deals with China's integration with the world economy, positioning its two key sectors such as textiles and telecommunications in world trade. The question is, how China's trade policy has gone through various policy changes to facilitate its integration with global market has extensively been discussed.

In this context, the issues that China had to grapple with immediately after its accession to the WTO are very important. The book aims to analyze some of these important issues. Most of the studies in the existing literature have dealt with China before joining the WTO and this study in particular focuses on China after joining the WTO. Theories of interdependence and sectoral approach have been employed as the framework to undertake the study.

The Context

China's integration with the world economy has undergone a paradigm shift with its entry into the WTO. From a closed economy till late seventies, it made a conscious and determined effort to reach out to the outside world through economic reforms and open door policy. It began to realize that establishing links with major industrial powers and participating in world economy were necessary requirements for economic progress. Its experience with developed countries in relation to protectionist measures and antidumping issues imposed on its economy made her aware about the need to integrate with the world economy. The provision of dispute settlement mechanism (DSM) is critical in the governance of world trade. Imposition of non-tariff barriers plays a debilitating role on China's exports whose intensity can be reduced once it becomes a member. It also realized that integration with the global economy would allow her having an important say in world affairs. It would be able to play a much more participatory role in world affairs. From playing a peripheral role to becoming a major player in world economy required adherence to a global regime, whose conditionalities were not easy to accept. China came under considerable pressure from the international community to adhere to a global trading regime not only in the economic sphere but also in the political sphere. Adhering to an internationally rule-based regulated regime was intimately related not only to the changes in the international context but also to China's own domestic situation and demands. Complying with such a regime necessitated number of institutional and structural changes. Thus, the process to join the WTO took considerable time.

China had to introduce reforms in its domestic institutions, policies, and decision-making mechanisms. Establishment of a well-defined legal architecture was the hallmark of the series of commitments it undertook. While China's increasing involvement in the world economy substantially enhanced its stature and image globally, it bound China to obey rules and regulations of the international economic community. While aligning to the requirements of this global trading regime, the Chinese leadership had to cope up with the pressures of an international order in transition. In its attempt to establish global competitiveness of its economy by joining the WTO, China remained wary of the WTO's impact on social, cultural and political milieu of China. It remained unsure about the extent of integration it should have with the world economy, especially in the field of telecommunications as protection of national security and sovereignty became the major constraint in integrating its telecom sector with the world economy.

In this context, its entry into the WTO provided a new dimension to world trade. As part of its terms of agreement, its economy became open to the outside world. Foreign players are keen to make an entry as they see huge prospects for them. World economy in the formal absence of China felt to experience a limited growth as China was consistently posing higher economic growth remaining outside the WTO. World economy, therefore, was negotiating since 1986 to bring China within its ambit. It knew a growing economy like China has a lot to offer for many developed as well as developing countries to make global economy growth-driven, balanced, and stable. Complementarily, the size, population, and purchasing power of China were proving to be the best bet for the world economy to maximize its trade gains. Similarly, China also enjoyed market access to its various trading partners, thus availing huge opportunities to expand its economic and business activities with the outside world.

Importance of China's Entry into the WTO

China's ambition to emerge as a strong economy in the world was adequately realized by the world economy from the time it launced its reform programme. It was fully aware of the opportunities available in world trade and was keen to be a part of it. Multilatral trading regime under a rule-based system provided China trust and confidence to integrate with the world economy. Similarly world economy driven by industrilaized countries like the US and the EU saw China a huge country with promising trade and economic growth. Its size, purchasing power and modernization provided impetus for the world economy to view to China as a global opportunity.

China's Importance for the World Economy

China's transformation into an economic powerhouse in the 1990s was crucial to its entry into the WTO. Its commitment to economic reform and gradual opening up helped her to project an impressive growth rate averaging around 8 per cent compared to other developing countries like India. The expansion of China's role in world trade also grew from a world share of less than 1 per cent in 1979 to 1.7 per cent in 1990 and 3.8 per cent in 2000 before its accession (WTO International Trade Statistics: 1999, 2000, 2001, 2002). Its exports and imports have also grown rapidly since 1979 at an average rate of 15 per cent. In I995, China was the sixth largest exporter of goods in the world and seventh largest importer accounting for 4 per cent of world merchandise exports and 3.4 per cent of world merchandise imports (Annual Report 1996 WTO Vol. II: 4). It continued to remain as the sixth largest exporter in 2001 and improved its position from seventh to sixth importer of the world in 2001 (WTO International Trade Statistics: 2002). This high growth coupled with a favourable investment climate and flexible labour laws have strongly driven China as a destination for the world economy to grow. With this growth in mind, developed as well as developing countries concluded that China's absence in the WTO would affect the pace of world economic growth.

Industrialized countries were particularly keen to see that China joined the WTO so that they would benefit from its growth.

Second, inflows of FDI, imports of low cost raw material and cheap labour allowed China to emerge as a global destination for production. This activity proplled the export prospects of China. Many of the advanced countries including the US benefitted enormously from this shift of global production to China, since imports of these goods helped to bring down prices in these countries. This shift in production to China at one level was welcomed by Southeast Asian nations. At another level it has also raised concerns for them because these countries began to feel that China's exports could crowd out their export opportunities (Athukorala 2010: 406) as there are apparent similarities in the export composition of these countries with that of China. This is an important reason why the ASEAN countries became interested to sign the FTA with China so that both benefit from this regional trade agreement. China sees this as a great opportunity to remain engaged as a constructive participant in the new round of global trade liberalization. This argument was further supplemented when many countries argued that the WTO so far has not been able to provide trade benefits that it had promised to aspiring developing countries at the time of their joining, that is why many developing and transitional economies had started scouting for regional trade partners to form effective regional agreements like FTAs. Chinese leadership recognized the economic advantages of such agreements and has even gone so far as to suggest that the signing of FTA with the Association of Southeast Asian Nations (ASEAN) in January 2010 was in the benefit of world economy to grow.

Third, the issue of transparency in China has always been a source of concern for the world community since its opening up. Its gradual rise in international politics became an apprehension for the world economy that it will not conduct itself in a responsible manner. However, China insists that entry into the WTO reiterates its commitments to abide by the multilateral rules and regulation, which the world economy follows. It is willing to play the trade game by international rules and it will help persuade the world, that its rise is an opportunity rather than a danger (Yong 2009: Personal Interview).

Fourth, it is argued that deeper integration and the complementary domestic economic liberalization will provide more opportunities for the Chinese people to engage in long gestation employment and some high-end manufacturing jobs (Broadman 2007:33) since China was developing as a manufacturing hub of the world. China will be able to meet the expectations of its huge population by raising their income and providing better living standards (Zhu 2009: Personal Interview).

Fifth, signing agreements with the WTO members regarding trade liberalization will further deepen integration with the WTO. Had it not joined the WTO, the country would have been left out of the mainstream of the global economy. Without liberalization and integration, China will not fully share the benefits of the free capital movements of multinational corporations (Yong 2009: Personal Interview).

Sixth, in a globally competitive world, China needs to prepare its industries to face tough competition. Protectionism for the domestic industry may not fetch the desired results anticipated from the current global regime. High tariff and non-tariff barriers only benefit specific industries for a specific period but impose high indirect costs on the economy as a whole. These costs are reducing the country's ability to keep pace with global competition. The country's industrial monopolies and recently reduced high telecom rates are often cited as evidence of these high costs. Entry to the WTO, therefore, is a favourable step for China to integrate with the world economy (Lei 2009: Personal Interview).

Seventh, only after the WTO entry can China effectively protest against the protectionist measures and unfair dumping charges, frequently imposed on the Chinese exports by its trading partners. Some experts, who argue for a delay in WTO membership, say that the country can gain the benefits of WTO through bilateral most favoured nation (MFN) status. The Ministry of Foreign Trade and Economic Cooperation (MOFTEC) team counters that saying only the WTO multilateral trade dispute mechanism can help China fight discriminatory treatment, and only membership can qualify the country for the benefits of the world trading system (Yong 2009: Personal Interview).

Eighth, "China was always eager to join the WTO because in the past it has suffered from serious harassment in trade relations with other countries; at least with the entry, it expects to get fair treatment and fewer trade disputes. While preparing for accession, it can continue with its domestic reforms which are also necessary for internal economic development as well as for external integration with the world economy," remarks Prof. Yin Xiangshuo (Xiangshuo 2009: Personal Interview).

World Economy's Importance for China

First, among the industrilaized countries it was apparent from the beginning that the US has large economic interest in China's domestic economy. It expected China to undertake deeper integration with the world economy so as to allow foreign countries to take initial advantage of its size, population and their purchasing power. As the US was globally competitive in services sectors like telecommunications, banking and insurance, it wanted to push these sectors to Chinese society and reap trade gains initially.[2] It served the economic interests well for the US and that is why the US wanted China to soon undertake the process of liberalization. By the 1990s China had already emerged as the most rapidly growing foreign market for the US goods and services. But it was still in the better interest of the US that once China joined the WTO and fulfilled its commitments, the access of the US firms to this market would be increased and the prospect for the bilateral trade relations would also be improved. In addition, the US was also keen to negotiate for increased access to its agricultural products and automobiles as China lacked competence in developing these products and this business activity would have widened its product market in China. Gradually China would have been a destination to spur the rapid growth of the US trade. In a span of eight years the US trade with China reached US$ 116 billion in 2000 from US$ 33 billion in 1992 (US Department of Commerce).

Second, many Chinese trade experts as well as policymakers believe that the WTO provides a wide scope to integrate its economy with the world economy. Its rules-based, transparent, predictable, and special provision for dispute settlement are uniquely placed to generate trust and confidence in countries who are interested to join it. The expectation hovers around the fact that more predictable access to foreign markets, which the WTO membership can bring, will result in strengthening the external sector of the country. Trade will prosper, member country will witness higher exports, country's GDP will be increased and many impending social problems such as poverty reduction, livelihood, rural employment, and food security will be tackled.

Third, it is sometimes argued that industrialized countries were keen to see China transforming from a planned economy towards a market-oriented one as this change will provide more flexibility and confidence to the world economy to deal with China. State intervention and rigidity of the system will gradually be reduced.

Fourth, China's entry will ensure transparency in the implementation of intellectual property rights as the Trade Related Intellectual Property Rights (TRIPs) has come under the ambit of the WTO. This has been a long-standing demand of industrialized countries that China seriously violates IPRs while indulging in scientific and technological innovation to spur its foreign trade and domestic growth. WTO member countries are keen to see this system implemented in China.

Lastly, China's entry into the WTO is expected to strengthen the trade and investment ties between China and Taiwan. Political tension between the two countries since 1949 will be reduced once both start operating at the multilateral level. Since economic reforms and open door policies, both the countries have tried to set aside their political differences to cooperate in a more constructive manner. China has taken initiatives in trying to establish three major links such as direct trade, postal and transportation facilities to accelerate their bilateral trade and other forms of cooperation between them (Tung 2004: 1). As a result, bilateral trade has witnessed a significant rise. Since 1993, China has become Taiwan's third largest trading partner, after the US and Japan. It has also become Taiwan's second largest export market after the US. In 2002, China became Taiwan's largest export market for the first time (*Ibid*: 2). This became possible because in the 1990s China became a major destination for production. Many Taiwanese firms had joined this production process and took advantage of this low-cost production network. According to the official statistics more than 50,000 Taiwan firms have invested in China and its entry will accelerate further investment from Taiwan to China.[3] Such progress in relations contributed to the gradual reduction of tensions between the two.

All these developments like the opening of direct trade, the elimination of Taiwan's ban on the import of a broad range of Chinese products and liberalization by the Taiwanese government of restrictions on the outflow of FDI to China have contributed to closer bilateral economic relations. These relations act as a powerful incentive to leaders on both sides of the Taiwan Strait to solidify their bond so that they would be able to take full advantage of this interdependent globalized world. Regular bilateral trade will establish an air of trust and confidence between them. Given the huge interest the US shows in internal affairs of China and Taiwan, such improved economic relationship between these two countries will help the US to further its own interest in the region.

China's accession to the WTO will be an important development. It will be mandatory for China to agree to internationally agreed set of rules and bind them to wide-ranging economic and systemic changes, in order to meet the commitments they have agreed to undertake as a part of WTO accession.

Review of Literature

The review of literature on the topic *China in the World Trade Organization: Implications for Textiles and Telecommunications* is divided into three broad categories. The first set of studies highlights the benefits that would accrue from China's accession to the WTO. The second set discusses the losses that China would incur. The third set looks at the challenges that China faces.

The first set of studies sharply focuses on the issue of China's accession to the WTO and analyzed the benefits that China would have once it joins the multilateral trading system in great detail. Studies by Yongheng Yang, 1996; Anderson Kym, 1997; Yongheng Yang, 1999 suggest that China joining the WTO would immensely benefit her as well as the world economy. Its major trading partners like the US, Japan, and the EU would find a big market for their wide variety of products. Joining the WTO will accelerate the pace of economic reforms and bring benefits to different parts of the country, and not merely allowing them to concentrate on a particular region. It will help China realize its goal of doubling its gross domestic product (GDP) by 2010 and taking its place among the world's largest economies (Panitchpakdi and Clifford: 2002).

Another study carried out by the Association of Southeast Asian Nations (ASEAN) suggested that China commands a distinct advantage over the ASEAN particularly with regard to future of FDI. It's a huge and dynamic market. The way its economic managers have steered the economy through the Asian financial crisis is commendable. Its political leadership is fully committed to economic reform. The liberalization of its market with the WTO accession will enhance the confidence of the investors and lower the cost of doing business in the country. It has much to benefit from the system (ASEAN Secretariat, China's membership in the WTO and its implications for ASEAN, November 2000).

In a study on textiles it was pointed out that China has benefited from the opening up of the sector. It became the world's largest exporter of textiles and clothing in 1995 and 2002. Its world share in textiles rose from 22 per cent to 30 per cent during this period (Nordas: 2004). 19 million people are currently employed in this industry which accounts for about 22 per cent of total employment of manufacturing industry. In 2005 China's exports in Textiles and Clothing (T&C) were US$ 31 billion and are expected to grow further (ILO: 2005).

Since December 2001 China has been a member of the WTO and enjoyed a wide range of benefits. These benefits included the 2005 quota phase-out, automatic quota increases after the phase out, as stipulated in the Agreement on Textiles and Clothing (ATC). The growth-on-growth provision under the ATC and China becoming a WTO member in 2001 seemed to signify that the country would receive benefits as other member countries had during the past six to seven years after implementation of Multi Fibre Agreement (MFA) in 1995. The changes that have taken place from 1995 to 2001 have had a tremendous impact on China's performance in the major importing markets. For example, the US T&C imports from China increased by 125 per cent in 2002. In the same period, apparel exports increased by 60 per cent. The Chinese exporters reduced their prices in order to gain a greater share in the market. They were able to do so, among other reasons, because quota rents were reduced and the Chinese enterprises increased their productivity by investing heavily in new machinery and technology (Knappe: 2003).

It is generally argued that the T&C firms in China will benefit from the reduction of import tariffs and the eventual elimination of export quotas (Zhang: 2000). The Chinese T&C sector will benefit from the WTO as China can import raw materials and machines at much lower tariffs, which will reduce the production costs and improve their competitiveness. The Chinese exporters will be able to export their finished products, without worrying about the availability of export quotas after 2005 (Zhong and Yang: 2000).

Accession to the WTO will provide the Chinese exports with a steady access to the world markets. It no longer has to depend on yearly renewal of the most favoured nation (MFN) status by the US and other major trading partners. This is likely to increase foreign investment in China resulting in increased output and exports than would have been achieved without accession to the WTO. There will be a surge in FDI as China will open its sub-sectors such as telecommunications, insurance, distribution services, retail, etc, (Agrawal and Sahoo: 2003).

The telecommunications market in China is lucrative and of considerable economic interest to powerful WTO Members. Recognizing this, China has taken several initiatives to open up this sub-sector in a strategic manner. China was already a major purchaser of foreign telecommunication equipment and by 1996-97, two telecommunications equipment firms, Motorola (China) Electronics and Shanghai Bell Telephone Equipment Manufacturing Co. Ltd. were among the top ten foreign-funded enterprises in China. In short, telecommunications investment opportunities are already being exploited successfully and are on a rapid path towards expansion (Janda: 1999). The telecommunications liberalization will foster higher economic growth, as it will effectively integrate the economic activities in the country. The importance it has in the trade facilitation will allow the leadership to exploit the potential of the sector sooner by ignoring the underlying political constraints on trade. It will help in securing a market economy faster as the sector promises to bring more capital (Yan Xu and Pitt: 2002). China's telecommunications is the fastest growing sector in the world in terms of mobile and Internet users. There is a great scope to benefit from this sector (Harwit: 2004).

The second set of studies paints a gloomy scenario for China as it enters the WTO. Many of these studies indicate that with the opening up and economic reform pursued since 1978, China has experienced a lopsided growth. For them, interior China has witnessed marginal or virtually no growth and as a result people living in these areas have been suffering from hardship and poverty. Demonstrations are increasingly common, reflecting the anger and frustrations of farmers with stagnant growth. They fear that with the entry of the WTO, the country will see a flood of imported industrial products, which will exacerbate their situation further. Meanwhile, some 25 million of the 85 million workers will see their jobs disappear at the state-owned enterprises as more efficient foreign companies will operate. More imported products will find place in China. This pessimistic scenario suggests that China will collapse. Though this scenario seems unlikely, it is still perceived that China's WTO accession is fraught with peril and promise (Chang: 2001).

Although the WTO is likely to have a positive economic and political impact over the long run, many worry that it will have an adverse effect, particularly in the short to medium term on social equality (both inter and intra regional), exacerbating differences between rural and urban areas, and forcing many people out of jobs (Fewsmith: 2001). In short, many believe that the WTO will spur greater inequality and aggravate unemployment at a time when 8-10 million new workers join the work force and 200 million rural workers need to be transferred from agricultural to non-agricultural employment. Fewsmith further points out that the WTO may cause unemployment and exacerbate regional inequalities because the East coast appears to be much better developed and positioned to capitalize the opportunities that the WTO presents. The Eastern part of China has advantages in terms of human capital, management, information, transportation, and infrastructure that other regions do not have, and hence will capture a lion's share of new foreign investment. People having higher education and better skills will find employment in high-tech and financial services coming to the Eastern region of China. This lop-sided growth is bound to create regional disparities. How China can control such social unrest without hampering its development is a challenge it needs to handle carefully. There will be larger dislocation and hardship in the near to medium term, but the gains would be materialized only in the long run (Fewsmith: 2001).

On textile front, the picture may not look too optimistic if removal of quota phase-out is taken into consideration. The impression that the phasing out of quota restrictions will allow the Chinese firms to increase their share in world market is somewhat incorrect. The export figures during 2000-2003 are showing an upward trend because the Chinese firms are able to exploit certain loopholes such as rules of origin (via transshipments and rerouting), and this loophole will soon be corrected as the WTO prepares to look into this provision more seriously. Besides, China will face strong competition from other Asian countries like India, Pakistan, Bangladesh, and Sri Lanka. China has already got into many trade disputes with major countries. That will have an adverse impact on this sector (Yeung and Mok: 2004).

Under the commitments in the telecommunications sector, foreign operators will be permitted to take a 25 per cent share in mobile telecom firms, which would be raised to 49 per cent after three years. In internet, paging and other value-added services, foreign firms will be allowed immediately to take 30 per cent stake in the Chinese companies in Beijing, Shanghai, and Guangzhou, which would be raised to 50 per cent in two years, when geographical constraints are lifted by end of 2003. Tariffs on many high-tech products like telecom equipment will be phased out and eliminated by 2005. State-owned telecom giants may be hit as competition between domestic operators heats up, with foreign investment beefing up their infrastructure and services. An increase in the number of network operators could bring more business opportunities to domestic equipment manufacturers. Lower tariffs on telecom equipment could have a limited impact as domestic manufacturers could not benefit from high tariffs (Global Policy Forum: 2000).

The third set of studies focuses on the challenges that China will have to grapple with once it becomes a WTO member. Prof. Li Yining (2000) holds the view that China should start to reconsider present laws in terms of attracting talent and supporting domestic private firms. Opportunities and challenges will emerge but China must make the most of every opportunity. To prepare domestic firms for China's entry into the WTO, the Chinese government must open its domestic industries such as telecommunications and banking wider to the domestic companies, before they are opened to foreign firms. Many people in China agree that the biggest challenge will be the one facing the government sector as there will be profound impact on the way China's economy operates and the way the Chinese government manages its economy. In this regard, the government's role will be shifted from looking after everything to macro-control and let the enterprises decide for themselves. This process will prove to be more difficult than expected and even painful. In the quest to join the global trading regime the issue of China's national sovereignty and the resolve to conform to international rules and regulations has always appeared contradictory and conciliatory by turns, but the movement has invariably been in the direction of eventual integration into the neo-liberal international economic order (Acharya:1999). The accession to the WTO creates fear of social unrest as its domestic economy, social institutions, and weak rule of law will undergo massive structural adjustment programme to conform to the international rule-based regime.

In the field of textiles, China will face challenges in terms of complying with international standards. This will be vital for developing and maintaining its international competitiveness. International standards such as ISO 9000, ISO 14000, SA 8000 and WRAP (Worldwide Responsible Apparel Production) concerning quality and environmental management are an immediate challenge for the textile industry. China is trying to meet such standards (Yeung and Mok: 2004). With the accession to the WTO, China has anticipated fierce competition that would set in, particularly at a time when the economy depends so significantly on the advancement of technology and the regulation adjustment process internally for telecommunications is becoming complex. The issues of ownership and foreign investors' entry occupy the centre of the debate. As China has signed the agreements, the sector will witness a massive opening. Dewoskin argues that within six years from the accession, the telecommunications sector will be opened up to 49 per cent equity to foreign investors forcing the Chinese domestic players facing a serious challenge (2001).

The WTO accession means for China a giant step forward in its long-term strategy to catch up with the advanced industrial world by following its principle of market socialism. The WTO offers significantly medium or long-term benefits to China by risking itself to a whole lot of social and economic challenges. On the other hand, China's trading partners, mostly the developed countries believe that they have equally risked themselves in trusting the ability of China's leadership to deliver on its commitments (Magarinos, et. al: 2002). China faces a wide variety of challenges in striving to promote national development and rise to the level of the industrial countries. The WTO accession has already demanded and will continue to demand the deployment of enormous and highly qualified manpower resources. For instance, China must amend no less than 177 domestic laws and regulations regarding customs administration, foreign investment, intellectual property and services to ensure consistency with the WTO obligations. These laws have to be revised and passed by the National People's Congress (NPC). Judges have to be trained; the legal institutions and procedures need to ensure that the laws are fairly and impartially upheld. In addition, there is a need to maintain the following: momentum of reform; address resource shortages and low productivity; reallocate high percentage of labour force; establish a social safety-net and attend the needs of educational, scientific, and technological demands of the system; and correct regional unevenness and deflationary measures.

The current study while taking into account the above literature makes an attempt to fill some of the gaps. For example, China's accession process, which took so long, is not completely based on economic factors alone. Political factors are equally important which form part of the current study. Existing literature does not focus adequately on the post-entry period. It delineates the changes that occurred after China's entry into the WTO in the textiles and telecommunications sectors. The sudden emergence of global financial crisis and its impact on China's textiles and telecommunications have substantially been analyzed to provide a new perspective on China as well as on the world economy. An attempt has been made by accessing various resources available in China and by discussing with a number of academicians, policy makers and trade and industry captains of China.

While making an attempt to analyze China's position in the world economy especially after joining the WTO, the study aims to examine certain significant dimension which has bearing on why China was keen to join the WTO. First, whether the expectations of benefiting from the global economy have been the main driving force behind China's entry into the WTO or its entry into the WTO will change the dynamics of the current negotiations. It is often observed that China would benefit substantially from its trade in textiles and telecommunications by joining the WTO.

Scope and Research Methodology

The book aims to delineate the implications of China's post-entry scenario. It covers two significant sectors of the Chinese economy, which are textiles and telecommunications. *First*, it analyzes how China's leading sector i.e., textiles in global trade regime under the WTO has performed. *Secondly*, it examines and assesses its growth and prospects. *Thirdly*, it provides an extensive account of trade liberalization of telecommunications service sector, its growth in terms of exports, employment, and contribution to its economy. *Fourthly*, it examines whether the terms of accession have proved to be more costly for China in terms of market access commitments, changes in the legal structure, and meeting the adjustment costs. *Lastly*, the role that China has played in influencing the negotiating dynamics since it became a formal member of the WTO. All these dimensions are central to the study.

The book further aimed to answer some of the pertinent questions that always generated curiosity among scholars such as what has been the nature of benefits that China and the rest of the world accrued from the WTO? As an emerging economic power, has China been able to influence the WTO negotiations, particularly after its entry? What has been the annual export growth rate in textiles after its entry into the WTO? How lucrative is the Chinese telecom market for the domestic as well as for the foreign players, and what have been the structural and policy changes that China has undertaken to liberalize this sector? While liberalizing the telecom sector how has the government handled the issue of security and national sovereignty? While phasing out the restrictions in telecommunications sector, did the Chinese leadership lose the freedom of exercising its option of regulation? How has the global financial crisis affected the Chinese economy with particular reference to its textiles and telecommunications sectors? What were the major challenges before the central leadership to tackle the crisis of such magnitude? What has been the response of China in handling such a crisis?

The study is carried out using both qualitative and quantitative inputs. Interdependence theories developed by Hirschman (1945), Keohane and Nye (1977), and Caporaso (1978) are applied to see how China has been able to achieve high economic growth and prosperity and emerge as a global economic power. The central arguments in these works are: (A) A notion that asymmetries in trade interdependence can provide a source of political power; and (B) dependence as a variant of interdependence characterized by a highly asymmetric form of transactions between two or more units are assessed in case of China to determine whether they held true. A sectoral approach is also employed to analyze and assess the trade gains and losses that China experienced, while liberalizing and fulfilling its WTO commitments in the two selected sectors. On carrying out the study, a huge database is used. Databases like the World Integrated Trade Solution (WITS), World Trade Online Database and China Customs were extensively used. Data from China as well as various multilateral institutions like the United Nations Conference on Trade and Development (UNCTAD), the International Monetary Fund

(IMF), and the WTO were also consulted. Available primary and secondary sources were examined. A field study in China and Hong Kong was undertaken to secure the first hand information as the study dealt with the direct government policies, state intervention and its impact on the Chinese economy and world trade. The field trip also helped to source the official data. Some interactions with eminent professors and scholars based at Hong Kong University of Science & Technology (HKU&T), Hong Kong City University, Lingnan University, Peking University, Tsinghua University and Fudan University, key trade and industry officials also did benefit the study.

Notes

1. http://stat.wto.org/CountryProfile/WSDBCountryPFView.aspx?Language=E&Country=CN. Accessed on 18 September 2014.
2. For more details see (Lardy 2001:http://www.brookings.edu/testimony/2001/0509foreignpolicy_lardy.aspx).
3. http://english.peopledaily.com.cn/200203/12/eng20020312_91986.shtml. Accessed on 10 April 2009.

2

China in the WTO

Theory and Praxis

China's entry into the WTO in 2001 marked a turning point in its drive for modernization. Its desire for modernization was apparent in the late 1970s. Economic reforms and open door policies initiated during this period aimed at addressing this major issue. The concept of 'Four Modernizations' which was designed to transform China into an economic power in the 21st century by introducing reforms in four major areas of agriculture, industry, national defense, and science and technology had thus emerged as the key strategy. While initiating modernization drive, the central leadership began to realize that modernization cannot be achieved with the domestic help alone. To make China economically strong, it needed to look to the West as a key source of support. As China was still ideologically not compatible with the ideology of the industrialized West, the central leadership had confronted with the dilemma of how to achieve the goal of modernization and economic development in a world economy that is dominated by the capitalist and industrialized countries. The cardinal question that remained was how to modernize without sacrificing its sovereignty.

For a developing country like China, whose economy was feeble and technologically backward in the early 1980s, the road to modernization without external assistance looked difficult as the Western powers, which were at the helm of providing external assistance, were not keen at the first sight to extend their support without visualizing a long-term interest in China. Therefore, in the post-Mao period China had to make efforts to adapt itself to this context by pursuing pragmatic policies of peace, development, and cooperation. During this period, it showed considerable skill and flexibility in terms of bringing in new adjustments to align itself to the new global trading regime. One of the striking features of its foreign policies has been its approach to join the global trading regime. It became the fundamental requirement for China to introduce reforms in economic, administrative and legal fields.

The period between 1986 and 2001 till the time China joined the WTO remained one of the most critical periods in its history. First, China actively participated in different international fora like the GATT, the UN, etc., and came closer to international norms and practices. Since end of the Cold War, China played a key role in global economy. It is the growing economic strength that catapulted it to the centre stage of world economy. The current degree of engagement and cooperation with a global regime, where various industrial and other countries are significantly involved, marked a point of departure from Maoist China of limited interaction with international community during 1949-1976.

With this brief backdrop, this chapter aims to analyze how China embraced the notion of interdependence and sectoral approach as the new principles of modernization and integration with the world economy. While conceptualizing theory of interdependence and sectoral approach, it simultaneously takes into account how such strategies were applied at the practical level to integrate China with the global economy.

CONCEPTUALIZING INTERDEPENDENCE AND SECTORAL APPROACH

Interdependence can be defined as the factor of reliance between units, nation states, or the governments. Though some forms of interdependence existed among countries for centuries, it became critical in the 19th and 20th centuries when nation states were striving for development. Some of these countries lacked all the resources like natural endowments, labour, capital, and technology that were required for making a country stable, independent and modern. Therefore, they had to depend on others. This core principle of reliance between nations to become self-sufficient and developed gave birth to the concept of interdependence. It became a dynamic concept of being mutually responsible to and sharing a common set of principles with others. It recognized the need of one nation state with other states at regular intervals and shared the productive activities to benefit each other. It supposedly implied that all nation states or governments are emotionally, economically, ecologically, and morally interdependent (Keohane and Nye 1977: 16). The principle of cooperation between countries was regarded as an important strand of this theory. It came to be visualized as the interconnectedness and the reliance on one another where social, economic, environmental, and political considerations played an important role. The concept of interdependence has received more recognition with the current phase of globalization. Global interdependence has intensified and accelerated through the growing use of information and communication technologies (Martinelli 2005: 242).

Likewise, sectoral approach came to be defined as a strategy to increase the voluntary engagement of a particular sector around the globe. This approach gathered momentum in the 1960s. After the devastation of World War II, when countries were contemplating on rebuilding their economies, some countries adhered to this approach as a viable mechanism to develop their economies. It gained prominence initially among the small economies, which popularly came to be known as 'microstates' by Dommen and Hein (1985:1). Countries like South Korea and Singapore were the successful examples of this approach.

However, looking at the success of countries like South Korea and Singapore as the major financial centres in the world, developing countries were inspired to pursue this approach. Sectoral approach is now actively pursued by many developing countries who find a number of advantages in undertaking it. First, it reduces administrative measures when implemented sectorally. Administration becomes easier when it is applied to a particular sector than to an economy-wide set up. In a sectoral set up, the number of concerned actors are few. Second, sectoral approach provides a well-informed database which is substantially developed even in developing countries to facilitate any major endeavour that the state intends to. Thus greater data availability builds confidence and provides accuracy to the entire conduct of business in that particular sector. Third, it develops a focused approach towards global technology transfer as most of the sectors in developing countries require technology to progress. Fourth, sectoral approach allows countries to locate their complementary strengths in a focused manner.

Theoretical Understanding of Interdependence and Sectoral Approach

The theory of interdependence gained prominence in international studies in the last few decades. In pursuit of peace, wealth, security, and development, various countries sought each other's assistance and cooperation. These interactions and engagements helped many nations to achieve their ultimate goals while others witnessed conflicts. Countries which embraced the notion of interdependence to integrate with the global system experienced several dimensions as far as their behaviour and requirements are concerned. Difference in specific needs of countries such as economic development, modernization, sustainability, strengthening security, achieving military might, peace and development resulted in various conflicts like war, external aggression, trade embargoes, etc. Such wide divergence of requirements among countries led them to confront various challenges when they operate in a globally sensitive and dynamic environment. This approach of interdependence led many scholars to analyze the kind of relations ultimately countries evolve.

The theory of interdependence generated several debates in international studies, especially in the second half of 20th century. Various scholars who worked on this area have arrived at a number of hypotheses. These can be broadly categorized as: i) trade reduces conflict; ii) higher trade interactions result in higher cooperation among states; and iii) higher levels of trade dependence will result in greater probability of conflict between states. Two schools of thought, namely liberal and realist focus on this debate. The liberals were far more optimistic compared to the realists. Some of the debates that grew out of this theory are analyzed here.

Liberal Perspective

A substantial part of the literature on interdependence theory emerged during the 1970s and early 1980s. Most of these studies came from the liberals who suggested that trade correlated with peace. A rigorous analysis of 30 pairs of states during 1958-1967 by a group of experts such as Polachek, Gasiorowski, Mansfield and Pollins concluded that greater levels of trade reduce the chances of outbreak of hostilities. For example, heightened trading activities between the US and the former Soviet Union from 1965 to 1975 significantly contributed to the lessening of tensions between these two super powers and led to the onset of détente (Pevehouse 2004: 252). Another study pointed out that heightened interdependence fosters cooperative political relations (Mansfield and Pollins 2001: 1). This arrangement gained greater currency with the formation of the European Economic Community, the proposal by the US during Richard Nixon's presidency for a constructive engagement with China, Willy Brandt's *Ostpolitik,*[1] and Henry Kissinger's conception of détente with the Soviet Union.

Albert O. Hirschman expressed a similar viewpoint. In his seminal work titled *The Passions and Interests: Political Arrangements for Capitalism before its Triumph* he suggested that increasing levels of trade leads to more interactions, which in turn create more potential for positive interactions between countries. This strand of theory was also advocated by Stein (1993: 249-250) who posited that interactions in trade result in the promotion of cooperation. This explanation highlights the hypothesis that increasing levels of trade dependence between states will result in higher political cooperation.

Consequently some other liberal theorists have argued that trade cooperation has reduced international conflict in a number of ways. First, economic trade replaces conquest as a means of exchange lowering the levels of conflict. What would have been achieved through war can now be accomplished through trade. Richard Rosecrance's concept of the "trading state" (1986: 31) is an example of this theory, which illustrates how trade and exchange can reduce the incentives to remain engaged in conflict. This process of trade and exchange encourages the states to develop specialization in the category of goods and services that would foster cooperation between states as both consumers and traders would like to be in constant interaction to avail the facilities of goods and services in the foreign market. These consumers and traders have an interest to avoid war because any interruption in commercial activity will prove too costly for them (Stein 1993: 279; Viner

1951: 261; Viner 1985: 12-14). Therefore the states are compelled to balance their interests *vis-à-vis* the interests of other states. In another significant work it is argued that as higher levels of trade have the capacity to reduce the war, it is practical to enter into a trading arrangement between the states than looking for a war (Morrow 1999: 89). It is also theorized that trade influences political relations among countries. It acts as a key factor in bringing countries together to resolve their political differences. Trade and political relations, therefore, have a direct correlation (Irwin 1996: 3). This kind of liberalism significantly focused on the aspect that higher levels of trade can minimize the economic based incentives for conflict leading to a better peaceful environment.[2]

Johan Galtung, a leading liberalist, argues that interdependence is "a style of cooperation that does not endanger new patterns of dependence." He further explained that this cooperation connotes the absence of total autonomy of the units involved (1979: 2). Similarly, Edward L. Morse has argued (1976: 118) "interdependence is the opposite of state autonomy, if autonomy is defined as the ability of a government to achieve its goal by itself." What he argues is that interdependence has gained currency and this is being pursued by the states to achieve modernization. According to him, modernization of a country has become important and it has elevated rising economic concerns to the level of high politics, which has been expressed in his writings; "the politics of wealth and welfare have overshadowed the politics of power and position" (1976: 86). Increase in interdependence among countries has taken place to satisfy their need for modernization. While analyzing the theory of interdependence between states, he has laid adequate emphasis on dependence aspect of the concept, explaining that it leads to loss of autonomy, incapability to control events, and vulnerability to pressures from outside. In addition, this dependence gives rise to dominance, to have an impact upon each other depending on the specific situation they are in. Morse points out that in an era of interdependence, one state may effectively intervene in another society by merely altering its own domestic policy.

Similarly, Christopher F. Gelpi and Joseph M. Greico (2001: 8-9) assess the behaviour of democratic and non-democratic states in relation to promoting economic growth through trade. The study highlighted that the standard model of trade has recognized the capacity of international trade integration needed to improve the aggregate growth rate of a country during the period in which integration is occurring. For example, a country that opens itself to global markets, according to the standard model, causes it to specialize in a narrower range of goods, the exact choice of which depends on the country's endowment of productive factors, local and world preference for and prices of goods, and the state of world technology. This selective product range of a country may in turn create opportunities for the enjoyment of increasing returns over some range of new productions, which in turn boosts the country's aggregate growth rate. However, declining economies of scale would eventually curtail the capacity of this specialization in product ranges through trade to raise the rate of economic growth for the country as a whole.

It is further elicited in the study that trade is a powerful mechanism for the expansion and deepening of markets, and thereby may by itself, encourage new investments in technology. It also gives rise to additional opportunities for small and medium enterprises (SME) sectors in a country to gain access to new technologies through these and other mechanisms. Trade can directly and indirectly enhance the productivity of the factors of production and contribute to national growth.

Another form of liberal approach was articulated by John R. Oneal and Lee Ray, (1997: 769-770) relating to the theory of interdependence where they have argued that two democratic countries were unlikely to be involved in a militarized dispute in the post-World War II era when they have deeper trade interdependence. Oneal is of the view that trade interdependence grew better when the dyads are democracies. The analysis put forth by these authors suggests that democracies are more peaceful while autocracies on most occasions tend to be involved in conflict. The chances of establishing peace between states are influenced by the level of democracy practiced under their regimes. Democratic pairs are less conflict prone but a high level of democratic framework in one state does not neutralize the dangers associated with an autocratic functioning of a strategic partner.

Realist Perspective

In contrast, realists do not hold interdependence as a direct source of conflict or a deterrent to conflict. However, they insist that rise in trade can become an important source for conflict between states. Albert O. Hirschman, who, earlier remarked that more trade interactions reduce conflict reiterating the liberal point of view, has provided another dimension. He pointed out that the rise in trade could also lead to conflict under circumstances, where the gains emanating from trade may not be proportional among the states. This disparity in gains can be a cause for asymmetrical advantages that the states may experience out of this exercise and which will lead to conflict among states. Any engagement between two countries will lead to problems as to who receives what in a given context. Opportunities of benefiting each other are limited in nature. More exchanges and interactions between the states according to the realist perspective will lead to more conflicts. They emphasize the view that interdependence leads to asymmetrical relations between states. As illustrated by Kenneth Waltz, "States that feel insecure must ask how the gain will be divided. They are compelled to ask, 'will both of us gain?' but who will gain more?"(Waltz 1979: 105). If one partner depends on a trading relationship much more heavily than the other partner, then the latter partner ends up in a state of dependence. Under such circumstances, trade may not act as a deterrent to conflict but becomes a source of tension. As the trading activities between states take place at a rapid pace, probability of dispute emerging over such economic issues becomes higher.

Interdependence indicates a pattern of interacting relationship between two or more units, where the interactions, exchanges, and transactions between and among these units are mutually beneficial. Many international theorists have defined this relationship to have reciprocal effects upon all the interacting entities. This would mean interdependence creates more dependence of some nation states on the others. It is argued that dependence acts as a variant of interdependence that is characterized by a highly asymmetric form of transactions between two or more units (Caporaso 1978:18-19).

However, interdependence as a viable mechanism for economic engagement received significant attention among scholars immediately after the Cold War. Close contact between important powers was characterized by economic interdependence rather than by dependence. This is amply demonstrated in Hirschman's work mentioned earlier. According to him, economic engagement is a long-term transformative strategy. As one state gradually expands economic interaction with another targeted state, the resulting (asymmetrical) interdependence creates vested interests within the target society and government. The beneficiaries of interdependence favour such an arrangement and they protect their interests by pressurizing the target government to accommodate the source of interdependence. Economic engagement is a form of structural linkage. The structural changes needed for the state to remain engaged in economic interdependence are domestic political change and foreign policy accommodation. It is a means to know other states' needs and suggest changes to achieve objectives of the state that is initiating the interaction. In a way, the initiating country is imposing pressure on the target country. This kind of engagement will lead to asymmetrical relationship between the two countries.

Economic interdependence is a process built over a period. According to Hirschman, it is injected in a careful manner to the target economy leading to a gradual, almost imperceptible transformation in domestic politics. The problem is that it is difficult to control the flow and effects of economic interdependence once a target economy begins to open to international economic exchange. Sometimes, the effects of interdependence are more likely to be shocking and disruptive than incremental and stabilizing. The experience of the "Asian tigers" during the 1990s illustrates this point amply. These countries opened their financial markets to find portfolio investment first flood in and then abruptly flood out, leaving collapsing currencies, plummeting growth rates, and beleaguered populations in their wake.

The overall arguments put forth by liberal theorists on interdependence are flexible in nature and provide a comfortable atmosphere for the countries to negotiate. An enhanced accommodative behaviour and a more open environment for outside interference on a country's sovereignty are the key dimensions of liberal tradition. These forms of liberal tradition are in sharp contrast to the realists who believe every action must be justified, and if they are in the interests of the state then they should be firmly pursued. Realists propagate the idea that interests should justify state's decisions. For example, interactions between the states must be less, because states are not at the same level of development.

This prolonged debate between liberals and realists on theory of interdependence has been sharply focused upon in a study (Copeland 1996: 5). Trade theories in new classical tradition or in multilateral trade liberalization, however, lack a way to fuse the benefits of trade and the costs of severed trade into one theoretical framework. Copeland has further suggested that the role of international institutions is important for a smooth conduct of trade. Such transparent trading activity through the WTO can invigorate the dependent state to look for theory of interdependence as a viable alterative for economic development.

Dependency Theory and State-Led Development

Among poorer and less industrialized nations, the notion of interdependence has been interpreted in a different way. The causal connection between modernization and interdependence seems reversed. Interdependence, instead of being an effect of modernization, is construed as a developmental strategy to accomplish national goal of modernization. An industrially backward country is keen to modernize but suffers from a weak economy, backward technology, scarce natural resources and inadequate capital. Hence it remains backward till the time it finds outside help on a sustainable basis to launch its modernization drive. The logical conclusion, therefore, is to look for external assistance or foreign aid from international financial organizations and foreign governments. Edward L. Morse has explained this as a developmental strategy that opts for "the fostering of domestic goals through international behaviour" (1976: 93) while exposing a poor country's fragile domestic economy to the vagaries of foreign economic penetration. This view coincides with the theory of dependency. This argument often took the form of state intervention, and a policy of industrialization was followed through import substitution which emerged in the 1950s. This view was advocated by Raul Prebisch (1959: 256), whose research had enunciated that the wealth of poor nations tended to decrease when the wealth of rich nations increased.

Andre Gunder Frank, an influential exponent of dependency theory, propounds a worldview which suggests that the wealthy nations of the world need a peripheral group of poorer states in order to remain wealthy. The poverty of the countries in the periphery persists not because they are not integrated into the world system, or not fully integrated as is often argued by right wing development economics but because of how they are integrated into the system. The poverty-stricken countries provide natural resources, cheap labour, a destination for obsolete technology and markets to the wealthy nations, without which they could not have prospered or have the standard of living that they enjoy.

First World nations tend to perpetuate a state of dependency through various policies and initiatives. This state of dependency is multifaceted involving economics, politics, education, banking and finance, sports, and all aspects of human resource development. Any attempt initiated by the dependent nations to resist or curb the influences of dependency will result in economic sanctions and/or military invasion and control. Such incidents may be rare. However, dependency syndrome is enforced actively by the wealthy nations by designing and controlling the rules of international trade and commerce. This kind of underdevelopment for dependent nations, according to Andre Gunder Frank, is a historical development and perpetrated with the rise of capitalism. For him: "contemporary underdevelopment is, in large part, the historical product of past and continuing economic and other relations between the satellite underdeveloped and the now developed metropolitan countries. Further more, these relations are an essential part of the capitalist system on a world scale as a whole" (Frank 1972: 3).

Dependency theory began to lose its influence around the 1980s leading to the prominence of another model. The State-led Development Model became popular around this time as a result of impressive economic growth achieved by countries like Japan and Newly Industrialized Economies (NIEs). Flying Geese Model which symbolized this State-led Development Model became an important paradigm shift in the approach that many countries followed. Japan was the first to adopt this strategy followed by first tier NIEs like Taiwan, South Korea, Hong Kong and Singapore. The overall significant of this model was that it followed a typical pattern of industrial restructuring and development of the countries where growth sequence was maintained as imports, then domestic production and finally exports. This was first highlighted by the Japanese economist Kaname Akamatsu in early 1940s, but gained popularity in the 1960s.

These countries soon followed a different agenda like more market friendly policies and more open to international trade and investment. These countries remained in the good books of the core nations and were not treated anti-Western. Drawing inspiration from the State-led Development Model of East Asian countries, many developing countries followed a policy of economic liberalization and sought greater integration into world markets. Onset of globalization around this period provided much needed impetus to these countries as it brought capital technology, skills, etc. to different parts of the world by creating a level playing field for all aspirant countries to benefit optimally from the globalization and policies of liberalization.

This argument further gained significance through the writings of liberal theorists like Robert Keohane and Joseph S. Nye (1977) who held the view that exposure to foreign shores may not result in the negative consequences for the country rather it infuses the countries to the global economic participation to spur their own development. Such participation does not reduce the country to a dependent status of international hierarchy. On the contrary, this interdependent developmental strategy through active participation leads to positive gains for the country as they participate in or take advantage of highly developed industrialized structure of international division of labour, free flow of capital and technology. Current world economy is experiencing such abundance of trade and investment taking place across countries and geographic regions and immensely reaffirming this aspect. Eckstein and Gourevitch have summarized such positive gains theoretically in a concise manner:

> Significant potential gains accrue to an economy that takes advantage of the international division of labour and specialization across national boundaries. These gains are rooted in the fact that certain types of goods (e.g., advanced technology) can be bought more cheaply abroad than they can be produced at home, and vice versa. These cost differences arise from specialization on the one hand and differences in resource endowments and in the accumulation of man-made skills and machinery on the other.
>
> Countries, like individuals, are quite differently endowed with supplies of product factors. Some areas have relatively more of one set of factors and less of another… Therefore, each area is best equipped to produce those goods that require large proportions of the factors relatively abundant there. It will tend to export such goods and import those in which other countries have a comparative advantage and which are therefore relatively cheaper abroad (Eckstein, 1977: 233-234).
>
> The relatively free play of world market forces, promotes growth and wealth for the investors and recipients alike. As a country is drawn into the world economy, the laws of supply and demand and comparative advantage initially give it the "supplier-buyer" role… but the country does not remain there. Foreign capital touches off a series of reactions leading to ever higher levels of industrialization. There are no inherent obstacles to the realization of parity or

> "maturity." The interaction of two unequal bodies leads to eventually their homogenization, to the elimination of inequality (Gourevitch 1978: 891).

Complex Interdependence

With the deepening of bilateral relations between countries and their opening up, relations among the countries became much more complex. During the eighties and nineties countries tried to forge better relations among themselves for mutual stability and prosperity. Keohane and Nye (1989) have developed the concept of complex interdependence to provide an understanding to this nature of relationship. According to them, "complex interdependence has three main characteristics: (1) state policy goals are not arranged in stable hierarchies, but are subject to trade-offs; (2) the existence of multiple channels of contact among societies expands the range of policy instruments, thus limiting governments' control over foreign relations; and (3) military force[3] is largely irrelevant" (Keohane and Nye 1989: 255). Interdependence does not only increase cooperation but may also lead to conflict. In a systematic study of cooperation among industrialized nations, Keohane (1984) pointed out that interdependence in the world political economy generates conflict. People, who are hurt by unexpected changes emanating from external factors such as increases in the prices that producers charge for oil or that banks charge for the use of money, turn to their governments for aid. Similarly, workers remain unemployed because of competition from more efficient or lower-wage foreign production. Governments, in turn, seek to shift the costs of these adjustments onto others, or at least to avoid having them shifted onto themselves. This strategy leads them to pursue incompatible policies and creates discord (Keohane, 1984). Although Keohane's analysis was based on a study of the discord and cooperation among industrialized nations before the mid-1980s, his perspective is quite relevant for examining current bilateral complex relationship evolving between many countries (Zhao and Liu 2010: 2).

Interactions among nations sometimes create unexpected relationship. Their interdependence often becomes complex in nature and largely leads to conflict. Nye and Keohane suggest that to avert conflict and develop reciprocal relations, various institutions have to play a positive role. This positive role leads to greater interstate reliance as a result it changes the nature of the relationships between states and the possible strategies that they then choose to pursue. Therefore, creation of such institutions is necessary to engage in development oriented and non-military exercise. As these institutions develop, states become increasingly reluctant to contravene institutional norms, and sacrifice the benefits institutions may create. However, Nye and Keohane have also stressed that states may still go against institutional rules if they perceive that they are not benefiting them.

In another important work Walter Carlsnaes, Thomas Risse and Beth Simmons have explained that the complex interdependence implies that the growing interconnectedness may lead to political processes that are different from those typically described by realism. Instead of international politics dominated by states that focus on security as their goal and armed forces as their security, in a situation of complex interdependence actors also include international organizations. In such a situation security and armed forces lose their relevance. As the world is becoming more integrated, notion of complex interdependence is getting more thickened. Today it can be reasonably stated that in the regions of the world that are very closely interconnected, complex interdependence seems to comprehend processes and outcomes of the world politics much better than realism. In the last three decades the roles of the most of the international organizations and institutions have increased in the era of complex interdependence (2002:241). With the increasing prevalence of complex interdependence, the number of international agreements between the countries has also increased.

Similarly, another significant dimension to the understanding of the theory of interdependence came from Harold K Jacobson, a prominent international theorist of modern era. In his famous work titled "*Networks of Interdependence: International Organizations and Global Political System*" *(1979)* he has analyzed the role of international organizations in a holistic manner where he has detailed their achievements in the fields of security, world economy, social welfare and human rights. He has shown how international organizations have become an integral part of world governance system and have carved out a perspective for the international organizations to play a crucial role in the economic field through interdependence to arrive at the final goal of 'individual development.' Economic growth is a key component of this development process is adequately emphasized by Jacobson (1979: 220). Continual introduction of technological innovation, capital and their application though have resulted in the growth of individual countries yet with the advent of globalization, world economy experienced trade transaction of new forms of products and services. To keep pace with such production and value addition, countries have increased their level of interdependence among states.

Jacobson found out that the effects of such interdependence have never been uniform and have varied with size and natural resource-endowment of states. However, such interactions continue to grow over the years. For the vast majority of states, economic growth has meant increasing interactions with other states. Most states that are now termed developed have had to import capital, raw material and technology from other states for their economic growth and this dependence on external sources of supply continue to exist in the present era reiterating the importance of interdependence.

With the recent growth and expansion of industrialization, trade with other states became an essential condition for achieving the advantages of specialization and economies of scale. Small states have been able to register better economic growth by relying heavily on foreign trade. Many countries including even the largest ones have also significantly depended on the external sources to increase their level of economic development (Jacobson 1979: 222). All these countries used transnational pool of scientific and technological resources and advancement. This dimension, as Jacobson suggests, is positive in nature, whereas interdependence has also provided less benign aspects. It has exposed countries to the harmful side effects of technology such as atmospheric and water pollution.

Interdependence adopted by the states has led to different forms of relations. Sometimes they are mutually supportive and symmetrical and more frequently they are asymmetrical and affect some states considerably more than others. That is because most of them are different in size and shape and having varied endowments. For instance, some countries are particularly dependent on import of particular raw materials such as petroleum, whereas others could be relying on export of certain commodities to one or a few countries for a substantial portion of their gross national products. This dependence is particularly vulnerable to shifts in external demand which under certain circumstances may not yield positive results. As a result exporting country might develop an asymmetrical relationship with the importing country. There are still some countries those rely more on trade with larger countries in order to increase their GDP bypassing their traditional trading partners (China and Hong Kong) to foster trade relations with the US. In this case the country seeking more reliance with the bigger country may enter into an unequal relation with the latter. Though interdependence means dependence, this dependence differs in degree and with respect to issues (Jacobson 1979: 222).

Interdependence, according to Jacobson, has been expedited among the states through interactions of various international governmental organizations (IGOs). The growth of activity, relevance and influence of IGOs continue to dominate channels of interdependence in modern sovereign states. He has explained how the modern sovereign state is entangled in a web of international organizations in a world system to pursue its goals of achieving economic growth, security and human welfare. The most important role of IGOs is their function of communication networks. In performing this role they have "become effective instruments in narrowing the differences among the countries concerning basic values and for working towards the development of a significant consensus (1979: 419)." This significant consensus developed among all the IGOs has been helpful in making the modern sovereign state powerful by achieving economic growth and social welfare. Thus, interdependence has been a powerful medium of global integration.

Speedy process of globalization has also resulted in the evolution of complex interdependence. This turbulent[4] globalization has given rise to an array of multiple trans-boundary forces and processes that reduce the government's control over what happens within national boundaries and enable a set of new political actors to project social, economic, and political influence over a long distance. The main drivers of globalization are technological innovation, economic interdependence, demographic transition, political diversification, environmental degradation/concerns, and ideational convergence. Globalization behaves as a double-edged weapon. It can promote cooperation but also may result in new conflict (Zhao and Liu 2010: 2).

The concept of interdependence has gained more momentum with many states firmly believing that the benefits from participating in a competitive world economy far outweigh the compromises they make in terms of political autonomy and independence. In an international trading regime characterized by interdependence, it is the ability and capacity of a nation to cooperate and accommodate than the ability to do it alone that merits emphasis. Gains that would accrue from this interdependent world would facilitate the process of economic development and would allow the poor to catch up with the rich. In the end all would benefit and prosper.

Sectoral Approach

Similarly, the theoretical basis of sectoral approach that evolved with the progress of trade liberalization provided a sound understanding on the economies that were interested in capitalizing trade gains from liberal world economy. Literature suggests that various countries have adopted the sectoral approach in many sectors of their economies. These essentially include agriculture, industry, and services. More recently several some countries have adopted sectoral approach even in sub-sectors such as IT. Such a specific sectoral approach on important sub-sectors like IT was initiated because with the increasing pace of global business activity, significance of IT as an important tool was recognized.

In addition, two types of sectoral approach can be noticed (Panagariya 2003: 3). First, one or more sectors may be identified and all members may liberalize imports within those sectors. This is sometimes called a 'zero-for-zero' approach. Second, each member may seek liberalization from its major trading partners in sectors of its comparative advantage in return for its own liberalization of sectors of comparative disadvantage. The sectoral approach to trade liberalization has witnessed major emphasis in world economy after the Uruguay Round of trade negotiations and establishment of the WTO. The first type of sectoral or 'zero-for-zero' approach has directed much of the liberalization taking place in the area of trade in services during and since the Uruguay Round. The member countries have identified broad sectors such as financial services or telecommunications and bargained market access within these sectors. This approach was later on applied to trade in goods during the first WTO Ministerial held in 1996 at Singapore. During this Ministerial, a group of countries signed the Information Technology Agreement (ITA) whereby they committed themselves to significantly liberalize and promote free trade in a set of technology products.

Under the second type of sectoral approach based on the theory of comparative advantage, all industrial products come under the negotiation but members negotiate with their partners sector by sector. In principle, this approach can be expected to yield an efficient outcome. Each member will seek liberalization in sectors and countries where its exports face the highest barriers. In turn, its trading partners will seek access to its most protected sectors. Thus, the bargain is biased in favour of lowering the highest tariffs. This approach may invite complex administrative procedure if trade patterns happen to be such that each country exports its goods to one set of countries but imports them from an entirely different set of countries. For instance, if India's exports go mainly to the US while its imports come from the European Union (EU), bilateral negotiations between India and its two trading partners become difficult. While it remains to be empirically verified, one suspects that under the current structure of trade and tariffs, this is not a significant problem. Goods subject to high tariffs in developing countries are largely imported from developed countries and evenly distributed over the latter. Conversely, major exports of developing countries face high barriers in all developed countries—examples include agricultural products and apparel (Panagariya 2003: 4-6).

Policy makers, economists and trade and industry leaders have passionately argued in favour of this liberalization approach (Rae *et al.* 2001: 294). It is pointed out that sectoral approach gained currency in recent years because movement of MNCs has significantly increased across the borders. Countries are opening up certain specific sectors to benefit from the entry of MNCs. As a result, countries are witnessing selective international product or services specializations with their technological capabilities and skills. Typically, a manufacturing process combining with high or medium or even low technology operations would find it appropriate to develop an integrated production structure wherein each unit specializes in the operations suited to its own level of technology and human skills.

Regional integration occurring in many parts of the world especially in East Asia and South East Asia after China has joined the WTO symbolizes such an approach. Regional integration would facilitate such venture even without formal integration. Individual countries may seek to enter into such sectoral initiative liberalization with other countries to ease production network and movement of goods. The Asia Pacific Economic Cooperation's (APEC) sectoral liberalization efforts are example of this approach (Rae *et al.* 2001: 295-296).

More recently, sectoral approach has also been initiated into handling the issue of global climate change. Sectoral approach is now on the international climate policy agenda, and has been discussed at the two recent United Nations Framework Convention on Climate Change (UNFCCC) and COP[5] meetings in Bali (2007) and Poznan (2008). They formed an important part of the negotiations that took place at the Global Climate Change conference in Copenhagen in December 2009. Sectoral approach involves organized action by key product producers in a specific industry sector and their host governments to address the greenhouse gas emissions from their products and processes within the UNFCCC framework. Specific actions taken would differ from sector to sector, dictated by the characteristics of each sector's structure and technologies. Actions would also differ from country to country, following the principle of common but differentiated responsibilities laid out by the UNFCCC. Thus a sectoral approach is not a *one-size fits-all* recipe, but a blend of policies and actions organized around each sector's unique characteristics and the location of production facilities. While focusing on the characteristics of each sector, a sectoral approach would not exclude actions across different sectors.

In advanced industrial countries, the service sector plays a crucial role in creating a robust economy. It accounts for a large portion of each nation's gross domestic product. Despite the increasing importance of services trade, the multilateral trading system began establishing rules to open markets in those sectors only in 1995, with the creation of the General Agreement on Trade in Services (GATS) at the conclusion of the Uruguay Round of trade negotiations. Decisions at the end of the round did provide for continuing negotiations in the services. Only with the renewed commitment to a new round of trade negotiations, undertaken in November 2001 at Doha, Qatar, serious individual sectoral negotiations have come into prominence. The urgency with which services sector needs sectoral liberalization is well founded by Peter Evans (2002: vii). It is analyzed that though services liberalization has come into effect late, yet there is an imperative need to expedite the liberalization process at sectoral level to integrate countries with the world economy.

Both at the national and at the international level, government policies often lagged far behind the changes in industry structure and competition forced by technological imperatives. Despite the solid and accumulating evidence of the benefits of both domestic and international liberalization of energy services markets, formal negotiations in the GATS have almost ignored energy as a service sector until quite recently. This is because the initial negotiations in the Uruguay Round did not count energy services as a separate sector and only a few countries made commitments regarding trade liberalization (primarily in oil field services). Since 2000, however, a core group of countries, led by the United States, Venezuela, and to some degree the European Union, has made a determined effort to clarify and expand the GATS classification system regarding energy services as a prelude to an effort to secure substantial liberalization commitments in the sector by the end of the Doha Round (Evans 2002: ix-x).

One of the most striking developments affecting the globalization of services during the past two decades or so has been the revision of government policies towards the services sector [United Nations Conference on Trade and Development (UNCTAD) and The World Bank 1994]. Two or three decades ago, governments of both developed and developing economies strictly controlled the extent and form of foreign (and often, domestic private) involvement in major services such as telecommunications, transport, banking and advertising, considered to be strategically, politically, or culturally sensitive industries, as well as in community services such as education, health and public utilities. The qualitative changes in service industries mentioned earlier, coupled, in some cases, with financial constraints affecting state-owned service enterprises have forced governments to review their protectionist policies and set in motion a process of liberalization of policies with respect to domestic as well as international production and provision of services. Sectoral liberalization of services has been given adequate priority by the individual governments. Domestic as well as foreign competition are increasingly viewed as tools for increasing the efficiency and productivity of service industries, which in turn are recognized as being critical for economic performance generally (Mallampally and Zimny 2000: 44).

Currently, many countries have laid down emphasis on strengthening knowledge economy as they found growth of this sector of economy is critically attached to the world economy. The knowledge economy is often considered to mean only high-technology industries or information and communication technologies (ICTs). It would be more appropriate to use the concept more broadly to cover how any economy harnesses and uses new and existing knowledge to improve the productivity and increase overall welfare. Sectoral approach to developing knowledge economy is a priority in several countries. In an era of globalization countries like China and India have steered their economies by identifying the sectoral strength in their economies. China with its manufacturing and industrial strength in computer hardware and India with business process outsourcing and IT services have excelled in world economy. This priority in sectoral approach has helped them to integrate globally into the knowledge economy (Dahlman and UTZ 2005: 32).

In another important study it is highlighted that how a country like Finland which was in the late seventies stood at the lower rank of OECD countries could significantly improve its economic growth in the late nineties. Its sectoral emphasis on strengthening the R& D sector has equipped it to compete with the economically powerful nations of OECD. It has made large R&D investment in the economy accounting for approximately 3.5 per cent of GDP, which is the second highest in OECD and the third highest in the world, just after Sweden and Israel. Increasing R&D has helped the economy coupled with national industrial and innovation strategies. These national strategies were important for consensus building, for example, by organizing economic policy programmes. Specialization in high-tech and R&D intensive production needs to be preceded by major structural change in economic and social structures. Recent research seems to indicate that poor countries get richer with this sectoral specialization (Dahlman, Routti and Antilla 2005: 5-6).

One of the important sectors that saw considerable emphasis in trade was textiles and clothing (T&C). Since 1974 the T&C sector was governed by Multi-Fibre Agreement (MFA), which put import restrictions on T&C trade and functioned as an important barrier for developing countries like China which had established their global competitiveness in this sector. In January 2005 MFA was phased out and the quota restrictions were lifted. This allowed a country like China to accelerate its exports in the world.

Intra Industry Trade

The sectoral approach to trade before the Uruguay Round of negotiations was largely addressing issues relating to Intra-Industry Trade (IIT) and continues to do so. IIT refers to exchange of trade within same products over a period of time. The concept is generally applied to international trade as same kind of goods and services are exported and imported. Products such as agri-food, textiles, automobiles, and IT services form part of the IIT. The traditional model of trade was set out by the models of David Ricardo and the Heckscher-Ohlin (Findlay 1995: 46) which tried to explain the occurrence of international trade between countries. Both models used the idea of comparative advantage and an explanation of why countries trade. However, many economists have argued claiming that these models provide no explanation towards intra-industry trade, as under their assumptions countries with identical factor endowments would not trade and produce goods domestically. Hence, over the last two decades as intra-industry trade has developed, many economists like Paul Krugman and Maurice Obstfeld have looked at other explanations.

Horizontal and Vertical IIT

There are two kinds of IIT. One is horizontal and the other one is vertical. Horizontal IIT refers to trade in similar products but with different characteristics or attributes, while Vertical IIT involves trade in similar products of different qualities.

Recent studies on IIT have brought to light rapid increases in vertical IIT and horizontal IIT. Krugman (1979: 469) has demonstrated that horizontal IIT is influenced by scale economies and preference diversity, while Falvey (1981: 497) has shown that factor endowment determines vertical IIT. Moreover, Jones and Kierzkowski (1990) and Deardorff (2001a) showed that locational advantage with cost of service links determines either inter-industry trade or vertical IIT. Thus, IIT must be decomposed into horizontally and vertically differentiated products and analyzed separately.

In the past twenty years, a number of theoretical studies have analyzed country and industry specific influences on intra-industry trade. Two of the most common assumptions made in the theoretical models of horizontal IIT are that trade is associated with imperfectly competitive product markets and that the output of relevant industries consists of sufficiently differentiated products. Both assumptions have important implications for the analysis of the gains from trade and trade policy. Spence (1976), Dixit and Stiglitz (1977: 297-298) and Krugman (1979: 470) and Lancaster (1980: 152) present a number of models of horizontal IIT based on monopolistic competition markets (Fung 1991: 391-392). Empirical studies argued that horizontal IIT plays a particularly large role in trade in manufactured goods among advanced industrial nations.

Over time, industrial countries have become increasingly similar in their levels of technology and in the availability of capital and skilled labour. Since major trading nations have become similar in technology and resources, there is often no clear comparative advantage within an industry, and much of international trade therefore takes the form of intra-industry specialization, that is probably driven in large part by economies of scale and other reasons rather than inter-industry specialization driven by comparative advantage. Shaked and Sutton (1984) show the mechanism of vertical differentiation based on quality under imperfect competition (natural oligopoly). They point out that international trade takes the form of intra-industry specialization that is driven by economies of scale, which is likely to be of practical relevance to high technology industries where the main burden of quality improvement falls on fixed research and development (R&D) costs, so that unit variable costs rise only slowly with quality (Chang 2008: 5-6).

In another study it is observed that, IIT arises because consumers who have different incomes look for different quality products, and because in a given country, the range of produced qualities does not correspond precisely to the demanded range of qualities. The pattern of IIT trade reflects differences in technology and in income distribution. This is observed more when the developing countries export low-quality, low cost varieties, while the developed countries export high quality, high cost varieties. This pattern is observed in many industries for example in textiles, toys, etc., (Flam and Helpman 1987: 821). Elaboration of this concept is also highlighted by many experts like Balassa, Grubcl and Lloyd, where they observe product differentiation was seen as an important ingredient in its explanation (1975: 42). Following the contributions of Dixit and Stiglitz (1977: 298) and Lancaster (1980: 153), product differentiation has become explicitly modelled in formal analyses of IIT (Greenway *et al.* 1995: 1506).

Global competitiveness of a particular industry became the driving force behind adopting this sectoral approach. The key inputs for an industry based sectoral approach are broadly the price, technology, capital, complementary trade policies, and global demand and supply. Theoretically, current sectoral approach draws a lot from the global value chain. With this specific emphasis of developing product specialization and global competitiveness of sectors, many counties are adhering to sectoral approach to trade liberalization. Post-entry phase has witnessed a focused sectoral approach where more and more member countries are joining through formal regional integration or through specific bilateral relations. China has also embraced this approach for its regional as well as global integration.

Praxis of Interdependence and Sectoral Approach by China

China adopted interdependence and sectoral approach as two viable strategies to fully integrate with the world economy. As it underwent a major shift in its approach from a socialistic pattern of economy to a market based economy through policy of economic reforms and open door, it gave a signal to the world that it wanted to be a part of the global economic community. With this objective in mind, it began its efforts in 1978, pursued them through 1980s and 1990s by embracing these strategies.

Praxis of Interdependence

As the influence of Maoism began to erode by mid-1978, the significance of self-reliance declined rapidly. A new kind of approach emerged on the horizon whose thrust looked closer to the Western theory of development. Since 1978, China has actively pursued the policy of interdependence with the outside world. The new approach reduced the significance of self-reliance. Concepts like “international cooperation”, “mutual benefit”, “equal exchanges”, and “supplying to each other’s needs” (Friedrich W.Y. Wu 1981: 468) began to shape the thought process of the Chinese leaders in their pursuit of modernization. Post-Mao leadership and the Western theorists of interdependence began to realize that the practice of interdependence will not only help China to modernize itself domestically but also will create more benefits such as securing peace, prosperity and dignity for the world.

Emphasis was laid on pursuing active integration with the global community. Deng Xiaoping was convinced that stability and economic development could only be achieved if China actively participated in global economy. To further this objective, during the 1980s, China entered into agreements with various counties in the field of economic exchanges and cultural relations. He emphasized that, "China should concentrate on economic development" by adhering to the policy of opening up to the outside world for its modernization and economic prosperity. He propounded the idea that "the policy of reforms and opening up will not be waived for hundred years" (Deng 1993: 350-351). According to him, "both planning and market are ways of developing productivity" (Deng 1993: 351). This needs to be harnessed by fostering need-based economic and overall cordial relations with developed and developing countries. These ideas led to a positive approach towards interdependence in China.

Initial support to this doctrine of interdependence as a part of the dominant strategy for China's modernization is also amply demonstrated in Hua Guofeng's *Report on the Work of the Government* (June 18 1979 p. 11), which he addressed to the Second Session of the Fifth National People's Congress:

> Economic exchange between countries and the import of technology are indispensable, major means by which countries develop their economy and technology. It is all the more necessary for developing countries to import advanced technology...in order to catch up with those economically developed... We hold that the development of economic, technological, scientific and cultural exchanges and cooperation among various countries on the basis of equality and mutual benefit will help to promote their friendly relations and preserve peace.

Such remarks created deep impression in the minds of the ruling elites of the Chinese state. A close examination of China's economic policies such as inviting foreign direct investment (FDI), acquiring foreign technology and adopting Western ideas in early 1980s adequately signified that the PRC was slowly inching towards the strategy of interdependent development. Such a strategy provided the necessary ideological justification for a policy change.

For its own development China required foreign capital for which it had to depend on developed countries. Developed countries and financial institutions needed a big market like China to expand their business and engagement. So, both benefited mutually from the system, which established interdependence as a viable option for mutual modernization and development.

Foreign trade soon gained prominence. Instead of relegating foreign trade to a secondary operation in the national economy, the new leadership under the stewardship of Deng regarded foreign trade as a key element of China's modernization. Earlier sensitive policy of depending on the import of capital equipment, up-to-date scientific and managerial know-how and skilled manpower was no longer remained a hindrance. Since late 1970s, China's participation in the world economy shot into prominence. More than 85 per cent of its foreign trade took place with non-communist countries in 1979 and 1980, out of which, 65 per cent was with developed countries. Its trade with socialist countries accounted for less than 15 per cent of its total foreign trade.

Unleashing of economic reforms and opening up to the outside world that started in 1978 brought several gains by which China attained modernization and fostered its economic development. Unprecedented economic growth and its emergence as a key economic power further deepened its cause of interdependence in the world. Such rapid economic and social changes fructified because China followed a more flexible and accommodative approach to world economy. Moreover, China's consistent efforts to integrate itself with the world economic order were noticeable when it made efforts in 1979 and 1980 to join multilateral institutions like the World Bank, IMF, and others. These institutions were keen to provide financial and other support to China. In return, China made structural adjustments to suit their requirements.

One of the major turning points in China's interdependent approach came when China negotiated to join the WTO in 1986. 15 long years of negotiations provided enough justification to follow a tradition that would reflect a more open, legal, predictable atmosphere to interact and exchange. China engaged in a variety of tough negotiations finally conceding to significant concessions demanded by developed countries to get an entry into the WTO. All these significant changes and developments provided justification in revisiting the theoretical understanding of China's relation with the outside world. Its engagements with international community in political, economic, and social spheres do highlight some liberal tenets of interdependence theory.

While the Chinese leaders might have resisted such high pressures regarding reforming and bringing in more transparency to the Chinese economy, yet they were also interested in access to foreign markets to gain foreign exchange and buy foreign technology (Sutter 1996: 18). At the time of opening up to foreign investment, some sections of the Chinese society were opposed to the idea of receiving foreign capital from Western countries because they felt that these powers would intervene in the internal affairs of the policy making and ultimately promote their own interests at the cost of country's economic development. They held a long debate over the issue i.e., whether external dependence for China in some ways could not be much helpful. However, the dominant view in the state was in favour of receiving foreign capital. The liberals in the Chinese society argue that foreign investment is regarded as the catalyst and may be the best and quickest way to develop the Chinese economy and strengthen the country as a whole whereas the conservatives expressed that such a step would end up in more social disparity and domestic apathy (Yong 2000: 2).

According to Prof. Andong Zhu: "Interdependence was a big strategy for China to connect to the outside world. It could get market access to the EU and the US by adopting a strategy of interdependence. Industrialized countries could boost their exports to China. It was mutually advantageous to both the trading partners" (Zhu 2009: Personal Interview).

Praxis of interdependence continues to be a central element in China's post-entry phase. This approach has been intensified especially after China had joined the WTO in 2001. There is unanimity in the leadership that interdependence is an appropriate strategy to engage with the world. According to Prof. Yin Xiangshuo: "Interdependence will be a mode of strategy for China as growth of China will squarely depend upon its mutual relations with the world." In the post-entry era, China continues to improve its performance in many fields. It has emerged as the second largest exporter and third largest importer in the world. Its trade to GDP ratio has increased to 69 per cent during 2006-08 from 22 per cent in 1986 at the time of its application to the GATT membership (WTO Statistics Database). Its merchandise world trade has reached US$ 1.28 trillion in 2008-09. It has received FDI to the tune of US$ 70 billion in 2007 from US$ 40 billion in 2001 at the time of its accession to the WTO (World Investment Report 2008 UNCTAD).

Through Joint Ventures

Very early on, China realized joint venture (JV) to be a viable option for investment. Soon the government promulgated the law: "The Law of the PRC on joint ventures using Chinese and Foreign Investment" in July 1979 which was immediately adopted by the Second Session of the Fifth National People's Congress and came to be regarded as a path breaking step as it would propel foreign investors to come in big numbers to China (*Beijing Review*, July 20 1979: 24). The advantage in the formulation of such a law was that it had no upper limit in the share of foreign equity in the joint ventures. Since the promulgation of the law there have been several contacts, consultations, and negotiations made between foreign investors on the one side and the Chinese government on the other (*Beijing Review*, April 20 1981: 16).

Continuous influx of Western capital, technology along with technical know-how and managerial skills began to contribute to the modernization process in a significant manner. The Government's policy of attracting foreign investment provided impetus to setting up Special Economic Zones (SEZs). Guangdong became an attractive destination for such investment. Within a short span, about 600 contracts for "compensatory trade", "cooperative production" and "processing trade" with foreign businessmen were signed (*Beijing Review*, March 3 1980: 8). This new initiative of joint ventures in the history of China and other forms of economic cooperation between China and capitalist countries consolidated China's approach to the world economy. The new trade practices introduced by the post-Mao China since 1979 which are now justified as "flexible methods commonly used in international trade" (*Beijing Review*, July 27 1979: 14) are sometimes interpreted as sort of an open acknowledgement of China's willingness to join, in a limited sense, the capitalistic global market. However, the policy makers and economic planners took a different view of the entire development. They rather insisted that China should flexibly apply the laws of supply and demand and comparative advantage in international trade to accelerate its domestic modernization (Yuan *et al.* 1980: 43-44). It is further argued by many theorists that by participating in international trade, a country is able to benchmark its division of labour. An active participation in international division of labour, would allow China to save its labour and at the same time speed up the contribution of China's productive forces.

In the post-entry phase joint venture activities grew significantly. Since China's entry and the government's relaxation of investment regulations, foreign investors have been choosing to establish more wholly foreign owned enterprises (WFOEs), which in the first three quarters of 2004 made up nearly 67 per cent of the value of new foreign direct investment projects in China. Before the entry, most of the JVs were in the nature of equity based or contractual based JVs. During the same year the US had invested in several projects through JVs in China. There is continuity in the policies relating to JVs such as government approval process, approval authorities, format of agreements, tax breaks, legal standing, and the means, laws, and authorities for dispute resolution after the entry. The JVs continue to be a preferred medium of doing business in China.

Through FDI

The Chinese leaders had also recognized the significance of FDI in their drive towards modernization and economic prosperity. In the 1980s and 1990s when China opened out in major way to participate in world trade it visualized foreign capital as an effective instrument to secure its faster economic growth and successful transformation in relation to establishing 'social market economy with the Chinese characteristics'. The Chinese leaders felt that the foreign capital has the necessary wherewithal in terms of providing monetary value, the required technology and the management practices, production techniques and a sense of heightened competition essential for achieving higher economic growth. It is this necessity, which prompted China to consider that foreign capital is much needed and important for speedy modernization as well as for it to gain access and increase share in world trade.

With the establishment of SEZs, China could invite large amount of FDI for its economic development and secures access to international trade. This happened at a time when major shift in the trade flows to developing countries was taking place. During the 1980s developing countries received about US$ 15 billion, about one third of the total world trade flows. In the 1990s developing countries' share continued to rise, though developed countries were still receiving more (Li and Li 1999: 32).

The contribution of overseas Chinese played a significant role in inflows of FDI into China. Most of the foreign capital, which flowed into China, came from the overseas Chinese. In 1987, 70 per cent of FDI came from Hong Kong, Macao, Taiwan, Malaysia, and Singapore. This share, however, declined over the years to 67 per cent in 1996 and 54 per cent in 1997. By 1995, it was also found that Hong Kong investors owned 96 per cent of Shenzhen's textile industry and 95 per cent of its garments industry. This indicates that the foreign inflows to China from these countries were considerably controlled by the overseas Chinese (Kanungo 2007: 13).

Since 1993 China has been the biggest recipient of FDI in the developing world. To maximize FDI's benefits in economic development, the Chinese government had employed a variety of favourable measures like providing tax benefits to foreign investors, creating an enabling environment, providing a legal based transparent regime, removing most of the restrictions on foreign investments, and finally allowing Foreign Invested Enterprises (FIEs) to increase their export volumes. These policies proved beneficial for these FIEs, which came in large numbers to invest in China. As a result, wholly foreign owned enterprises (WFOEs) replaced joint ventures as the most popular form of FDI in China. The FIEs have become major players in China's industrial restructuring. Their relatively large contribution to domestic investment and to manufacturing output, their higher capital intensity and labour productivity compared to domestic firms, indicate potentially strong effects on China's industrial structure and efficiency. While contributing decisively to China's export performance, the FIE production is also geared towards more domestic consumption. China's share in international trade has trebled, rising from less than 1 per cent in 1980 to more than 3 per cent in 1999. China has become the second largest recipient of FDI, after the US, with cumulated inflows amounting to more than US$ 300 billion at the end of 1999. By 2001 at the time of its entry into the WTO, China had accumulated about US$ 450 billion (China Statistical Yearbook 2003). It continued to register increasing amount of FDI surpassing most of the countries in the world. In 2008 it had accumulated FDI to the tune of US$ 899 billion.[6]

The post-entry phase changed the map of FDI in China. Most of the investors felt confident as China's investment regime became rule-based, transparent, legally-binding, and predictable. China emerged as a favourable destination for FDI. Multinational enterprises (MNEs) across the world continued to pour in to organize their production activities in accordance with their corporate strategies and competitive advantages of the host country. Through this process, the MNEs secured market access to China and could multiply their exports by using China as a globally competitive base. For example, the MNEs from Japan are willing to move their production bases to China to remain competitive in the face of rising wages and an appreciating Japanese yen. They also supplemented their business activities by increasing their production for domestic consumption. Source countries that enjoyed this advantage are mostly drawn from East Asia such as Hong Kong, Taiwan, Japan, South Korea, and also include industrialized countries like the US, the EU and Canada. These activities flourished in China due to emphasis on the efficacy of interdependence.

In 2001, at the time of China's entry into the WTO, Hong Kong was the biggest foreign investor totaling about US$ 205 billion followed by the US amounting to US$ 40 billion. Japan and Taiwan were at the third and fourth places respectively (Ministry of Commerce China 2003: 131). Asian investors continued to lead investment in 2004 and 2005 with the US coming in at fifth position (UNCTAD World Investment Report 2006). FDI continues to be a key input in China's integration with the world economy. During the 1990s and till 2004 China continued to experience maximum inflows of FDI into its traditional manufacturing sectors like textiles, toys, leather products, etc. However, the trend has changed towards technologically intensive sectors like equipment manufacturing, electrical machinery, telecom, high-tech mobile industry, and entertainment. After joining the WTO in 2001, the government's decision to permit China to be adequately used by multinational corporations as an export platform has made the country a major competitor for other Asian export-led economies such as South Korea, Singapore and Malaysia.

Through Exports and Imports

In the last two decades China has accomplished rapid economical growth based on trade expansion. The Chinese export sector has averaged over 35 per cent of the total production output of every year since mid-1980s (Moore 2002: 2). The FDI has been instrumental in such significant export growth. Trade has enabled the inflow of foreign technology, know-how, and has, in addition, built up capital for development of production and infrastructure. In recent years China has increased not only its export of labour intensive goods like textiles, toys or leather products but also increased its production of technology-intensive products such as electrical machinery equipment, computer hardware, telecom products, etc. (Fukao *et al.* 2003: 3). According to OECD statistics, products categorized as electronic machinery equipment have experienced the highest export growth in China during 1992-2003. China's exports to the world have witnessed a continuous rise, registering US$ 1.4 billion in 1995 while they touched the US$ 2.6 billion mark in 2001 at the time of its entry into the WTO (World Trade Atlas Online Database, 2009).

Since the opening up of the Chinese economy in 1978, China's exports have gone up rapidly. From 1978 to 2005, exports have increased more than ten-fold (Swedish Institute of International Affairs, 2005) and since 1996 China has contributed one quarter of the global growth in international trade. It is currently one of the largest trading nations after the US, Germany, Japan, and France. Since the early 1980s the Chinese authorities have used a *dualistic trading regime* combining export promotion together with relatively strong import protective measures. Import protection normally hurts the export sector by raising cost of capital and imported intermediate inputs required for production. Thus in order to neutralize this effect, export-orientated industries have been subject to tariff exemptions on imports. Since the mid-1990s, however, the level of protection has been progressively lowered (Lemoine 2000: 9). China's entry into the WTO has heralded a new beginning and also amply demonstrates its desire to continue the drive towards trade liberalization. However, with a much more open economy, foreign competition for the Chinese products has increased and will intensify more in the future. According to Lemoine (2000: 55), China follows the classical theory of comparative advantage. It is argued that 75 per cent of China's exports come from sectors where it has a comparative advantage like textiles, toys, minerals, etc. This ratio has, however, progressively diminished since the 1990s because of high demand in technology intensive products. Lemoine (2000: 55) found that China has a comparative weakness in sectors that are capital and technologically intensive (machinery, engines, etc). Trade patterns, however, show that it is in these sectors that exports are growing most rapidly lately, particularly since 2004-05 (World Trade Online Database, 2008).

Empirical findings also show that FDI plays an important role in China's export sector. A survey by Organization for Economic Co-operation and Development (OECD 2005c) indicates that, foreign investors dominate the export sector accounting for over half of all overseas trade (Moules: 2005). International division of value added production chains is getting more and more common as international companies are searching for cost reduction and economy of scale in production. Intermediate goods account for an increasing part of international trade as countries specialize in segments of production in which they have a comparative advantage. This is especially true for China since it has been recognized as one of the cheapest locations for production and has developed a specialization in labour intensive stages of production. The share of processing products in the total volume of trade has increased faster than overall trade since 1980. Currently a large segment of China's manufacturing industry is internationalized with respect to their capital, supplies, and outlets.

Similarly its imports had also significantly gone up during 1995-2005. China's total imports from the world were to the tune of US$ 1.3 billion in 1995, which went up to US$ 2.4 billion in 2001 (World Trade Atlas Online Database 2008). Imports have played a key role in China's domestic production, technology upgradation and export promotion drive. Raw material and intermediate products have been often necessary inputs into processes that yield finished goods, which can then be sold outside to promote China's exports. Segmenting total imports in 2001, importation of primary goods amounted to the US$ 45.74 million, or 18.78 per cent of total imports and importation of manufactured goods were to the tune of US$ 197.81 billion or 81.22 per cent of total imports. By 2005, importation of primary goods had increased by 222.91 per cent to register US$ 147.71 billion, representing 22.38 per cent of 2005 total imports, whereas importation of manufactured goods had increased 158.96 per cent to reach US$ 512.24 billion, representing 77.62 per cent of 2005 total imports (National Bureau of Statistics of China, 2006). This trend continued till 2008. Since the beginning of 2009 the total value of foreign trade has declined. The customs statistics also show that the total value of foreign trade reaches US$ 124.95 billion in February, down 24.9 per cent. Among them, the exports were to the tune of US$ 64.9 billion, down 25.7 per cent, while the imports were US$ 60.05 billion, down 24.1 per cent (General Administration of Customs, China: 2009).

Imports of primary goods in 2005 were more in demand than the manufactured goods, which suggests that production in China is becoming increasingly important relative to the Chinese consumption, though both are growing considerably, given the use of many primary goods as major inputs to produce finished products for exporting. China's major importers are Japan, Taiwan, Hong Kong, Korea, Thailand, and the US. It's a growing trend that China is importing more from its neighbouring countries. The WTO accession has encouraged China to import many of its "metals and petrochemicals from Korea; electronics from Singapore; light manufactures, petrochemicals, machinery, equipment, and electronics from Taiwan; and metals, petrochemicals and other manufactures from Japan" (Guoxing 2009: Personal Interview). Following the accession, newly-industrializing economies were well poised to provide China with its growing demand for services in transportation and communications, while the already-established Hong Kong was well prepared to provide a host of financial services.

The revised Foreign Trade Law, issued in April 2004, provides for trading rights to be granted automatically through a registration process for all domestic and foreign enterprises and individuals. After pressure from the US, tariff-rate quotas (TRQs) on protected agricultural products were expanded in line with the WTO obligations. To promote foreign trade China has undertaken a huge programme of aligning national technical standards with international standards. As a result in 2005 about 1,416 national standards had been abolished. The post-WTO phase continues to witness liberal foreign trade policy which has led its trade to GDP ratio to increase to 69 per cent in 2006-08 from 22 per cent in 1986, at the time of its application to the GATT (Statistics Database WTO). Its merchandise world trade reached US$ 1.28 trillion in 2008-09.

Through Multilateral Institutions

China has been an active participant in multilateral economic arrangements. It is establishing its trade cooperation at bilateral, regional, and multilateral levels. In the 1980s, it had taken the initiative to join the Pacific Economic Cooperation Council (PECC) and finally joined it in 1986. It remained committed to promoting economic cooperation and interaction, collaboration on various matters of common interest in a range of fields and jointly develop resources "so as to realize the economic potential of the Pacific Basin and make it a prosperous, progressive and peaceful region"(Klintworth 1995: 489). China's commitment to multilateralism was further heightened when it became a participant in the Asia Pacific Economic Cooperation (APEC) process in 1989-1990. It was convinced that the APEC is a forum, which will provide opportunities to countries in the Asia-Pacific region and can challenge the hegemony of the US. The Chinese government remained committed to opposing protectionism and supporting free trade and investment. China believed that multilateralism is a medium that promotes spirit of interdependence (Wang 2000: 481).

China's participation in multilateral fora and support for free trade and investment has come a long way from the time that China viewed multilateral organizations as instruments of perpetration of imperialism and out rightly rejected those ideas or be a party to them. It had even adopted interdependent approach to economic prosperity much before it initiated its process of accession to the WTO. For instance, its close economic and trade relationship with Hong Kong is a clear example of this strategy. "Hong Kong is a window for China. China benefited by fostering close alliance with Hong Kong and Hong Kong's entrepreneurship and business and industrial houses invested in China for their business expansion and profit making," says Prof. Lok Sang Ho (Ho 2009: Personal Interview). Prof. Hong Song said: "Hong Kong played a key role in China's economic development. China would not have developed without the assistance of Hong Kong. So China had followed interdependent approach much before for its economic development." (Song 2009: Personal Interview).

Countries from the Southeast Asia and other parts of the world identified China as a market of billion people with rising income. China experienced its market reforms producing favourable external results like raising its export growth. Such interdependence suited both sides (Guoxing 2009: Personal Interview). The ASEAN, Australia and New Zealand had also taken deep interest in forging regional cooperation with China to benefit from the world economy (Song 2009: Personal Interview).

In the post-entry phase towards end of 2006, China had signed Comprehensive Economic Partnership Arrangement (CEPA) and, free trade agreements (FTAs) with Hong Kong, Macau and, the ASEAN, Chile, and Pakistan respectively. It signed FTA with New Zealand in 2008; negotiations with Australia, the Gulf Cooperation Council, and southern countries of Africa are still in progress. Prominent among the FTAs that China has signed with different countries is The China-ASEAN FTA. The Framework Agreement on Comprehensive Economic Cooperation, signed in November 2002, provided for the establishment of a China-ASEAN Free Trade Area (CAFTA) for goods trade by 2010 for the older ASEAN members, including Brunei, Indonesia, Malaysia, the Philippines, Singapore and Thailand; and by 2015 for the newer ASEAN member states such as Vietnam, Laos, Cambodia, and Myanmar. The Early Harvest Program, implemented on 1 January 2004, specifies that China and all older member countries of the ASEAN should phase out and eliminate mutual import tariffs on almost all agricultural goods by 2010.

The enforcement of the Agreement on Trade in Goods of July 2005 signals the operational phase of the Free Trade Agreement. The China-ASEAN Free Trade Area is one of the largest free trade areas in terms of population, gross economic output and trade volume. By the end of 2005, the GDP of CAFTA reached US$ 2971.1 billion, and the total value of imports and exports reached US$ 1394.8 billion. The development and maturation of this free trade area will have significant impact on the Chinese and the ASEAN economies as well as far-reaching implications for the economy and trade structure of the whole world (Huanguang Qiu *et al.* 2007: 78). Countries are entering into regional agreements with China with the expectation that they would gain adequate market access to a large country to trade in a variety of products. These countries through regional agreements would exploit each other's strengths to maximize gains.

Praxis of Sectoral Approach

The sectoral approach became an integral process of China's trade liberalization. The ambition has clearly been to catch up with advanced industrialized countries rapidly. China's entry into the WTO was also crucially dependent on how fast China aligns its various sectors of the economy to multilateral conformity. The emphasis on a sectoral approach to the Chinese economy gained momentum in the 1980s. With the failure of planned economy and onset of globalization, the need to integrate with world economy through market mechanism became a primary concern. Accession to the WTO pushed China to consider sectoral approach as a strategy to align with the global economy. Policy prescriptions of Bretton Woods Institutions and acceleration of globalization gave more thrust to this approach.

It is a known factor that every country cannot produce all types of goods and provide all services in abundance, but can specialize in certain products and develop comparative advantage to benefit from world trade; China realized this in great measure. It accorded priority to this strategy. Sectors like electrical machinery, office equipment, hardware, textiles, toys, banking, telecom, etc., were given adequate boost by the Central and provincial governments in terms of liberalizing policies such as easy access to foreign capital, favourable taxation policies, a conducive legal regime and favourable labour laws, etc (Ho 2009: Personal Interview).

Sectoral trade has high potentiality in the current world trade as countries are following liberalization in a selective manner in specific sectors such as telecom, office equipment, finance, textiles, and electronics goods. Three key sectors of the Chinese economy namely agriculture, manufacturing, and services adopted this strategy.

Agriculture

Agriculture has traditionally been the mainstay of the Chinese economy, food security, and livelihood. Over the last twenty-five years, China's agriculture has been transformed from a tightly controlled, centralized system of commune-based farming into a household based system. This approach was driven and encouraged by markets rather than by government's planning and targets. In response to this change, the 1980s witnessed surge in agricultural output, increase in rural incomes, and substantial improvement in market integration. Production, distribution, and marketing of crops and livestock products remained free from significant government intervention. Agriculture was also seen as an important vehicle for foreign exchange earnings through exports. This role began to lose its importance when industrial exports supplanted agriculture as the key foreign exchange earner.

Towards the mid-1990s its contribution to GDP substantially declined. It largely remained as an employer for a vast rural population. From a share of 30 per cent to its GDP at the beginning of reforms in 1980, its share came down to 16 per cent at the time of its entry into the WTO. In 2007 its share got further reduced to 11 per cent. Similarly its declining role in international trade was also striking. Its share in total exports was 50 per cent in 1980, which fell to 10 per cent during its accession to the WTO (China Statistical Yearbook, various issues). This declining importance of agriculture has been caused among other reasons due to explosion in population growth, unavailability of cheap loans to farmers, lack of modern technology to raise productivity, and limited land resources. Such drawbacks shifted China's comparative advantage from land intensive economic activities like agriculture to labour intensive manufacturing and industrial activities like textiles, toys, electrical equipments, leather products, etc.

However, accession to the WTO demanded further liberalization in agriculture. Sectoral accession commitments to agriculture began with the reduction in tariff rate. China reduced its tariff from 40 per cent in 1995 to around 15.8 per cent at the time of its entry into the WTO. Currently it is 9.8 per cent. It promised to reduce it further by the end of 2010. While reducing its tariff for imports it took measures to protect its own agricultural products and domestic market by resorting to mechanism of tariff-rate quotas. It implemented tariff-rate quotas for the key commodities like wheat, rice, corn, vegetable oil, and wool. China's other commitments were also significant and far-reaching. It agreed to provide non-discriminatory treatment to all the WTO members on farm products. China eliminated dual pricing practices and pitched for early removal of price controls. Developed countries were keen to see China undertaking trade liberalization early so that primary sector is liberalized initially to provide them huge advantage to export their farm products to a big market like China. It succumbed to that pressure and undertook commitments to remove export subsidies on agriculture. China made compromises with the privileged position of State-Owned Enterprises (SOEs) and increased the scope of private traders in the marketing of agricultural products. It removed a significant number of non-tariff barriers. It bound all tariffs to provide a predictable trade in agriculture.

However, its post-entry phase has witnessed a marked change to its approach to agriculture. It has taken up the issue on global front by demonstrating significant activism in agricultural negotiations in the Doha Round. It has fought for the issue of agriculture sectorally in many important fora demanding elimination in agricultural trade distortions. Distortions caused by domestic support and export subsidy provided by developed countries are making the Chinese agricultural products globally uncompetitive. As a result, China is unable to secure a fair share in global agricultural trade, which is contrary to the expectations of joining the WTO. It pursues with other developed countries to remove barriers for its growing labour-intensive agricultural exports. It has an interest in banning developed countries' export subsidies and significantly reducing their trade-distorting domestic subsidies. Hence, it joined the G-20, led by India and Brazil and continues to support the G-20 at the WTO negotiations. During the last eight years of Doha negotiations China has been able to influence the key negotiators like the US and the EU that the fulcrum of negotiations should be evenly balanced to benefit both the developed and developing countries.

Manufacturing

China's manufacturing sector has undergone a rapid process of growth and transformation since the reform process and Open Door Policy started in 1978. Industry has remained at the core of its modernization programme. The government has taken keen interest in mobilizing resources to spur the industrial growth in the country. The industry has registered a high growth of 11. 8 per cent between 1979 and 2000 compared to an average GDP growth rate of 9.6 per cent during the same period. Till 2007 China's economy grew at 11.4 per cent, but towards end of the 2008 it had declined to about 9 per cent and continued to further decline in the context of global financial crisis (Statistical Yearbook of China: 2009).

China's manufacturing sector has emerged as a major production hub for multinational corporations and became an attractive destination for FDI. Continuous rise in industrial growth had strengthened China's belief to join the WTO. Thus China's WTO entry became a watershed for industrial reforms. The WTO accession demanded immediate need for certain adjustments such as removal of protection from inefficient industries, establishment of market discipline, better access to latest technology, and insistence on developing a legal and regulatory framework necessary to monitor foreign investment and establish a well functioning market economy.

To remain in conformity with the accession process, China implemented series of measures to liberalize the manufacturing sector. It brought down its tariff reductions on industrial products to below 10 per cent level. It removed a number of non-tariff barriers (NTBs) like licensing, quotas, and tendering requirements. It phased out other restrictive policies like state control and bureaucratic procedures to speed up the acceleration process of industrialization. It created an enabling atmosphere for the foreign investors to feel confident and safe about their investment in the country. Industrial policies were also focused on shifting natural resources from agriculture towards manufacturing. With this change in policy during the 1980s, Township and Village Enterprises (TVEs) became the driving force behind industrialization and played a major role in the promotion of light industries. They became the backbone of labour intensive industries like textiles and apparels, toys, footwear, etc.

These reforms transformed the industrial sector from almost complete reliance on state-owned enterprises (SOEs) to one where non-state small and medium-sized enterprises played a crucial role. The rise in non-state enterprises has occurred due to removal of entry barriers to industries that have been long monopolized by the government protected SOEs. As competition got intensified in the market, numbers of TVEs were also increased. The composition of industrial sector has also slowly changed with the rise in income and growing demand towards other products like consumer durables, lifestyle products, fashionable apparel products, leather, beverages, etc. Domestic demand for electronics and telecommunication products has gone up, creating a market for highly technology intensive industry to flourish. As a result of this transformation, China has developed a highly diversified industrial structure encompassing a wide range of industries from light labour industries to technology intensive industries to capital-intensive industries like steel, petroleum processing and automobiles.

On the manufacturing front, China has been quite active after its entry into the WTO. In the on-going non-agricultural market access (NAMA) negotiations at the WTO (manufacturing sector), China's interests are manifestly aggressive. It wants greater access for its manufactured exports in both developed and developing countries. It has been able to attract large amount of FDI by providing a secured atmosphere to investors and has been able to innovate and upgrade its products for exports. It has introduced new management systems to help increase productivity and emphasised on raising personal income and consumption so that its manufacturing sector is also given a push for domestic growth.

Services

In the field of services, China followed a sectoral liberalization policy. Major service sectors like telecommunications, banking, and insurance were opened up to outside competition in a phased manner. In telecommunications at the time of accession, a number of operators were present in the Chinese market reflecting a regulatory structure inherited from prior reforms in 1999. The most significant entity in the sector was China Telecom (CT), originally part of the Ministry of Posts and Telecommunications and established as a separate entity in 2000. The CT controlled about 99 per cent of China's main fixed line phone capacity. China Unicom, the major mobile phone operator established in 1994 was ranked second in the competition. With reforms and liberalization of the sector, a series of enterprises with regulatory approval came to operate in various telecom markets. These include a satellite operator ChinaSat, a broadband IP network developer China Netcom, China Telecommunications Broadcast Satellite Corporation, Jitong, and China Railways Communications. Till 2004, the two large state-owned providers (China Telecom, and China Unicom) dominated the market.

The main commitments stemming from China's WTO accession involved partial removal of limits on market access (especially the right to establish) and the removal of limits on national treatment. Foreign investments were allowed in the sector, but initially with geographical restrictions, and with limits placed on the ownership level. China promised to remove geographical restrictions and raised the foreign ownership limit to 49 per cent for most services in two years, i.e., by 2004, and for value added services like mobile telephones in five years, and for international services in six years. China opened up its service sectors sector-wise. It lifted all restrictions in a time frame of 5 to 6 years after its entry into the WTO. Sectors like banking, insurance, legal and telecommunications were carefully monitored and followed a process of gradual liberalization.

Sectoral approach found a deeper meaning when China initiated its current services negotiations through a positive list approach in the WTO. It is currently following such an approach in various WTO negotiations. This positive list includes telecom, finance, real estate, tourism, etc. As part of the WTO accession, China has also signed the WTO Telecommunications Agreement, which provides free entry to foreign service providers in its market by 2007. This placed China on par with OECD economies where, in recent years, foreign providers frequently and freely access foreign markets and large rate reductions have occurred.

China's post-entry scenario in services is still protected. Services barriers have come down more slowly than goods barriers, and perhaps more slowly than expected, after the WTO accession. High and discriminatory capital requirements discourage entry for foreign services providers in sectors like telecommunications, insurance, and construction (though capital thresholds have been reduced in banking). Licensing procedures have become more transparent and regular, but problems persist, especially in telecommunications, financial services, and express-delivery services. Equity and operating restrictions are prevalent in insurance, securities and telecom. Telecommunications is dominated by three SOEs, all having close links to the Ministry of Information Industry. No joint venture involving a foreign-invested enterprise has been licensed since the WTO accession. The government promotes domestic services sectors through foreign-investment restrictions in telecommunications services. However, as part of the commitments, the Government will be compelled to remove protection in services in due course. In practice, China remains more protected in services than it is in goods trade.

Summary

China's membership in the WTO marked a major step towards its integration with the world economy. It secured its rights over the economic and trade opportunities those were earlier enjoyed by other member countries. WTO members equally found access to China's market with a sense of security as China had to operate in a rule-based multilateral trading system.

China's adaptation to interdependence was visualized as a strategy to attain its immediate national goal of modernization and catch up with the rest of the world. Its integration with the world economy was done in a gradual manner. Foreign trade played a key role in opening up its economy to the world. Its comparative advantage in manufacturing sector helped it to occupy a unique position in world economy, where other countries were deeply attracted to maximize their trade gains by enjoying economy of scale, favourable environment for FDI and size of the market. China became the world's manufacturing hub. Similarly, sectoral approach became an integral part of China's overall strategy to join the international trading community. Three key sectors, viz., agriculture, manufacturing, and services experienced structural adjustments and institutional changes. As the role of agriculture witnessed a gradual decline towards mid-1990s, policy focus had shifted towards manufacturing. Comparative advantage in manufacturing was given a boost by diverting national resources, technology, skills, and management practices. Concerns shown by the government during this period were also noticed when they created an enabling environment for inflows of FDI, production, tax regime and treatment towards MNEs. The services sector slowly gathered momentum. China followed a cautious approach to liberalization of services sector. Barring agriculture, manufacturing and services have noticed upgradation in many respects. Technology, labour productivity, capital flow, and incomes have advanced much more rapidly in industry and to a lesser degree in services than in agriculture.

A significant aspect of China's integration with the world economy has been its informal and formal integration between pre and post-entry phase. During pre-entry phase China followed policies which had some semblance of liberalization and opening up without any multilateral rule based system attached to them. It designed policies to attract FDI, invite MNCs and make China a manufacturing hub. During this period it lacked a well regulated legal regime, which had become a major constraint for the foreign investors to operate in China. The primary liberalization thrust, especially in the 1990s, was in the domestic economy and unilateral in nature which was well steered by the Chinese leadership. The Central leadership used the WTO-accession negotiations as a strategic lever to consolidate and accelerate national reforms. In the post-entry phase, China became more rule-bound. With this discussion on China's entry into the WTO focusing on interdependence and sectoral approach, the next chapter explains China's process of accession to the WTO. It delineates the structural adjustments and institutional reforms that China undertook to accede to the WTO.

Notes

1. A policy aimed at improving relations with East Germany, Poland and the Soviet Union
2. Several scholars of the seventeenth-century held the view that, the disruptions in trade relations were a possible justification for entering into a conflict with a neighbouring country. See Irwin 1996, pp. 22-23.
3. Regarding the military force, Keohane and Nye have explained that military force is not used by governments toward other governments within the region or on the issues when complex interdependence prevails. It may, however, be important in these governments' relations with governments outside that region, or on other issues. Military force could, for instance, be irrelevant to resolving disagreements on economic issues among members of an alliance, yet at the same time be very important for that alliance's political and military relations with a rival bloc. (Keohane & Nye1989: 25 and 255).
4. This turbulent globalization is explained by Rosenau in his book *Turbulence in World Politics*. According to him "the turbulent model" has created the boundaries between domestic and foreign affairs nontransparent and porous.
5. Conference of the Parties, an annual UNFCCCC meeting held to discuss and negotiate further progress under the Kyoto Protocol
6. See MOFCOM 2010: www.fdi.gov.cn/pub/FDI. Accessed on 14 September 2010.

3

China in the WTO

Process of Accession

This chapter analyzes the process of China's accession to the WTO in detail. First, it points out the barriers that China had to face to join the WTO. Secondly, it takes into account the commitments and changes that it had to make to get an entry and carry them out further in joining the WTO. The chapter endeavours to answer questions such as what more China did than other developing countries to accede to the WTO (did the terms of agreement prove to be more costly for China vis-à-vis other developing countries?). Thirdly, it depicts how China domestically prepared itself for the accession. It describes the internal decision making process besides detailing the agreements and disagreements over the critical issues that led to the signing of bilateral agreements with the major trading partners like the US, EU, Canada and other countries, as these were mandatory for its accession. Lastly, it provides a summary assessing the significance and difficulties that it had to face to accede to the WTO.

Barriers China Faced to Enter the WTO

China faced number of trade barriers while trying to join the WTO. Tariff reduction constituted an important facet of such trade obstacles. Bringing it down to a single digit level in sensitive sectors like agriculture and Non-Agricultural Market Access (NAMA) was a great challenge. During the negotiations industrialized countries had asked for substantial tariff reduction in these sectors while protecting their own sectors through agricultural and export subsidies. Tariff barriers were raised essentially to provide protectionist measures to different sectors of the Chinese economy. China before negotiating for entry into the WTO had maintained a high tariff wall in agriculture knowing fully well that it is heavily dependent on agriculture. Similarly non-tariff barriers (NTBs) are imposed by importing countries to curtail significant export drive of the exporting countries to protect their own sectors. China had faced number of NTBs while trying to enter the WTO.

According to Nicholas Lardy (1994:110), China, in some respects, is one of the more open economies in Asia: "Its economy is more open than that of other East Asian economies at comparable stages of economic development and in certain respects is even more open than they are now." What, then, are the main barriers or obstacles for China's accession to the world trading system? Many differences cropped up between China's position and the demands made by the US. Firstly, it wanted a gradual adjustment whereas the US wanted a rapid change. In relation to gradual vs. rapid change dynamics, it was the tariff reduction that held the centre stage of negotiations. In the area of tariff reduction, China has reduced its average tariff rate from 47.2 per cent to 21.5 per cent in less than six years; but it was still high compared to other developing countries in the WTO. China has indicated a willingness to cut its average tariff rate to 15 per cent in three years for industrial products and six years for agricultural products; but the US wanted a 7 per cent tariff rate as a precondition to accession, and the EU wanted an 8 per cent rate. With regard to the trading license system, China had offered to phase out the then existing trading license system in five years, but the US tried to push it for two to three years. The US and the EU countries had demanded that import licensing system must be sufficiently liberalized early. The existing export and import policies have been liberalized in China. In addition, the OECD countries wanted China to open up its distribution sector within a few years but China did not want it till 2020. Finally, with regard to discriminatory industrial policies, China initially refused but later on accepted to treat them at par, which is otherwise known as *national treatment* in the WTO's parlance. The US, the EU and Japan wanted China to change these policies upon accession, but China however, subsequently implemented these conditions in the assumption that it would get an early entry.

Secondly, the US and other developed countries wanted to have special safeguard options to protect their own industries against future import surges from China, but it did not however, initially accept these conditions. Industrialized countries were aware that it had comparative advantage in the world market in many manufacturing products, especially in the area of low technology sectors like textiles, toys, footwear etc. Developed countries wanted to protect their industries against China's surge in imports; hence they wanted to impose safeguard measures. As a condition of accepting China into the WTO, the EU wanted to have the right to impose "safeguard" tariffs or quotas on China's exports. China objected to this as a violation of the MFN principle, which is fundamental to the functioning of the WTO. It understood that as a precondition, the safeguard option would undermine the objective of its accession. China would be easily discriminated against even as a member of the WTO. It eventually had to agree to such demands of the developed countries.

Thirdly, China was keen to maintain protective measures for its "infant industries" as a developing country but the US did not agree to grant the full range of protective measures to China as it did to other developing countries. During the process of negotiations, it insisted joining the WTO on *developing-country status*, but the US wanted China to enter the system as a developed country. As a developing country, China can take longer time to liberalize international trade and have more time to protect its "infant" industries. By the World Bank's definition, China is a developing country but the US, however, argues that China is an "export powerhouse" (Chong: 1995) and it is so big and significant in the world market that it cannot be treated as a regular developing country. In short, the US wanted China to liberalize trade and foreign investment before it became a member of the WTO. The US and other OECD countries pointed out that China was still not a market economy.

However, a full market economy was not a necessary precondition for accession into the GATT/WTO. When Poland joined the GATT in 1967, it was a centrally planned economy. Poland undertook no tariff reductions, but pledged to increase imports from the Western market economies by 7 per cent per year. When Hungary entered the GATT in 1973, its tariff rate was 32 per cent and it promised to reduce it to 21 per cent. Compared to these countries, China is a far more open and decentralized market economy, in terms of importing goods and attracting investment from developed countries. Its imports from the world market grew at almost a 17 per cent annual rate. Its average tariff rate was already reduced to 21.5 per cent in 1999 which further came down to less than 10 per cent in 2007. More importantly, it has been carrying out a market-oriented reform for more than two decades. It has also announced that it was slowly giving up its central planning in favour of a market economy with the Chinese characteristics. According to the Chinese negotiators, the WTO demands were much greater than they were in the late 1980s when China's economy was much less open and free. As Lardy (1994) has pointed out: "It is time to recognize that the US has already demanded and received more from China in terms of economic reforms than was demanded of other comparatively developed countries when they entered the GATT." Regarding the *developing-versus developed-country argument*, it is true that China is a large exporting country but it should not be penalized for its good performance. The GATT's definition of a "developing country" (or less-developed country) is based on standards of living, not on export performance. Therefore, the US interpretation of China's case is untenable. It is clear that China has experienced a much more complicated entry process into the GATT/WTO than many other countries. Now, the question is, why did the US and other WTO member countries push so hard and demand so much? There are both economic and political reasons. Economically, China was growing at a rapid pace and becoming increasingly important in the Asia and Southeast Asian region. Politically, it is too independent and is still led by a Communist Party. From an economic point of view, the recent growth in China's economy and the rapid increase in exports have made developed countries feel jittery about the future challenge from China. The earlier situation of the US in the early 1980s having trade deficit with Japan in a way haunted the leaders of America and the US felt that with the current exports of China to the US, China might become another Japan. To prevent such a scenario from emerging, the US wanted to access the Chinese market before this concern became a reality.

A World Bank study pointed out that under the Uruguay Round of trade liberalization, China's exports to the US, the EU and Japan would increase by 40 per cent (World Bank: 1993). Many WTO member countries believed that China would receive large benefits by joining the WTO. This belief gives a strong incentive to the US and other countries to use this opportunity to demand more from China. Politically, the US and other developed countries wanted to ensure that China's market-oriented economic reforms continue. After the collapse of the former Soviet Union, China remained a powerful country in Asia. In order to have their sphere of influence in China, the US and some other OECD countries were interested in China joining the WTO. This would increase their market access to China and shape its trade structure. Besides, as a developing country and a former planned economy, China had a large number of inefficient industrial sectors. To avoid sudden social and political change, it had adopted a gradual approach in its economic reforms. The Chinese government too realized the cost of slow reform in its state-owned enterprises (SOEs), but social stability too remained a top priority for the then political regime under the leadership of Deng and Jiang Zemin.

Process of Accession

China has been more than keen to join the multilateral trading system; first the GATT and then the WTO. This is evident from the fact when China had initially become a founding member of the GATT in 1945. However, after the Chinese revolution in 1949, the then KMT government was defeated and was driven out by the communists from the mainland. It had left for Taiwan where it established its regime as the Republic of China (ROC) and had then announced its withdrawal from GATT in 1950. Since the establishment of People's Republic of China (PRC) in 1949, China remained engaged in its nation building by resorting to indigenous planning and acquiring support from the former Soviet Union. With the Sino-Soviet rift in the 1950s, China's relationship with the former Soviet Union turned sour and China distanced itself from her. It remained a closed society having limited interaction with the outside world. Only around the mid-1980s when it became economically stable and strong, it wanted to integrate itself with the world economy. It was convinced that integration with world economy is a necessary condition to remain economically powerful. Such considerations enhanced the urgency for joining the world trading system governed under the WTO. China's leadership came to view membership in the WTO as central to the country's economic future.

China's application to join the GATT was a positive step and is now moving in the right direction (Zhu 2009: Personal Interview). It is also the continuity of reforms, which projected China as moving closer to capitalism. This dimension interested particularly the US and other developed countries to look favourably towards China as a potential partner in the global trading regime (Yong 2002: 20). It was also felt that the practice under which every year China had to negotiate with the US for renewal of Normal Trade Relation (NTR) had created too much irritation in the Sino-US trade relationship. Once it becomes a WTO member such renewal will not be required (Lei 2009: Personal Interview). China was a major exporting country even before joining the WTO when exports were contributing two thirds of its GDP. With the entry into the WTO, it is expected to perform better in terms of exports as it will gain market access to most of the countries. Such a step is in the interest of China (Lei 2009: Personal Interview). China's accession to the WTO became a necessity for China, as it will remain a part of the international community where it can fight for its trade disputes. Besides it will be able to attract more FDI for its economic growth and internal development (Ho 2009: Personal Interview). China's initiative to launch economic reforms from early 1980s was an important consideration for major industrialized countries to seek its entry into the WTO. Its accession in 2001 is still heralded as a significant step towards global integration (Song 2009: Personal Interview).

China's process of accession had found positive expressions from various quarters such as Foreign Invested Enterprises (FIEs) already operating since Eighties and some sections of corporate sector who had developed global competitiveness then (Tao 2009: Personal Interview). The Protocol of Accession was a long-standing process as it involved a whole lot of political and economic programmes such as structural adjustment, establishment of transparent judicial system, economic reforms pertaining to internal domestic preparation, handling of human rights issues, and bilateral negotiations. The terms of China's Protocol of Accession to the WTO reflect a series of development that have been unparalled in its history. Its overall commitments have been much more far-reaching than those who acceded to the multilateral trading regime under the WTO. As a condition for membership, it was required to make protocol commitments that substantially exceeded those made by any other member of the WTO, including those that have joined since 1995. The Chinese leadership has increasingly come round to the view that one of the principal benefits of becoming a member of the WTO is the increased competition it would bring to China's domestic market. Increased competition is seen as an essential additional source of pressure on the government institutions, state-owned banks and enterprises forcing them to undertake badly needed structural reforms. The arduous process of accession which involved 15 years of hectic negotiations revolved around the major trading partners of China such as the US, EU, Canada, Japan, etc.

The WTO Procedure for New Membership

The accession to the WTO at the same time is no less bureaucratic as the country has to pass through many tests. *First*, the government applying for membership has to describe all aspects of its trade and economic policies that have a bearing on the WTO agreements. This is submitted to the WTO in a memorandum, which is examined by the Working Party dealing with the country's application. This Working Party dealing with accession procedures is open to all the WTO members to seek any clarification from the acceding country. *Second*, when the Working Party has made sufficient progress on principles and policies; parallel bilateral talks begin between the prospective new member and individual countries. These talks cover tariff rates and specific market access commitments and other policies in goods and services. *Third*, once the Working Party has completed its examination of the applicant's trade regime, and the parallel bilateral market access negotiations are complete, the Working Party finalizes the terms of accession. These appear in a report, a draft membership treaty ("Protocol of Accession") and lists ("schedules") of the member-to-be's commitments. *Finally*, the decision is taken when the final package, consisting of the report, protocol and lists of commitments, is presented to the WTO General Council or the Ministerial Conference. If a two-thirds majority of the WTO members vote in favour, the applicant is free to sign the protocol and to enter the organization.

Establishment of Working Party

A Working Party was established on March 4 1987 to start the process of China's re-entry into the GATT. The Working Party was assigned with the task of examining and evaluating China's trading regime, defining areas and timetables for negotiation and adjustment, and preparing a report for the GATT Council. The Working Party met for the first time in October that year. The Working Party had conducted several meetings about twenty by 1989. Soon after the Tiananmen Square massacre, it was suspended and was not reconvened until 1992, when, it made serious efforts to re-enter the GATT. The Working Party held a number of meetings and completed the general hearing and assessment of China's trading system. Negotiations on the commitment and conditions for entry into the GATT also started in 1992 with other GATT members as it was mandatory for the acceding country to conclude bilateral negotiations with other countries. More significantly, China accelerated its reform programme in the direction of a market economy. Following the conclusion of the Uruguay Round in 1994, China launched a major campaign to join the GATT. Like the 23 founding members of the GATT, it had shown keenness to become a founding member of the WTO. China had launched a nationwide propaganda to promote the internationalization of the economy and disseminate knowledge on the GATT. During this period China made many adjustments to carry forward its accession to GATT/WTO.

Domestic Preparation

China was engaged with two sets of domestic preparation. First one was in the sphere of commitments and the second one was relating to the structural and institutional adjustments required to accede to the WTO. First, in order to acquire the right to the WTO membership and to comply with the WTO rules and standards, China made numerous commitments before and after joining the WTO. These can be divided into two broad categories. First, adherence to the international rules and practices and second, to gradually open up its market to the outside world. Commitment to international rules and practices demanded certain fundamental structural changes to be addressed with immediate effect. Challenges that unfolded through these economic reforms and opening up process became daunting for the leadership. First, the market economy that China was forced to evolve as part of the WTO requirement was based on the rule of law. Industrialized countries spearheaded by the US had seriously objected to the prevailing legal regime of China. Lack of transparency was highlighted in major negotiating forums as a serious drawback in the functioning of the state.

During the 1980s and the 1990s lack of adequate of rules was felt in the functioning of administrative procedures. The planned economy pursued for several decades had concentrated on 'rules of men'(Yongtu 2002: 27). When negotiations for the WTO began, an urgency for revising these laws gathered significance. Establishing rule of law became an essential element for the new economic system. It is in this regard that China's commitment to international rules and regulations became an integral feature of its economic reform process. As China began to revise its rules and laws according to the requirement of the WTO, it had to engage in an extensive clean-up of its existing legal system. This change in the legal system had propelled the Chinese leadership to look for reasonable legal measures to protect its domestic industries and the domestic market. It resorted to the so-called "Safety Valve" mechanism which was directed to be set up concurrently with the lowering of tariffs and opening of the market once China is in the WTO (Zagha *et al.* 2005: 142). These measures include modifying and drafting anti-dumping regulations, anti-subsidy regulations, and special safeguards.

Secondly, in its opening-up to the outside world, China figured as a premier location for FDI among the developing countries, with a yearly average of

US$ 40 billion in the 1990s. Today the FDI plays an important role in China's economic development, contributing 50 per cent of its imports and exports, 20 per cent tax revenue, 30 per cent of its industrial output and, more importantly, generating more than 20 million jobs every year. It is of paramount importance to keep up the volume of FDI and improve the quality of the investment. In spite of all the efforts already made by the government, including an array of preferential treatments, there is still much room for improvement in China's investment environment. The chief concern that an increasing number of foreign investors had, was whether their investments would be protected in the absence of a transparent, predictable and stable legal environment, and called for an early action from the Chinese government. The importance of FDI is well known to the government. Hence, the establishment of a transparent, legal regime became a pressing concern and the WTO accession provided a timely framework to improve the business environment for FDI flows.

Non-Discrimination

China committed itself to provide non-discriminatory treatment to all WTO Members. With respect to the right to trade, all foreign enterprises, including those not invested or registered in China, will be accorded treatment no less favourable than that accorded to enterprises in China. In its Accession Protocol, China has also agreed to undertake additional commitments in order to ensure smooth application of non-discrimination principles including eliminating dual price systems, phasing out restrictions on trading, and introducing more administrative arrangements (Protocol of Accession WTO: 2001).

Improving the Environment for FDI

Recognizing FDI as a tool for economic development, the Chinese leadership had taken several measures to attract FDI. The measures that were introduced included improvement in the political and legal environment, and enhancement of legal administration level. Promises were made to make legal system steady, consistent, and predictable. It was proposed that efforts would be made to further simplify the examination and approval procedures for foreign investment, and adopt a standardized examination and approval system. A sense of legality and openness in relation to administrative environment for foreign investment was promised to be fostered. Such services include efficient and transparent government services, reform of administrative approval systems, and sound legal and business environments. All these administrative and policy changes formed part of China's accession, which have been stipulated in the provisions of the Protocol of Accession. Some of them are discussed below.

Transparency: Transparency is crucial to ensure certainty in business. It is understood that foreign investors would demand transparent laws, regulations and other elements of the operating environment. In view of the specific conditions of China, the protocol on the accession of the PRC states that:

- China undertakes to enforce only those laws, regulations and other measures that are published and readily available to other WTO members;
- China shall establish or designate an official journal for the publication of all laws, regulations and other measures, and provide a reasonable period for comment before such measures are implemented (except those involving national security and those whose publication would impede law enforcement); and
- China shall establish a designated enquiry point to provide timely information on relevant laws and regulations.

Independent Judicial Review: China in the late 1990s advocated that a transparent legal framework should entail equal access to the law for companies in their commercial activities. These activities should not just be ones between companies, but also activities by companies against the government. In this connection, the protocol states:

- China should establish or designate and maintain tribunals and contact points for the prompt review of all administrative actions relating to the implementation of laws. Such tribunals should be impartial and independent of the agencies entrusted with administrative enforcement;
- If the initial right of appeal is to an administrative body, there should always be the opportunity to choose to appeal the decision to a judicial body.

Uniform Application: As implementation of national laws by the national government has been one of the pressing concerns of foreign investors, China has committed itself in the protocol to a special section on "uniform application." This is not only important to eliminate conflicts between local regulations and national laws but also essential to root out all kinds of local protectionism at various levels. The section provides:

- China should apply and administer all its laws, regulations and other measures of the central government as well as the local ones in a uniform, impartial and reasonable manner;
- China's local regulations, rules and other measures shall conform to the obligations undertaken in the WTO Agreement and the accession protocol.

In a nutshell, it is argued that China's WTO commitments to observe international rules would help China to build a market economy based on the rule of law, on order and one with a transparent, stable and predicable legal environment. All these are not only fundamental for China to move to a truly market-driven economic system but also hold importance in the perspective of building an image in the outside world as an orderly, transparent, and predictable market for potential investors, and also help in avoiding unnecessary trade disputes with the rest of the WTO members.

Two-Way Process

China's commitments to a gradually more open market have thrown up some concerns. China realizes that in an interdependent world both partners have duties to respect and show concern towards each other. It believes that market opening is a two-way process. As an increasingly important trading country in the world, China can not just take advantage of the markets of others; it has to open its own market. This is the principle of mutual benefit and it has no scope for discrimination. It is also of fundamental importance to reduce trade related frictions and disputes. However, China has held the view that the opening of the domestic market, especially by developing countries should be a gradual process. The extent of opening should be in line with the level of development of the individual countries concerned. That is why China insisted very firmly on developing-country status for itself during the whole period of negotiations. China has successfully convinced its negotiating partners that market opening is not an objective by itself. Rather it should be a favourable condition for market growth and be conducive to domestic economic development. China and its negotiation partners, especially those from developed world have come to a common understanding that only a gradual opening of the Chinese market can bring a win-win outcome for all parties concerned. However, China insists following provisions need to be looked into while negotiating for entry.

- In financial services, the capital market in local currency will not be opened to foreign competition;
- In telecommunications and life insurance, only 50 per cent foreign ownership is allowed. Management control by the foreign partners is excluded (Report of the Working Party on the Accession on China: (http://docsonline.wto.org/DDFDocuments/t/WT/ACC/CHN49A2.doc);
- In agriculture, China should be entitled to grant a higher level of subsidies as compared to developed countries (8.5 per cent *vis-à-vis* 5 per cent ceiling for the latter).

In addition to the afcrementioned, many arrangements for the transitional period have been stipulated to ensure a gradual opening. Here are some examples:

Services

- In telecommunications, geographic restrictions on paging and value-added services will be phased out two years after the WTO accession, while the phasing-out period for mobile and domestic fixed line services will be five and six years respectively.
- In banking, foreign banks will be allowed to conduct local currency business with Chinese enterprises two years after entering and with individual Chinese citizens after five years ((Report of the Working Party on the Accession on China: http://docsonline.wto.org/DDFDocuments/t/WT/ACC/CHN49A2.doc).

Such mutual agreements have shown the level of maturity reached in each and every sector under negotiation. It was believed at the time of negotiation that these arrangements would not jeopardize the development of these industries. On the contrary, they would promote their development by means of healthy and appropriate competition from outside. Secondly, China believes that the main benefit of opening up to trade and investment flows is to catalyze change in the Chinese domestic industries not just to generate foreign exchange. It is opening up not only to satisfy the consumers' demands for a wide range of products or services but also to enhance the competitiveness of its domestic industries.

As a result of the WTO market access negotiation, China has made the most significant offer of opening up the service sector. The service sector is relatively undeveloped in China, accounting for only 35 per cent of its gross domestic product (GDP)—a lower ratio than in some developing countries and even more so with respect to the developed countries, where the service sector accounts for 65-85 per cent of the GDP. From the Chinese Government's standpoint, the services sector has more opportunities for employment. Therefore, the Chinese government is determined to restructure the economy and make special efforts to develop its service sector industries. Its experience in developing some of its most advanced manufacturing sectors such as electronic home appliances has led the government to believe that the Chinese service sector will also follow the same road by opening up to foreign competition. This is the reason why so many major market openings are slowly taking place in banking, insurance, telecommunications, distribution, tourism, transportation, and professional services.

It is widely believed that the opening-up of these service sectors will generate several opportunities, especially middle-and high-income jobs, which is important to ensure work prospects at home for the talented young Chinese rather than compelling them to seek jobs abroad. The paramount consideration of creating more jobs is not only reflected in opening up the service sector, but also in some of the major manufacturing sectors. The impact of the refusal to accept the WTO commitments has been costly for China. It was given the status of 'non-market economy,' which gives advantage to the other WTO members to impose anti-dumping duties at their whims. Due to lack of opening in services sector, China has not been able to integrate better in services markets of world economy. Insurance and telecommunications facilities are still costly and not available to the poorer sections.

Dual Pricing Practices

China practiced dual pricing as well as differences in treatment accorded to goods produced for sale in China in comparison to those produced for export. Price controls will no longer be used for purposes of affording protection to domestic industries or services providers. Within three years of accession, all enterprises will have the right to import and export all goods and trade them throughout the customs territory with limited exceptions reserved for state trading.

Agriculture

As part of its commitments relating to agriculture, China's average tariff on agriculture imports fell to 15 per cent from 22 per cent in trade-weighted terms, affecting mainly wheat, maize, rice, and vegetable oil. It was also agreed that the tariff should be further reduced to 14.5 per cent on agriculture in 2004, and eliminate non-tariff barriers like quotas, liberalizing trading rights, and export subsidies (Yang 2003: 7). Sensitive and livelihood sectors like agriculture being opened to international market had aroused public anger. However, final decision of joining the WTO convinced the Chinese people, that such entry provides a real opportunity to restructure its agricultural sector, which has been the least opened and lags relatively behind other industries in the reform process. Compared with advanced countries, China's agriculture does not enjoy comparative advantage in producing some foodstuffs from wheat, corn, soyabeans and other vegetable oil crops. China has only 7 per cent of the world's arable land (Mitra 2003: 88) but has to feed 20 per cent of the world's population. In addition, many areas of China are short of water supply. Therefore, as some agricultural experts argue it should import more grain as this is tantamount to the import of scarce land and water resources. Given its dimensions, even if it imports the full tariff-quota volume of grains (about 22 million tons a year), such imports would still amount to less than 5 per cent of its total production of these crops. This means that food security could be guaranteed even in the very unlikely event of a food embargo.

China is resolute in restructuring its agricultural sector so as to move to its more competitive areas such as fruits, vegetables, and meat as the WTO membership will bring greater access to foreign markets. The WTO entry certainly exerted a major influence on the government to introduce a more rational and fair policy towards agriculture strengthening it with better infrastructure and services and by alleviating the financial burden and increasing the incomes of the farmers. The development of the agricultural sector after the WTO accession could prove that the WTO entry was a turning point for China's agricultural policy and the driving force behind a new phase seeking to achieve world standards of competitiveness. China believes that another key benefit of opening up to world trade and investment flows is the nurturing of new industries in order to generate massive employment, which is critical for China's sustainable economic development as well as social stability. In addition to taking on the obligations of the WTO agreement relating to agriculture, China made several additional commitments in its accession agreement, that will help to rectify numerous agricultural policies upon accession or after limited transition periods. For example:

- China has committed not to provide export subsidies;
- It has also committed to a cap for trade and production-distorting domestic subsidies that is lower than the cap permitted developing countries, and that includes the same elements that developed countries use in determining whether the cap has been reached;
- It has also lifted long-standing ban on the importation of agricultural products such as corn, wheat, citrus products and meat (during the course of the US-China bilateral negotiations as a sign of good faith); and
- It hast implemented tariff-rate quotas that provide significant market access for bulk goods of special importance to the American farmers such as grains, soyabean oil and cotton upon accession.

It has also agreed to eliminate import monopolies maintained by state trading enterprises on agricultural goods such as wheat, rice and corn, and to permit non-State trading enterprises to import them.

While free trade would improve on account of reduction of tariffs, it may be thwarted due to the application of non-tariff barriers (NTBs). Various NTBs include: Sanitary and Phytosanitary Measures (SPS), rules of origin, technical barriers to trade (TBT), labeling, product standards, etc. China has undertaken obligations of the WTO agreement relating to SPS, TBT, etc.

Sanitary and Phytosanitary Standards (SPS) and Technical Barriers to Trade (TBT)

As a part of the commitment, China is committed to apply science-based SPS standards to all agricultural goods, including grains, meats, and fruits. China is required to ensure that its conformity assessment bodies operate with transparency, apply the same technical regulations, standards, and conformity assessment procedures to both imported and domestic goods and use the same fees, processing periods and complaint procedures for both imported and domestic goods. In addition, It must ensure that all of its conformity assessment bodies are authorized to handle both imported and domestic goods within one year of accession. While taking on the obligations of the WTO agreement relating to rules of origin, China specifically agreed to adopt internationally harmonized non-preferential rules of origin, once they were completed. China also confirmed that it would use rules of origin, equally for all purposes and that it would not use rules of origin as an instrument to pursue trade objectives either directly or indirectly. By the time of its accession to the WTO, it was required to establish a mechanism to provide, upon request, an assessment of the origin of an import or export.

China is committed to the phase-out of trade-distorting non-tariff measures (NTMs) such as quotas and licenses covering hundreds of products. Most of these NTMs must be eliminated upon accession, while the remainder of them must be eliminated within three years after accession. China signed a series of accession commitments, of which other important ones are the following.

China Specific Safeguard

China's accession agreement includes a unique, China-specific safeguard provision allowing a WTO member to restrain increasing Chinese imports that disrupt its market. This mechanism will be available for 12 years after accession.

Textiles Safeguard

The accession agreement also includes a special textiles safeguard, which was available for 7 years after accession (until December 31, 2008). This safeguard covers all products subject to the WTO Agreement on Textiles and Clothing as of 1 January 1995. Under the WTO commitments, China had to further reduce its average tariff rate to 10 per cent by 2005. On 1 January 2004 China lowered it average tariff rate by 0.6 percentage points to 10.4 and then to 10 per cent. China also signed another important agreement known as the WTO Information Technology Agreement (ITA) which will result in the elimination of IT products.[1]

China continued to implement its further commitments after joining the WTO as it was a part of the accession commitments. During 2006-2007, China further lowered its tariff rate, increased market access to trade in services, and enhanced the transparency of its trade policy. During the same year, China reduced the tariff rate of 187 items in accordance with its accession commitments. Until 1 January 2008, China's overall tariff level had been reduced from 15.3 per cent at the time of accession to 9.8 per cent, among which the average tariff rate of industrial products had been cut from 14.8 per cent to 8.95 per cent, and the rate for agricultural products from 23.2 per cent to 15.2 per cent.

Such long-standing commitments and intense negotiations establish that China joined the WTO under difficult circumstances. That is why it is argued that the terms of agreement that China had to agree to for accession to the WTO have proven too costly for her as against other countries. Prominent reasons for this delay and onerous agreements are explained here to provide significance to the study.

First, developed countries' insistence on reducing agricultural import tariffs to less than 15 per cent whereas for other developing countries this remained higher around 22 per cent. Second, after the accession China was forced to commit to implement a series of tariff cuts to allow private enterprises to participate in trade activities, and to eliminate NTBs by 2004. Third, in addition, China committed to establish tariff-rate quotas (TRQ) for wheat, corn, rice, soyabean oil and cotton with gradually increasing quota levels; which means limited amount of products of the Chinese exports can enter developed countries market at lower rate and then products will be exported at a higher rate. This was bilaterally agreed under the Sino-US deal during its negotiations for accession whereas the US has not imposed such measure against other developing countries. Fourth, agricultural subsidy was a focal point in the negotiation process where China had to agree to limit domestic agricultural subsidies to 8.5 per cent of the value of production (i.e. less than the 10 per cent limit allowed for developing countries under the WTO Agreement on Agriculture) and to eliminate all agricultural export subsidies upon WTO entry. Fifth, transitional product-specific safeguard mechanism as provided under the WTO Agreement on Safeguards, a country may impose restrictions on imports if it can demonstrate that they cause or threaten to cause serious injury to domestic firms producing similar products. Special safeguard mechanism for China's textile and clothing exports was imposed for eight years from the date of accession unlike for the acceding countries. Sixth, under the WTO agreement, other members can invoke "non-market economy" provisions to determine dumping cases for 15 years following accession. Non-market economy provisions imply that domestic prices cannot be used as a reference point and make it much easier to reach a positive finding in an antidumping investigation. A third country's domestic price may be taken into account to locate the case of dumping. Seventh, in relation to Trade-Related Investment Measures (TRIMs*)* foreign investment approvals will no longer be subject to domestic mandatory requirements (e.g., technology transfer or local content requirements). Eighth, trade liberalization commitments in services are extremely large relative to almost all other countries and they are more often subject to qualifications and reservations than those of other developing countries. Lastly, a special WTO procedure, the Transitional Review Mechanism (TRM), was established to review China's compliance with the WTO agreement. China's Protocol of Accession provides that, the TRM will review China's compliance on an annual basis in the first eight years of WTO membership. Reviews are conducted separately by sixteen WTO sectoral councils. Rather than simple "pass or fail" tests, these reviews are opportunities for stocktaking on past progress and areas for further efforts (Rumbaugh and Blancher 2004: 8).

Structural and Institutional Changes

Second set of domestic preparation engaged China to introduce changes to orient itself to requirement of the WTO. China introduced a series of reforms in line with the GATT rules. Its bold reforms programme included a series of structural and institutional changes in its foreign trade regime. First, to begin with China had to bring in decentralization of foreign trade. Prior to the reform, the Ministry of Foreign Trade conducted and controlled all trade. Since 1988, foreign trade has been decentralized and handed over to local authorities and foreign trade corporations (FTCs). In 1980, the Central government controlled about 98 per cent of the total trade. By 1991, only 11 per cent of foreign trade was still controlled by the Ministry of Foreign Trade and Economic Cooperation (Garnaut and Huang: 1995; Zhang: 1993). China promised that it would cease to exercise control on all trading rights after it became a member.

Secondly, China undertook the demand set in by the US and EU to eliminate export subsidies. In 1991, the Chinese government abolished all explicit export subsidies. From then onwards the Foreign Trade Corporations (FTCs) were responsible for their own losses. Thirdly, foreign investors demanded transparency in the investment regime. China issued a Foreign Trade Law on 1 July 1994 to make regulations more transparent. It also started to change the method of allocating license from bureaucratic application procedure to open competition. Fourthly, reforms in foreign exchange market converted the Renminbi (RMB) official exchange rate to the market rate and abolished the dual exchange rate system on 1 January 1994. In spite of China's regular efforts and keenness, the bilateral and multilateral negotiations were not producing satisfying results till 6 November 1995. The US attitude toward China was firm: "China must follow the rule of the WTO if it wants to join the international trade body," remarked the chief US negotiator, Charlene Barshefsky (Chong 1995: 18). The US insisted that China must meet all the WTO's rules for accession. On 10 November 1995 Barshefsky provided a "road map" for China's accession.[2] China found it as a positive initiative but admitted that the US is trying to negotiate too hard (Wen 1996: 5).

However, after conclusion of a successful meeting with Charlene Barshefsky in 1995, China made a constructive move by applying formally to the WTO. As the WTO became the successor to the GATT, it became mandatory for China to apply formally again to accede to the WTO. On 7 December 1995, the Government of China applied for accession to the

Marrakesh Agreement establishing the World Trade Organization ("WTO Agreement") pursuant to Article XII[3] of the WTO Agreement. Following China's application and pursuant to the decision of the General Council on 31 January 1995, the existing Working Party on China's status as a GATT 1947 Contracting Party was transformed into a WTO Accession Working Party effective from 7 December 1995 (WTO: Report of the Working Party on the Accession of China).

During 1996-97 negotiations between China and the US witnessed significant exchanges relating to memorandum on China's foreign trade regime, which is the basic document to be debated in the negotiations forum. Many queries relating to transparency in foreign trade regime were asked and China had to clarify them in due course. China argued that the US was obstructing China's accession to the WTO for political reasons and that China's economic system was much closer to the WTO requirements than what the US seeks to portray. To this recalcitrant attitude of the US, many experts like Panitchpakdi and Clifford (2002: 18) had felt that "China is too big to be changed and too important to be ignored. Keeping China outside the WTO, which no longer prevents it from playing a major role in real global trade, has become more costly for the multilateral trading system."

Members of the Working Party welcomed China's accession to the WTO Agreement and considered that its accession would contribute to strengthening of the multilateral trading system, enhancing the universality of the WTO, bringing mutual benefits to China and to the other Members of the WTO and ensuring the steady development of the world economy. Even the then US Vice-President, Al Gore had pledged his support for the Clinton Administration's China Trade Bill and vowed to persuade the Congress to permanently normalize trade relations with China. He pointed out: "If China joins the WTO and has normal trade relations with other members of the WTO and not with us, then our ability to get improvements in the WTO in the future is limited." He also emphasized that he would work with the administration's economic team "in trying to bring people together around a formula that gets a majority." Thomas J. Donohue, President and Chief Executive Officer of the US Chamber of Commerce, stated in an article in the *Journal of Commerce* that: "business must win" the congressional approval of permanent normal trade relations because "billions of dollars" and "millions of jobs" are at stake (*Beijing Review* 27 March 2000: 7).

Decentralization of the Administrative System

As China embarked on a progressive path, it undertook a number of initiatives to reform its central administration. The initial outlook of the Chinese planners was quite conservative and they resisted any kind of decentralization taking place in the power structure as that would dilute their authority. When the move for entry into the WTO was initiated and was discussed, the idea of decentralization came to the fore. In order to break the monopoly run by the central planners, China's reformers introduced local and other central players into the process and allowed the new players to push for decentralization. This strategy is defined as "playing to provinces" by Shirk (1993: 47-50). It is essentially meant that the government approved industrial ministries had to find their trade companies specialized in the trade of industry related products. The first one came in the provinces of Guangdong and Fujian in 1979, and then it spread to other coastal provinces in 1982. By June 1984, the industrial ministries had set up 23 general trading companies with 52 subsidiaries. More importantly, the trading rights of provinces by then had greatly expanded. Gradually in early 1990s these trading companies had spread to all other provinces. The new policy delegated to local trading companies, the power to do business in all categories of products. By June 1984, local trade companies increased to 125 and the direct trade plan was replaced by directive on foreign currency earning.

In the realm of state trading, only state-owned companies were qualified to establish foreign trade companies. The government carried forward reform of state trading sector in order to improve efficiency of the whole sector. These reforms included contractual system, separation of government from enterprises, increase of foreign exchange earnings retention to firms, and gradual withdrawal of state subsidy. Further, reforms took place in the area of expansion of trading rights to manufacturing sector. In 1987, China made a decision to accelerate export processing, to improve market share of 'Made in China' products. Export processing firms gained trading rights which were restricted to processing and export. More importantly, foreign invested enterprises (FIEs) automatically received trading rights limited to their own products and parts needed for further manufacture of products. The expansion of trading rights to manufacturing enterprises significantly boosted China's exports and FDI into the country.

With the accession process in progress, substantial liberalization of trade regulations became a necessary condition for China's entry into the WTO. This led to dilution of power exercised by the agencies. Especially under the General Agreement on Trade in Services (GATS) and the Agreement on Trade-Related Investment Measures (TRIMs), the agencies were in charge of liberalizing the procedure felt further dilution of power and authority. Internal bureaucracy had initially resisted the opening up of China to the world economy, because, this not only demanded liberalization in trade in goods but also in services and investment. These broad areas of negotiations involved a large number of economic agencies in the Central Government that were drawn into the WTO negotiations.

The bureaucracy in China is characterized by overlapping jurisdictions partly due to its sheer size (Yong 2002: 21). Before the launch of the government restructuring in 1998, there were more than 40 ministries, commissions, and agencies, and more than half were directly related to economic and industrial affairs. For example, the State Council Commission on Tariffs (affiliated with the State Economic and Trade Commission, or SETC) and the General Administration of Customs had together undertaken responsibility for tariffs but they had to consult with other agencies when setting new rates. In other words, they had to deal with pressures from other government agencies that wanted to protect domestic industries. The power to determine quotas was divided between the Ministry of Foreign Trade and Economic Cooperation (MOFTEC) and the State Planning Commission (SPC). The MOFTEC was in charge of export quotas while the SPC took care of import quotas. Its bureaucracy had undergone substantial transformation as part of the requirements for accession to the WTO.

The Role of US in China's Entry into the WTO

Though reforms were mandatory for China to kick-start the accession process, yet the political dimensions between China and the US significantly influenced the pace of accession process. The process began smoothly in 1987 but took a dramatic turn in 1989. The Sino-US relationship changed significantly when the Tiananmen incident broke out in 1989. China developed strained relationship with the US thereafter. It's not only the US Government, but also the US trade and industry advocated about the use of economic and political pressure to bring about structural change in China's domestic political and economic systems. The American measures that were imposed on China included ban on exports of military and nuclear technology, restriction of loans to China from international financial institutions and restriction on export financing, linking renewal of MFN status with improvements in human rights conditions, threats of economic sanctions for violation of intellectual property rights (IPRs), textile export restrictions and insistence on tough conditions for China's entry into the WTO. These measures combined with the US policy towards Taiwan had severely damaged the prospects for China to get an early entry into the WTO. Simultaneously, in the 1990s when the former Soviet Union disintegrated and the end of Cold War was announced, the US emerged as the only superpower. However, the US was fully aware that the rising economic power of China would put up a formidable challenge for her in the Asian region. A Chinese historian saw the problem in terms of hegemonic transitions: "Some Americans are afraid the power structure will change fundamentally, their economic advantage will be hampered and their strategic sphere of influence will be lost. Historically, most of the old powers have held such a mentality towards rising new powers," (Shi Yinhong 1997: 10).

While the US viewed bilateral economic disputes over Intellectual Property Rights (IPRs), market access, technology transfer, and China's entry into the WTO as part of normal economic negotiations between the countries, China felt that these were tough negotiating positions which were part of a strategic effort to impede China's economic growth.

Meanwhile, the American business community had also put pressure on China by siding with the Congress to block China's exports to the US. This business community wanted the Chinese government to buy their aircrafts and wheat. They linked it up with the renewal of MFN vote, buying billions of dollars of the American goods in order to gain Congressional support for renewal of China's MFN status. American business lobby had also exerted pressure on Clinton to de-link MFN renewal with the human rights issue. For example, the business community forced the then Clinton administration to press for enforcement of Intellectual Property Rights (IPRs) as an important precondition for China's entry.

However, these conditions never deterred China from striving towards global integration. Ross Madelyn argues that China has consistently practiced economic nationalism in the international arena, and that the "driving force behind all of China's foreign economic relations—to make China stronger, more modern, more self reliant—has not wavered" (Ross 1995: 437). Therefore, the Chinese reformers have used competition from imported goods to force the Chinese enterprises to become more efficient and have encouraged foreign investment in order to improve the Chinese technology and management practices. The determination was further strengthened when it began its full participation. Long Yongtu, Assistant Minister, Ministry of Foreign Trade and Economic Cooperation (MOFTEC) led the Chinese delegates in March 1996 in their official negotiations with the WTO members. Besides on 1 March 1996, the Chinese Premier Li Peng, while addressing the first Asia-Europe Meeting in Bangkok reiterated the need for mutual cooperation between China and the WTO. He observed:

> Work together to counter trade protectionism, eliminate trade discrimination, oppose imposition of trade sanctions and promote trade development. WTO ought to be a truly universal and open organization. However, it will be incomplete without the participation of China, a country with about one fifth of world's population (*Beijing Review* 1996: 10).

While pursuing an active relationship with the US was well understood, China also gave importance to establish a good relationship with other important partners like the EU, Japan, ASEAN, South Korea etc. The idea of economic security was high on China's agenda. It was convinced that economic security would be maintained provided it kept favourable working relations with these entities instead of depending excessively on one country. The efforts to maintain economic security are intended not only to protect China from the unpredictable impact of international economic shocks but also reduce its vulnerability to foreign economic pressures. The Chinese leaders during this process of negotiations for accession to the WTO had borrowed financial loans from the multilateral, bilateral and private sources in order to prevent any single lender from enjoying too much political leverage.

This balance helped China to compensate in the face of the US efforts to suspend World Bank loans after the Tiananmen Square massacre. China also followed a similar pattern in trade. It diversified its trading activities with other partners like the EU, Japan and South Korea. China tried to reduce its dependence on the US market and broaden its economic base with Japan, the EU and South Korea. Thus it played skillfully its market card (Wu Xinbo 1998: 144). Nonetheless, such efforts became complicated by trade liberalization which had reduced to an extent the Central government's control over the foreign trade conducted by Chinese enterprises, especially by foreign invested enterprises (FIEs). These professional enterprises make their decisions based on the reflection of market behaviour and not on the policies of the Government. China also made increasing efforts with the Russian government during 1990s to develop a strategic partnership. Such efforts, however, did not produce the much desirable results as the markets and not the governments determined the relationship (Saunders 2000: 71).

Despite rhetoric about diversifying markets, China's dependence on foreign trade with the US steadily increased in the 1990s. Total exports witnessed a rising trend from 1995 touching US$ 24 billion to register US$ 184 billion in 2007 (World Trade Atlas Online Database 2007). China ran a trade surplus with the US in 1990s, signifying the US to be the fastest growing export market in the world. Most of these exports were labour intensive, low value added goods such as textiles, shoes, toys, and other consumer goods. In many cases production was managed by the FIEs, which import components from abroad, use inexpensive Chinese labour to assemble the products, and then export the finished goods to markets in the US, the EU, Japan, and other parts of Asia. Many of these factories have moved from Hong Kong, South Korea and Southeast Asia to China to exploit the cheap labour.

As China found the US to be its biggest market for its trade expansion, it could not ignore the US even if it found the imposition of commitments too harsh. Besides, when China was rising as one of the significant trading countries in the world, it depended heavily on FDI. A bulk of FDI came from the US, so China had to agree to many of the demands imposed by the US. When the Asian financial crisis occurred during 1997-98 and the FDI from Southeast Asia got reduced substantially, the FDI flows from the US, however, became the major source of foreign capital for China. To boost its bilateral trade around this time China had developed interest in lowering tariffs, to reduce the costs of imports and utilize them for expanding export markets (Fewsmith 2000: 269-273) to places like the US and the EU. China concentrated on markets like the US and EU to sustain its rising exports. During this time, the US involvement gained more importance. It is also significant to note that most of the non-American investment that China received went to the construction of various factories which exported heavily to the US. Therefore, the loss of access to the US markets at any point of time would also have a negative effect on China's ability to attract FDI from other countries. All these dimensions played a critical role in China's acceptance to the terms of the agreement with the US to enter into the WTO.

Political Constraint in Sino-US Negotiations

The Sino-US relation has witnessed many ups and downs in the last three decades since 1978. The nuclear issue of North Korea, Taiwan factor and human rights issue were some of the major events which created constant frictions between China and the US causing many political obstacles for China to join the WTO. North Korea's proliferation of nuclear programmed has caused enough consternation in the US establishment. The US was consistently pursuing to form a world opinion to stall the nuclear programme of North Korea. It had demanded that such proliferation is not in the interest of the world community, rather poses enough danger to the world. To further its objective, the US had sought the help of China in curtailing the nuclear activities in North Korea. However, China was clear that it is North Korea's internal matter and it should not intervene in other's internal affairs. With the fall of Soviet Union, North Korea had come closer to China and found it a reliable ally. Under the pressure from the US, China remained firm in its position of not joining the world community to completely isolate North Korea on security issues. China never wanted to see the South Korea taking over the North. This would fulfill the objective of the US to hegemonize the region. China wanted to observe that North Korea is still an independent nation having its own ideology and ethos. Similar ideological solidarity between North Korea and China had established a special bond. The US government had remained critical of this relationship. This relationship was a source of constant tension between China and the US and played a damaging role during the 1980s and 1990s in China's negotiation process with the WTO.

The Taiwan issue which has long been a key factor in the Sino-US relation also played a critical role during the period of China's negotiations with the US. Establishment of Kuomintang government in Taiwan after its defeat in the hands of the communists in China in 1949 remained a bone of contention between China and the US. It was only towards the late 1970s when the US and China came to an understanding to establish diplomatic relations between them that issue of Taiwan received some positive responses from China and the US. On 15 December 1978, President Carter expressed that "normalization between the US and China will not jeopardize the well-being of the people of Taiwan" and that "the US will continue to have interest in the peaceful resolution of the Taiwan issue" (Chai 1986: 1309). Continuous involvement of the US in its internal affairs and arm sales to Taiwan had constantly irritated China. Deep interest in establishing a pluralistic society with democratic governance was the long-term interest of the US. Besides influencing the geopolitics of Taiwan Strait, it was important that it maintained relations with Taiwan by selling arms to Taiwan. This attitude of the US was strongly criticized by the Chinese leaders when they observed "as for the way of bringing Taiwan back to the embrace of the motherland and reunifying the country, it is entirely China's internal affair" (Tsou 1986: 169).

While both nations pledged to resolve the problem of normalizing their relations, the Taiwan issue remained unresolved. During the negotiations the US maintained that after normalization it would continue to sell limited amount of arms to Taiwan for Taiwan's own self defense. The US asserted that the well-being and security of Taiwan were matters of continuous concern, and therefore it is essential for the US to look into such security issues. China had strongly opposed to this idea. It maintained that sale of arms to Taiwan would be detrimental to peaceful liberation of Taiwan and would exercise an intimidating influence on the peace of East Asia. This disagreement over the Taiwan question, as stated by Chinese President Li Xiannian during his visit to the US in July 1985 had become "the biggest obstacle" in the growth of Sino-US relations (Shi and Shih 1993: 119). He further went to say that the US has increased its arms sales to Taiwan both in quantitative and qualitative terms. In the 1982 Joint Communiqué, the U.S. promised that arms sales to Taiwan "will not exceed, either in qualitative or in quantitative terms the level of those supplied in recent years since the establishment of diplomatic relations between the United States and China" (Qimao 1987: 1171) and it will not seek to carry out a long term policy of arms sales to Taiwan. The US had not agreed to these provisions of the communiqué. China had vociferously criticized this policy of the US and till the late 1980s the Taiwan issue remained a major impediment in the Sino-US political relations. During this time the Taiwan issue slowly lost its focus because by then the US had diverted its energy and resources towards Vietnam. During the pro-democracy movement the US had again diverted its attention towards China. Violation of human rights and trade embargo during this period aggravated the Sino-US relations. China believed that the US has used human rights issue as a diplomatic tool and provoked confrontation. By posing as a protector of human rights and formulating resolutions, the US seeks hegemony. China insists that the US has also raised this issue to curtail its international image.

As the tensions mounted between the two countries, economic reforms in China were stalled and programmes of exchange and cooperation between China and the US were suspended. Disagreement at highest level called off the WTO negotiation process. The sudden collapse of the Soviet Union and Washington's hostile attitude convinced China that the political relations have considerably worsened. Towards the early 1990s, the Sino-US relations had deteriorated. The US imposed broad sanctions against China which included suspension of official and military exchanges between the two governments, a prohibition on the US trade financing and investment insurance for China-related projects, and an embargo on exports to military and police entities in China (Yang 2004: 2). Among all these sanctions economic sanctions were used for a longer period as a means to derail the rising influence of China in the world. It was meant to teach the Chinese leadership to respect the human rights conditions. Though the Bush Senior administration imposed limited sanctions, the Congress had called for tougher action. As the revocation of MFN status to China depended on the Jackson Vanik Amendment's requirement, the American Congress could easily find institutional means to impose more sanctions on the Chinese government. But with the rise of bilateral trade between China and the US rising, China made efforts to improve its political relations with the US. Politically US$ 18 billion of US exports to China had become more significant than US$ 55 billion of the Chinese exports to the US (Saunders 2000: 77). This development led the US government to change its policy from confrontation to cooperation. Finally, in May 1994 after long hesitation and much debate President Clinton renewed China's most favoured nation (MFN) trading status with the US and announced that the issue of human rights in China would no longer be a consideration for this annual exercise in the future. This so-called de-linking decision signaled that Washington was ready to move beyond Tiananmen and seek a new, broad and stable basis for ties with Beijing. The relationship improved rapidly and the intensity and quality of the exchanges and cooperation improved significantly between the two countries. In February 1995, after a long stalemate in negotiations, the US and the Chinese governments reached a major agreement on the protection of intellectual property rights in China (Huang 2000: 271-272).

These signs of interdependence revived further hope in a mutual agreement. Two meetings were convened in February and May of 1997, wherein both sides made compromises so that the negotiations made some progress. China showed some flexibility on human rights issues which raised interest in the US to show flexibility on the time requirements during the adjustment period.

President Bill Clinton's visit to China in 1998 strengthened that objective of confidence building and mutual agreement. Clinton also expressed hope that current American policy-makers will seek a prosperous, cooperative, more politically tolerant China and its future relations will be inextricably intertwined with the West and rest of Asia. Clinton's visit accelerated political negotiations between the two countries and made China open to the outside world. The pressure of opening up various sectors to the outside world was too overpowering for the Chinese Government than protecting China's SOEs, as there was always a section of society, which opposed China's opening (Yong 2009: Personal Interview). With Clinton's visit political relations witnessed favourable development and bilateral trade between two countries grew significantly. Clinton maintained that through this favourable political ties America can save hundreds of thousands of jobs by maintaining trade with China, which has an enormously favourable balance of trade and foreign exchange reserves totaling US$ 140 billion in 1998 (Elegant 1998: 2).

Such positive signals from the US Government gave some hope to China. In late 1998 and particularly in early 1999, China became much more cooperative and yet determined (Fewsmith 2000: 268). The Chinese leaders realized that China cannot remain outside the system for very long. This new thinking reflected a maturing of the Chinese society which looked at the US and the EU in a more positive way.

Zhu Rongji's visit to the US in April 1999 was solely directed at expediting that process. By then, he was openly articulating the view that China's membership in the WTO could be a lever for promoting domestic economic reform. At a joint press conference with President Clinton in Washington Premier Zhu stated: "the competition arising (from WTO membership) will also promote a more rapid and healthier development of China's national economy."

The Sino-US relationship suddenly took a nasty turn in 1999 because of the bombing of Chinese embassy in Belgrade by the US. The incident again soured the relationship between the two nations. However, regular efforts were made to revitalize the relationship. On July 25 1999, the Chinese Foreign Minister Tang Jiaxuan met with the US Secretary of State, Madeline Albright while attending the ASEAN Regional Forum (ARF) meeting in Singapore. On September 11, 1999 President Jiang Zemin and President Bill Clinton held an official meeting during the APEC Informal Leaders Meeting in Auckland, New Zealand where the two sides stated that China and the US should continue to build constructive strategic partnership gearing towards the 21st century.

Signing of the Historic Deal

During 10-15th November 1999, the Chinese Government delegation headed by Shi Guangsheng, Minister of Foreign Trade and Economic Cooperation of China and the United States' Government delegation headed by Ambassador

Charlene Barshefsky, the US Trade Representative and Gene Sperling, Director of the National Economic Council of the US held negotiations in Beijing on the issue of China's accession to the WTO. On November 15th the two sides signed the Bilateral Agreement between the Government of the People's Republic of China and the Government of the USA on China's Accession to the WTO. The Chinese leadership believed the signing of the aforementioned agreement with the US will help accelerate the process of China's accession to the WTO and the development of China-US economic cooperation and trade relations. Responding to this success, President Jiang Zemin emphatically announced: "Where there is a will, there is a way" (*Xinhua* 1999). The two sides are looking forward to close cooperation in the WTO in the future so as to help ensure the sound development of China-US relations and the prosperity of the world economy (*Xinhua* 1999). This policy laid the foundations for China's accession to the WTO.

The US ambassador to China, Joseph W. Prueher supported China's accession to the WTO and permanent normal trade relation (PNTR) status in the policy briefing sponsored by the National Committee for the US-China relationship. "It is articulated that China's WTO accession will serve America's long term political, economic and military interests, so we need not take our eyes off the ball." He also said that the US should support the economic reform and the rule of law in China and put forward human rights dialogue and military-to-military contact between the two countries. According to the US Trade Representative, Charlene Barshefsky: "China's WTO accession is one of the most important American trade and foreign policy goals" (*Beijing Review* 2000: 5-6). Meanwhile, the US President, Bill Clinton told in a press conference that the US will face 20 years of regret if Congress fails to vote for the trade deal with China on the country's accession to the WTO. While appealing to the Congress to approve the legislation, Clinton also underscored the fact that the "matter is of huge national interest." The US trade representative, Barshefsky expressed hope that China's entry into the WTO will be the most significant step in order to strengthen peace and security for the US and for the rest of the world (*Beijing Review* 2000: 4). The US President also mentioned that the US-China agreement on China's entry into the WTO was a "win-win deal for America" and American products will get better access to China's market in every sector from agriculture to telecommunication (*Beijing Review* 2000: 5).

Further, Mike Moore, former Director-General, WTO observed that China's accession to the global trade body may not be affected by the US decision on permanent normal trade relations (PNTR) with China. He said: "If the United States decides not to extend PNTR to China, it is possible that China will join the WTO without the US approval." Warning the US Congress against rejecting the Clinton administration's trade agreement with China,

Moore said that the US risks losing the benefits of the agreement, if Congress rejects PNTR with China. He stated: "Never before in history has one country lifted so many of its people from poverty," and "A policy of greater openness in China has been instrumental in lifting 120 million people out of extreme poverty over the past 20 years." According to the US President, Bill Clinton, it would be "very unwise" for Congress to deny NTR with China: "From a national security point of view, it would be a very, very unwise and precarious move to say that the US does not care whether China is part of the world community or not." He pointed out that China is going to enter the WTO whether the US votes to give normal trade relations every year or not during his speech in the Conference of the Independent Insurance Agents of America. He further clarified: "There are 1.2 billion people in China and, increasingly, more and more of them will be able to buy what Americans sell" (*Beijing Review* 2000: 5). US Senate voted in favour of PNTR on September 19, 2000. According to the Ministry of Foreign Affairs and Foreign Trade and Economic Cooperation, the US House of Representatives' passage of a bill granting China permanent normal trade relations (PNTR) status was wise but certain provisions within the measure are not addressed. The provisions, in effect, interfere in China's internal affairs under the guise of human rights and allow for a Special Commission on the Human Rights and Labour to be set up in China to assess the ground level situation in China, according to the Foreign Ministry spokesperson Zhang Qiye. She emphasized that the settlement of PNTR was an obligation of the US, in accordance with the rules of the WTO and is the prerequisite for implementing the bilateral trade agreement signed six months ago. Jiang Hu, spokesperson, Ministry of Foreign Affairs and Foreign Trade and Economic Cooperation stressed: "China reserves the right to react on the issue in the future" and "We urge the US side to correct its mistake so as to ensure the healthy and smooth development of China-US economic cooperation and trade" (*Beijing Review* 2000: 5).

Meanwhile, in the Ninth National People's Congress (NPC) and People's Political Consultative Conference (CPPCC) held in Beijing during 3-15 March 2000 concluded that the Chinese laws and regulations concerning foreign trade and investment should conform to international practice. The spokesman of the conference Zeng Jianhui on this occasion remarked: "China is making full preparations to join the WTO, and is studying related laws and regulations on foreign trade and investment to adapt its legal framework to new requirements" (*Beijing Review* 2000: 4). The US Trade Representative, Charlene Barshefsky pointed out that in 2000 during the negotiations that former Cold War suspicions were being laid to rest in the cause of global cooperation as the US—the leader of the free world—helps 'communist central planning regimes' integrate into rule-based world trade. In Barshefsky's assessment China's accession would aid world prosperity and stability

(Barshefsky 2000: 5). The Sino-US bilateral agreement deal led to the discussions on the signing of bilateral agreements between China and other important countries. China signed bilateral agreements with other countries as a part of the WTO accession mandate. Its signing of bilateral agreements with some major trading partners like the EU, Canada, Japan etc., are discussed in the following passage in detail.

It was observed that the signing of the Sino-US bilateral deal had a strong impact on the successive agreements. "One element that contributed pressure on China and members to conclude bilateral accords rapidly was the US administration's agreement with China—as a quid pro quo for China's market access concessions—that the US would provide China with permanent MFN status thus eliminating the annually renewed conditional MFN provided under the Jackson-Vanik amendment to the US Trade Act" (Gertler 2003: 62). This development gave rise to China signing twenty-one bilateral negotiations by February 2000. China made consistent efforts to complete market access negotiations with most of the countries and then proceeded to clear her outstanding issues with the Working Party.

Negotiations with the EU

The EU has been a strong supporter of China's accession to the WTO, expressing the view that a WTO without China was not truly universal. This view fostered strong trade ties between the EU and China leading to the emergence of the EU as China's third largest trade partner, next only to Japan and the US. According to statistics of the China General Administration for Customs, the total volume of bilateral trade between China and the European Union was to the tune of US$ 57 billion and US$ 69 billion in 1999 and 2000 respectively. China's export value was US$ 40.90 billion, a growth of 7.1 per cent year on year, while its import value was US$ 35.72 billion, increasing by 15.8 per cent year on year. The continuous rise in bilateral trade has propelled the relations between the two to expedite the Chinese accession to the WTO.

On the issue of accession, there were several negotiations between China and the EU. In one of the important negotiations, discussions covered the outstanding issues on market access for the industrial goods, while negotiations also included issues like tariffs, phasing out of quotas and subsidies on farm products. The second round of the discussions focused on the services sector which included telecommunications, banking, tourism, insurance, security, brokerage, law, and accounts. The Minister of Foreign Trade and Economic Cooperation, Shi Guangsheng informed that both sides have agreed to meet again in order to finalize the agreement. He told that "China will never make any commitment which it cannot keep but we will try our best to satisfy certain countries requirements" (*Beijing Review* 2000: 4).

The third round of talks between China and the European Union (EU) ended in Beijing in 2000. A statement issued by the Ministry of Foreign Trade and Economic Cooperation stated: "The negotiations were positive, constructive and fruitful, and both sides made a great effort." The EU Trade Commissioner, Pascal Lamy, who led the EU delegation, stated that he will report back to the 15 EU member states as well as European Parliament to "assess how best to approach a future round of negotiations" (*Beijing Review* 2000: 5). In these negotiations China agreed to reduce import tariffs and other NTBs. China also accepted to ensure that the investments by the EU companies in China will take place in a more attractive and predictable business environment. These negotiations eventually culminated in signing the bilateral agreement between China and the EU on May 19, 2000 at Beijing.

Negotiations with Canada

China signed bilateral accession agreement with Canada in 1999. China committed to improve market access to agricultural products from Canada. Products included canola, canola oil, barley, wheat, feed, and North American ginsheng. China, in order to protect its own industry, would apply for Tariff Rate Quotas (TRQs) in politically sensitive sectors. A TRQ is a tiered tariff structure under which higher tariffs are applied to imported goods that exceed an established quota. The two Canadian products affected by such quota are canola and canola oil.

In the services sector, the liberalization of financial services will be made open in five years from the date of accession in which geographic and customer restrictions will be phased out. Foreign banks will offer services to foreigners and the Chinese customers in local or foreign currencies. Greater access will be given to life insurers who will benefit from the gradual removal of restrictions and an expanded scope of operations within 50 per cent foreign ownership restriction. This increased advantage to life insurers will provide better services to the subscribers. In the negotiation process Canada has demanded that in priority agricultural goods tariff reduction should come down to 5.2 per cent from 12.5 per cent over the three years from the date of accession. Canada seemed to have demanded heavy concessions from China in relation to market access. Similarly on industrial goods it will bring down the tariffs from 10.3 per cent to 4.5 per cent.[4]

Negotiations with Other Countries

China had signed accession agreements with different countries as a part of its WTO requirement. The accession agreement was signed between China and Australia during the visit of the Australian Foreign Minister, Alexander Downer in July 1999 announcing that the two countries decided to conclude their bilateral negotiations on the issue. They declared the official conclusion of the bilateral market access negotiation between China and Australia in relation to China's accession to the WTO. Australia supports China's early accession to the WTO, and China appreciates this support. President Jiang Zemin told Downer, during their meeting, that China and Australia, as influential countries in the Asia-Pacific region, share wide-ranging common interests in maintaining peace and stability, and promoting prosperity and development. China stands willing to make joint efforts with Australia to develop long-term stable and sound bilateral relations oriented towards the 21st century. (*Beijing Review,* 2 August 1999, p. 7). China and Australia are ready to strengthen cooperation in multilateral international organizations and on major issues, and will work for the establishment of an equitable and rational, international economic and financial order. This was the common consensus reached by President Jiang Zemin and Prime Minister, John Howard in September 1999 in Canberra. The two leaders agreed during their meeting to establish a 21st century-oriented relationship between the two countries of long-term stability, healthy development and all-round cooperation. Howard declared that the Australian Government regards its relationship with China as one of country's most important and that Australia attaches great importance to working with China in all sectors. Howard also expressed Australia's support for China's entry into the WTO. The two leaders attended the signing ceremony of five agreements and memorandums of understanding on consular affairs, mining, and combating crime (*Beijing Review* 1999: 6). China has already concluded bilateral negotiations with over 10 WTO member states by 1999. During this period it was reported that among the 134 WTO members, 36 countries have proposed to hold bilateral negotiations with China.

The painstaking talks on China's entry into the WTO came to an end in August 2001. The Working Party under the Chairmanship of Mr. Pierre-Louis Girard met on 17 September 2001 and concluded its work, marking the end of all negotiations concerning China's accession to the economic super-group. All agreements reached at the informal working party were submitted to the formal Working Party meeting for approval (*Beijing Review* 2001 p. 4).

China will adopt an even more broad-based opening-up pattern than before, remarked Premier Zhu Rongji at the Sixth World Chinese Entrepreneur Convention. Zhu added: "We will open up our service sector step by step, including banking, insurance, telecommunications, trade and tourism, and explore new forms and channels to use foreign funds." He further pointed out that China would closely combine its efforts to attract foreign funds from those (world entrepreneurs) with whom it can readjust its funds to build industrial structure, develop China's western region and deepen the reform of State-owned enterprises. The imports of advanced technologies and development of modern managerial expertise will also be a focus (*Beijing Review* 2001: 5). The accord on China's entry into the WTO was approved in the formal meeting of the 18th Working Party on China's accession, clearing the way for Beijing to join the world trade body within months. "International economic cooperation has brought about this defining moment in the history of the multilateral trading system," told WTO Director-General, Mike Moore at the conclusion of the meeting of the Working Party on China's Accession (*Beijing Review* 2001: 5). Given the timing of the fourth WTO Ministerial at Doha in-mid November 2001, it was agreed that these documents may be sent to Doha Ministerial, instead of tabling them at General Council in Geneva for approval of the ministers. In accordance with established procedure, the Ministerial approved the Decision on Accession and the Protocol on the terms of China's accession on 10 November 2001.

The WTO finally opened its door to China, and the Chinese delegation signed a membership protocol with the WTO. Shi Guangsheng, head of the Chinese Delegation to the fourth ministerial conference of the WTO noted the following three basic conclusions: First, participation in the multilateral trading regime with a positive stance is the only way the various countries will be able to better share the benefits of economic globalization. Second, the participants will be able to do their best during this globalization process only by establishing an economic and trade regime in line with the international practices and specific economic situation thereby safeguarding their financial security while opening up to the outside world. Third, the multilateral trading system will be able to maintain its vigour only by constantly adapting itself to developments in the world economy and fully reflecting the interests of all parties, including those of developing countries (*Beijing Review* 2001: 4).

As one of the provisions of the WTO suggests that the acceding government becomes a member of the WTO thirty days after it has accepted its Protocol of Accession which China did on 11 November notifying the Director-General of the WTO that the standing Committee of National People's Congress had ratified the terms of accession.

Thus after prolonged negotiations, China became the 143rd member of the WTO on 11 December 2001. "This is an historic moment for the WTO, for China and for international economic cooperation. With China's membership, the WTO will take a major step towards becoming a truly world organization. The near-universal acceptance of its rules-based system will serve a pivotal role in underpinning global economic cooperation," said WTO's Director-General, Mike Moore, commenting on the approval of China's accession (WTO, 2001). After the approval of China's accession, the head of the Chinese delegation, Shi Guangsheng, Minister of Foreign Trade and Economic Cooperation, said: "We need to invite all members to formulate the international trade rules of the new century through equal participation and consultation so as to enable more developing countries to share the opportunities and interests brought about by the economic globalization and to avoid the further widening of the gap between rich and poor and protect some countries against being marginalized" (WTO, 2001). Soon after joining the WTO, China agreed to undertake a series of important commitments to open and liberalize its regime in order to better integrate with the world economy and offer a more predictable environment for trade and foreign investment in accordance with the WTO rules. China's future commitments will indicate how it is going to benefit from the world economy.

Summary

Recognizing the importance of joining the WTO, China made a conscious decision in 1986 to join the multilateral trading system. The advantages the Chinese leadership had conceived from such a system looked apparent for her. First, it would represent international recognition of its growing economic power. Second, it would be able to play a major role in the development of new international rules on trade in the WTO. Third, multilateral trading system would provide China access to the dispute resolution process in the WTO reducing the threat of unilaterally imposed restrictions on the Chinese exports. Fourth, it would make it easier for reformers in China to push for liberalization policies if they could argue that such steps are necessary to fulfill China's international obligations. Fifth, China has sought WTO membership as a means to obtain permanent normal trade relations (PNTR), or most-favoured-nation (MFN), status from the US on a permanent basis. Renewal of that status every year is no longer required. Sixth, it witnessed huge opportunities in international trade which it can exploit by joining the WTO for its own economic growth and development. At the same time world economy will have access to promising market which remained isolated for long. Finally, China wanted to influence the multilateral trade negotiations in the WTO.

China's attempt to the join the WTO has never been easy. Barriers it faced to join the WTO were far more onerous in nature compared to other acceding countries. Tariff reduction to minimal level for industrial products and more so for agricultural products had become critical for her. Imposing special safeguard measures and forcing it to join as a 'developed country' member were the major barriers, which China had to negotiate for long years. Allowing it to function as a 'non-market economy' till the end of 2015 continues to be an important barrier for China in its drive for integration with the world economy.

China joined the WTO by paying a huge price. This is reflected in the commitments that it made to join the WTO. It agreed to abide by those long-standing commitments to become a member. On agricultural front it promised to forego all export subsidies and accepted a cap on domestic subsidies that is lower than normally available to other developing countries. It agreed to an across the board commitment on services in addition to trade in goods. It succumbed to the pressures of negotiators by allowing the foreign investors to distribute their products in China and gradually eliminate all kinds of restrictions that would make business for foreign investors easy and promising. From a developing country's perspective, China's overall commitments to join the WTO had been some of the most radical and onerous so far. World economy was equally aware about the economic and trade potentialities of China so much so that it never desired China to be out of the multilateral trading regime for so long. Its current standing in the global economy to a large extent complements this attitude as China is a major player in international forums like the WTO, G-20, and G-33 and in various global climate change summits like the Copenhagen climate change conference in 2009.

China's long-drawn process of accession finally secured its WTO membership. Its integration with the multilateral trading system provides her equal opportunities vis-à-vis other countries. Its intention of emerging as a globally competitive economy led her to integrate and compete globally through various sectors. The following chapter focuses on textiles and examines in detail how the sector has responded to internal changes and external growth and competition.

Notes

1. Under the ITA, developed countries are bound to eliminate tariff on IT products by 2002 and developing countries by 2005 on some products.
2. "It doesn't matter whether you are Bangladesh or Brussels. There are rules. These will be the rules for China."—Ms. Charlene Barshefsky, United States Trade Representative, Chong (1995).
3. Accession process set out in the WTO is dealt under Article XII of the Marrakesh Agreement, which led to the establishment of the WTO.
4. For more see Ministry of Foreign Affairs at http://www.fmprc.gov.cn/eng/gjhdq/dqzzywt/2633/2634/t15542.htm. Accessed on 10 January 2010.

4

China's Textiles Sector

Performance and Challenges

Textiles[1] sector occupies a special significance in China's economy. Considered as a pillar industry, its contribution to the economy in terms of foreign exchange earnings and employment is noteworthy. Currently more than 20 million people are employed in the sector, representing 22 per cent of total employment in the manufacturing industry. Besides, another 80 million are estimated to be indirectly dependent on this sector.[2] With its abundant supply of low-cost and skilled labour, China has become a large producer and exporter of textiles and apparel.

This chapter aims to examine the overall performance of the sector in the context of China's integration with the world economy. The chapter is divided into four sections. Section II analyzes the positioning of China's textiles sector in the pre-WTO phase, focusing on policy changes introduced by the Government and the role FDI played in the sector. Section III deals with how the textiles and clothing (T&C) sector is placed in a global perspective and how it has performed in relation to exports after joining the WTO. Section IV analyses the challenges and future prospects for the textiles sector. Section V provides the summary.

Textiles Sector in Pre-Entry Stage

Economic reforms and open door policy initiated in the late seventies gave a new direction to China's economy. The leadership began to realize that China with its gradual and pragmatic economic policies could improve its industrial performance at domestic and international levels. It chose the T&C industry as one of its domestic industries for promotion. There were two reasons for this choice. First, China had basic infrastructure and experience in this industry. Second, this industry (mostly textiles) is a labour-intensive one and it did not require very advanced technologies. It could exploit comparative advantage since the country had a large population and abundant labour force. This advantage encouraged the Government to embark on a reform programme in

1979, aiming at a strategic integration with the world economy by following a 'dual track' policy. This policy focused on liberalizing FDI and sourcing imported inputs for select industries like textiles to become matured enough so that it could take on the global competition.

Since the early eighties, China's industrial drive has adopted a three-pronged strategy. *First*, the government aimed at developing endogenous productive capacity through SOEs or government support by paying attention to science and technology policy, and then linking the SOEs with the private sector or research institutes. *Secondly*, domestic T&C industry with the government support remained alert to integrate itself with the world economy. The industry has gradually and strategically integrated into the world market in order to have access to technology, capital, skills, raw material, and world market. *Thirdly*, the government followed a gradualist approach to adjust to the market economy. In the eyes of the policy makers market and government policies were to supplement each other and as the economy progresses gravity of each would change. Deng Xiaoping had referred to this strategy as "crossing the river by feeling each stone" (Deng Xiaoping Selected Works Vol. 3: 51).

As a part of this strategy, China launched a policy called "Six Priorities" to promote the T&C industry. Under this policy, the industry enjoyed favourable treatment in six areas: supply of raw materials; fuel and power; innovation and its transformation and infrastructure construction; bank loans; foreign exchange, imported foreign advanced technology; and transportation. As a result, the industry's output rose rapidly. From 1979 to 1982, the average annual growth rate of the total value of T&C output was 13.2 per cent. China could attain such growth because of continuous economic reforms, improving living standards, foreign trade expansion, and continuous increase in demand both in domestic and foreign markets. The Chinese products began to impact significantly during the early 1980s in international markets, as a result manufacturing industry; especially the T&C sector drew more attention from the Government.

Around 1980 China had moved away from the traditional stereotype model of a developing country dependent syndrome where dependence on exports of primary commodities was strong (Todaro 1994: 229). During early 1980s, manufacturing exports started soaring up and reaching almost 50 per cent of China's entire exports as against 24 per cent from resource-based products, and 26 per cent from agriculture. This share of manufacture further rose to secure 62 per cent of China's exports in 1995 and continued to experience high growth consistently at that level in 2001 and 2002 (Martin and Manole 2008: 207-208). The textiles sector had figured prominently as a potential manufacturing sector having vast opportunity for its expansion (Zhu 2009: Personal Interview). It had huge demand for domestic consumption as well as for exports. The government had subsequently laid emphasis by creating industrial clusters in this sector to expand domestically as well as to push its export demand.

Subsequent adoption of establishing industrial clusters in textiles popularly known as Special Economic Zones (SEZs) to boost the sector was given state preference. These T&C clusters are located in the Eastern coastal region, the most industrialized area of China, covering the Pearl River Delta (PRD) and Yangtze River Delta (YRD). These areas contribute significantly to the growth of national GDP as well as cater to the growing demand of exports. Zhejiang, Guangdong, Jiangsu, and Shandong provinces and Shanghai municipality are the five top exporters of China's textiles, representing 80 per cent of total textiles output.

Opening up to the outside world had accelerated the opportunities for exports. Gradually T&C clusters in China focused their orientation towards exports. Raw materials and processed apparel products are often cheaper in China and their quality is increasingly confirming to the global standards. This led the Government to realize that the T&C has immense potential in the world market and supportive policies must be formulated to give the sector a boost. Textiles exports in China had earlier greatly benefited from the rural reforms that took place in the late 1970s. Sharp rises in the cotton production in the 1980s provided abundant supply of raw materials for textiles production. The fact that the Chinese economy was fairly closed during the early 1980s, value-added domestic inputs became quite vital for domestic production, to help exports match the international standards.

Between 1979 and 1984 cotton production nearly tripled with the input of technology coming from abroad through foreign direct investment (FDI) thereby increasing the volume from 2.2 million tonnes to 6.3 million tonnes (State Statistical Bureau, 1985). By 1988, China's market share had peaked accounting for more than 22 per cent of total textile exports originating in developing countries, or 7 per cent of the world's textile exports. As for clothing exports, China's market share has continued to increase. By 1994 it accounted for 26 per cent of clothing exports originating in developing countries, or 16 per cent of world clothing exports. In 1994, China overtook Asia's newly industrializing economies (NIEs)—Hong Kong, South Korea, and Taiwan—as the world's largest clothing exporter.

Around the mid-1990s China emerged as a significant player in world textiles. It registered the highest exports of T&C in the world in 1995 and also in 2002 soon after its accession to the WTO. Its world market share rose from 22.5 to 30 per cent over this period in the clothing sector and from 16 to 22 per cent in the textiles sector. By the late 1990s China had become one of the world's largest textiles producers and exporters. The production and exportation of textiles became vital both for its economic development and foreign exchange balance. It also helped to create a balanced supply and demand, and sound trade patterns for textiles in the world market (Yongding, Bingwen and Hongren, 2000: 437).

The T&C industry in pre-WTO era looked quite promising. China consistently figured among the top 20 exporters in the world from the mid-1990s. In 1995, it exported textiles worth US$ 3.8 billion to the world taking into account products-textiles fibres, yarn, fabrics and clothing classified under Standard International Trade Classification (SITC)[3] Nos. 26, 65, and 84. During 1996-2001 it experienced certain fluctuations in its exports to the world. Towards the last quarter of 2001 at the time of its entry its total exports of T&C registered US$ 5.4 billion showing an annual average growth rate of 6.3 per cent over 1995 (UNCTAD Statistical Hand Book 2007).

From the mid-1990s onwards, China's major export destinations have been countries like the US, Japan, Germany, Hong Kong, Singapore, Italy, etc. Since 1995 its exports to the US had witnessed a progressive rise. In 1995, it exported US$ 3.1 billion to the US and reached US$ 4.53 billion in 2000. Between 2001 and 2002, the jump in exports is significant which suggests that opening up and joining the WTO has helped to integrate better with the world economy in the T&C sector. Similarly, the Chinese exports to Japan have been steadily rising from US$ 8.7 billion in 1995 to US$ 13.5 billion in 1998. But in 1999 and 2000 the growth in exports has come down bordering about US$ 11 billion. China's exports to Germany between 1995 and 2001 have seen several ups and downs. In 1995, it exported US$ 956 million worth of products to Germany, but in 1996 it registered a decline by bringing it down to US$ 845 million. Similarly in 2000, US$ 1.09 billion worth textile products were exported whereas in 2001 it amounted to 961mn. Singapore, a neighbour and an active partner in ASEAN imported substantially worth US$ 749 million in 2000 and US$ 718 million in 2001 from China. Hong Kong, another important trading partner of China and a major commercial hub in East Asia also saw some fluctuation in its import growth from China on T&C, registering 12.9 billion in 2000 and 10.2 billion in 2001 (World Trade Atlas Online Database 2009).

Similarly, it can also be observed that few countries have consistently performed better in terms of percentage share of world exports of T&C. China, Turkey, Mexico, and India are some of the countries whose shares have steadily risen in the global market. China has been a frontrunner in the percentage share of exports. From 1995 it has shown a steady rise, registering 11.04 per cent to 12.12 in 1997 to 11.77 in 1998. Its share in 2000 was 13.86 and in 2001 it went up to 14.58 (UNCTAD Statistical Hand Book 2007: 17) which means China's T&C sector remained globally competitive through out. China' exports in pre-entry period are also analyzed from another trade database (WITS COMTRADE Database). In this analysis, performance of the EU as an important trading bloc having 25 member states has been explained.

The analysis found that the EU's imports from China on T&C (Articles 61, 62 and 63 of HS code[4]) noticed a rising trend. In 2000, it amounted to US$ 3.31 billion and went up to US$ 3.39 billion in 2001. Similarly, under categories 62 and 63, the EU's imports from China went up from US$ 4. 41 billion to US$ 4.79 billion and US$ 0.83 billion to US$ 0.87 billion. Imports of USA on same products from China witnessed a rising trend. Under HS code 61 imports registered US$ 2.38 billion in 2001 from US$ 2.14 billion in 2000. Likewise, under HS code 63 it went up marginally from US$ 1.18 billion in 2000 to US$ 1.29 billion in 2001 (WITS COMTRADE Database). By 2001 China had begun to dominate the world scene by registering US$ 48 billion, leaving behind most of the competitors in the T&C sector (World Trade Atlas Online Database 2008). In terms of employment, this sector continues to hold promise for its people. The T&C sector in China exuded confidence and growth. China's T&C industry has matured from early phase of its industrialization till date and continues to contribute significantly to the world trade. It had the largest share of world trade in textiles and clothing. It captured US$ 16.14 billion (10.2%) and US$ 30.07 billion (18.1%) in world exports of T&C respectively in 2001 (Statistical Year Book of China, 2001). The overall steady growth in T&C before joining the WTO had necessitated urgency in the government's functioning to plan out strategy to join the WTO. Its preparation to join the WTO had called for several measures to be taken up in China. Key actors like the Central Government; trade & industry, have played a prominent role. Institutional and structural changes were brought about in various sectors keeping in view the requirements of the WTO. Policy changes were made at different stages. Such important changes are explained below.

Structural Changes in the Policy-Making Bodies

One important change has been the abolition of the Ministry of Textile Industry which has been in charge of planning, production as well as policy-making for the national textile industry. The Government is mainly responsible for setting guidelines for the industry development, exercising macro control and making adjustments. Presently, the State Development and Reform Commission (SDRC) is responsible for monitoring and controlling the economic operations of the industry as well as establishing plans for the industrial development. The Ministry of Commerce (MOFCOM) is in charge of areas for textile trade policy, and the State-owned Assets Supervision and Administration Commission (SASAC) is managing and supervising the state-owned assets in the textile industry, particularly the restructuring and rationalization of state-owned enterprises. The China National Textile Industrial Council (CNTIC) was separated from former Ministry of Textiles and made into a non-governmental intermediate organization, mainly responsible for guiding the industry in improving its performance and providing consultancy services for the industry.

Another significant development in the textiles sector has been the establishment of the China Textile Academy (CTA) which remained originally affiliated to the Ministry of Textile Industry. This was opened under the initiative of the Central Government and was founded in 1956 to develop skills for large scale domestic production. It was only around the mid eighties that this academy significantly contributed to the skills development and provided coordination and planning to the domestic textiles enterprises to expand growth of textiles in the country. The success of CTA generated interest in the Central Government to widen its role in the economy. In 1999, the CTA was transformed into a large-scale high-tech enterprise directly under the Central Government and developed into the biggest and comprehensive Research and Development (R&D) institution and high-tech enterprises group in China's textile industry. It is equipped with advanced and professional instruments, facilities, and production workshops for trial.

Government Policy Towards State-Owned Mills in the Textile Industry

By the end of 2001 and the early part of 2002, state-owned economic component had a diminished role in China's textile industry. State-owned enterprises in the whole textile industry were 2,723 in total, accounting for 11.5 per cent, whereas non-state-owned enterprises are numbered at 20,877, occupying 88.5 per cent. The non-state-owned enterprises tend to perform better than state-owned enterprises. During 1986-1999 non-state enterprises like the Town and Village Enterprises (TVEs) contributed much more significantly to the total output accounting for 61 per cent of total textile output and 98 per cent of clothing output (Yang 1999: 7). The performance of textile enterprises varied geographically and across sub-sectors. Profits earned in western and central China were much lower than those earned in the eastern China. The government was aware of the textile industry's problems and yet had withdrawn subsidies for the loss-making state-owned enterprises such as preferential tariff and value-added tax treatments. In the wake of competition, SOEs were unable to deliver. Huge staff concentration and non-performance led to the closure of many SOEs in this sector. Protests against incidents of such lay-off were wide spread.[5]

The Central Government's full intention of joining the WTO, however, propelled the industry to undergo certain restructuring. The overall principles of industry restructuring were as follows. Inefficient and unprofitable state-owned enterprises in all sectors of the textile industry were phased out. Big and medium sized state-owned enterprises were restructured into joint stock enterprises by listing on the stock market, joint venturing with foreign investment as well as developing mutual share holding. Medium and small sized enterprises having high debt ratio, but with advanced equipment, better management and market for the products were encouraged by the government to revitalize them through assets restructuring for reducing the debt ratio. The government also encouraged other medium and small enterprises that were financially in an advantageous position and were regarded crucial to the growth of the textiles sector. These small enterprises were given favourable treatment over large because they were still found competitive in spite of high debt ratio. It helped them through schemes like resorting to foreign trade development fund as well as discounted interest rates for technological upgradation.

Chinese Government's Policy on Domestic Wool Usage

Wool has been a major input for China's success in garment industry in the world. Realizing this, the Government had taken certain major steps to promote its production. Although China itself has the world's largest sheep population (143 million), it is strongly dependent (70%) on imported wool for its wool textile industry. Though it produces a variety of coarse and semi-fine wool types that are generally of a low quality; hence used mainly in carpet manufacturing. It is said that the Ministry of Agriculture wishes to see more domestic wool to be used by state-owned wool textile mills but this seems to be difficult given that 95 per cent of wool textile mills are non-state-owned. So there are no specific favourable policies in place for domestic wool usage. Production of wool has been stepped up in 2005 as the world witnesses more trade in this sector. Production in wool industry has increased year on year with accumulated production of wool yarn increasing moderately by 3.5 per cent and wool fabric growing by 17.7 per cent respectively.

Performance of wool industry was rising steadily in the same period. Sales revenue of 1233 above-scale wool spinning and weaving mills and 1523 above-scale wool knitting mills have strongly lifted by 32.3 per cent, 32.1 per cent year on year; total value of export shipments has increased by 25.0 per cent, 27.3 per cent and 10.8 per cent respectively; accumulated production/ sales ratio reached to 95.94 per cent, 98.52 per cent; profit gains sharply increased by 40.4 per cent and 40.7 per cent as well. This is a strong indication of the industry moving in the right direction. Domestic sales being the key driver for industrial development, the industry's growth rate of sales revenue has exceeded that of export value indicating a stronger domestic market for the industrial sectors. Exports also gradually experienced high growth. In contrast, exports of wool yarn and wool knitwear have slowed down with traditional destinations of Hong Kong and Japan taking lower volumes. Overall, in the field of T&C, a rising market share for China was noticed around the time it completed its accession to the WTO. During the 1990s it increased its market share in the EU (WITS Database), Canada, and the US, but the surge that most of the people had expected didn't take place. This is evident because higher tariffs as well as quota were still restraining China's trade with them. Beginning 1 January 2002, China felt the pressure of reducing the tariffs imposed by developed countries.

FDI in Strengthening the Sector

One of the key elements of China's economic reform process has been the encouragement of FDI. In the textiles, the FIEs are not as important but still account for about 20 per cent of the industry's total number of firms in output and in value-added services (Fung *et al*, 2002, pp. 14-15). It was predicted that the FIE's contribution in this sector will see an upward trend (Zhu 2009: Personal Interview).

China has also been a major recipient of FDI from the Japan. In fact, the Japanese firms started investing in China as early as 1981. Textile sector is the third largest in terms of cumulated FDI. It received 200.4 billion yen direct investment from Japan from 1989 to 2001 (Xing 2004: 6). Investment came heavily into this segment because garment industry is labour intensive and China enjoys comparative advantage in the international division of labour. Both could reap huge benefits by producing textile products in China due to its rich labour endowment. These direct investments from Japan have been export-oriented and they helped immensely in promoting China's manufacturing exports. Most of "Made-in China" products available in the Japanese domestic market carry Japanese brands, and many products under Japanese MNEs' brands in global market are made in China. For example, the Japan Wool Textile Company Ltd. produced garments in a plant located in China for exports. Japanese investment in textiles industry was fairly strong during late 1980s and early part of the 1990s. This reflects a clear strategy behind the Japanese investment in China, making it as a cheaper production base essentially to cater to its domestic market and for world exports.

Another significant characteristic of the Japanese direct investment in China is that these investments are actively engaged with reverse imports, which refer to the products made at overseas Japanese plants and exported to the Japanese market. Rising yen and shrinking domestic demand have compelled many Japanese firms to relocate their domestic production to China, and in some cases simply outsource their production to the Chinese firms. The Fast Retailing Co., which designs, distributes, and markets UNIQLO brand products in Japan, produces the products in its China's affiliates, or subcontracts to China's domestic firms. Thus China has emerged as the most popular destination for the Japanese direct investment since the middle of 1990s. According to the survey of JETRO (2001), among the Japanese firms with overseas production facilities, 54.4 per cent of them have production facilities in China, the highest among all foreign countries. Around this period, China was emerging as an ideal location for regional investment.

China sourced more than 80 per cent of its textiles raw material imports from Japan, Hong Kong, Chinese Taipei, and the South Korea. In addition, China also sourced most of its inputs like technology and skills for its domestic clothing industry from these countries.

In 2005-06 China received FDI to the tune of US$ 60 billion, out of which the textiles sector received about 10 per cent. The FDI in T&C continues to increase in China. Most of the investments came from Hong Kong and other South East Asian countries, and not so much from the US and EU. In 2007 China received FDI worth US$ 1.8 billion in the T&C sector, which is about 2.5 per cent of total FDI it received from the world (Guoxing 2009: Personal Interview). According to many trade experts in China, FDI has played an active role in promotion of China's T&C sector. "It has brought in technology, skills and capital to upgrade and revitalize the sector to take full advantage of industry's integration with the global industry," according to Prof. Wang Guoxing (Guoxing 2009: Personal Interview).

Textiles Sector after its Entry into the WTO

Accession to the WTO in 2001 opened up a plethora of opportunities for China's exporters of T&C products in the global market. Having obtained the WTO membership it became a beneficiary of the global trading in apparels, more particularly the Agreement on Textiles and Clothing (ATC). China could now position herself to take advantage of the phase-out of the quota under the third phase of the ATC (which was put into force on January 01, 2002) and could look forward to the benefits accruing from the final quota phase-out (which was implemented on January 01, 2005). Many observers (Tatsufumi 2007: 7, Knappe 2003: 18, ILO 2005: 30) believe, China is well poised to take full advantage of the opportunities of the global market once the quota-free regime was in full effect.

China's potentiality in T&C was known to the world. By becoming a member in the first year of joining it had improved its global share from 13.86 to 14.58[6] and had increased its volume of exports from US$ 48 billion in 2000 to US$ 49 billion in 2001.[7] Its global competitiveness came to be well recognized by other competitors. The reasons for this success were due to a number of factors. Besides exchange rate manipulation, there was a host of other explicit and hidden policies, which according to the ILO report, gave China a competitive edge vis-à-vis other countries. China's 13 per cent tax rebate on T&C products, government subsidies given to the state-owned textile and apparel enterprises (which, interestingly, comprises 52 per cent of the textile sector and 25 per cent of the apparel manufacturing sector in 2003 and 2004), and availability of "free credit" for both the public and private enterprises provided, China significant opportunities to undercut other competitors. The T&C trade invites particular attention in China because it is one of the largest sectors and its contribution in terms of export and employment is significant. The peculiar structure of earlier global textile architecture before 2005 was so restrictive in nature, that many developing countries whose potential to perform better could not get reflected in their economies. China is one such country.

As is well known, T&C exports from developing countries to the industrial countries are subject to high tariffs, hovering around 8.9 per cent for the US and 12.4 per cent for Canada (WTO 2001: 11), and are also subject to a system of bilateral quotas that were developed under the MFA. Though agreement was reached in the Uruguay Round (1985-94) to phase out quotas against developing countries' exports of T&C, yet it did not help China to enjoy those advantages because by then China had not acceded to the WTO. The major turning point came on 1 January 2005 when the abolition of quotas was implemented. During this course of development some other WTO members like the EU, Canada, etc., retained the option of trying to restrict China's exports using a range of provisions under China's WTO Agreement (Bhattasali *et al.*, 2004, p. 28) including the product specific safeguard in China's WTO Accession Agreement. In addition, developed countries had the provision of targeting and obstructing China's exports under anti-dumping actions to which it is vulnerable because of the non-market economy provisions (Messerlin 2004: 108). China remained under pressure even after it had acceded to the WTO.

It started bearing the liabilities of cutting tariffs further after joining the WTO. According to the commitment, the average duty of T&C was gradually reduced from 17.8 per cent in 2002 to 11.4 per cent in 2005. In 2002, the average reduction was 2.45 per cent. The average duty level in 2005 was reduced by 6.4 per cent compared to that of 2002, with a reduction range of 36 per cent. By 2005, all duties had reached the binding level except for one duty number. After the duty reduction, the "ladder" duty pattern (from low to high) was created for products from raw materials, medium products, and manufactured products. Upon joining the WTO, China had also abolished the import quota and licenses for products under 42 duty numbers, i.e., wool, acrylic, terylene, etc. From 2002, all import quotas and licenses for textiles, raw materials, textile garments, and textile machinery were abolished. Apart from tariffs, China cannot re-adopt or implement any other non-tariff measures after entering the WTO, unless a large volume of foreign products are dumped or the domestic industry suffers serious damages. Thus, pressure on China continued. Based on the agreement of the WTO, animal and plant products underwent a quarantine inspection. In 2002, the tariff quota for wool was 264,500 tons and for wool yarn, 72,500 tons. These figures jumped to 287,000 tons and 80,000 tons respectively in 2004. From 2002, the number of companies appointed to trade in wool, wool yarn, and acrylic also rose gradually. By 2005, trading rights were relaxed. While cotton imports continued to be traded by state-owned enterprises, non-state-owned enterprises continued to have the cotton import rights. The Government slowly abolished the State-owned trading rights system of silk by increasing and expanding trading rights to non-state sector. By 1 January 2005, the Government completely abolished all active restrictions on silk exports, including all procedural fees. After the WTO accession, the state-owned trading system of the "two yarns and two fabrics" and silk, and raw silk were amended, and trading rights were opened to all enterprises. Exports of raw cotton fabrics to Japan and South Korea were exported under a quota, and export licenses were applied according to relative regulations.[8] Such pressures propelled China to augment its technical skills, financial resources and infrastructural development to sustain its export growth and explore new opportunities in world market.

China's Export Scenario in Post-Entry Period

The changes that have been introduced from 1995 to 2001 have had a tremendous impact on China's performance in the major importing markets. For example, US T&C imports from China increased by 125 per cent in 2002, a trend that continued in the first three months of 2003. In the same period, apparel exports increased by 60 per cent. The Chinese exporters reduced their prices in order to gain a greater share in the market. They were able to do so, among other reasons, because quota rents[9] were reduced and the Chinese enterprises increased their productivity by investing heavily in new machinery and technology (Knappe 2003: 20). China had soon become a dominant player in the T&C markets. By becoming a member of the WTO, it could promote its trade within a short span. China exported 19.3 and 5.9 per cent of textiles to Australia and South Africa respectively in 1995. The corresponding market shares had expanded to 35.2 and 18.5 per cent in 2002. It also became a dominant trading nation in the clothing sector with a respective market share of 54.3 per cent in Australia and 29 per cent South Africa in 1995. By 2002 it could register as much as 70.4 and 56.3 per cent in these markets (Nordas 2004: 16-17).

China's T&C sector in the post-entry phase looked promising. From Figure 4.1 it is understood that in 2001, the year it joined the WTO, its exports to the world reached US$ 36.1 billion (products based on HS codes 61, 62 & 63). It continued to witness significantly high growth touching US$ 62.5 billion in 2004 and thereafter registering US$ 130.1 billion in 2008, thus signifying global dominance in the world market. From the Figure 4.1 it can be noticed that Hong Kong was the nearest rival touching US$ 26.8 billion in 2008 and the major industrialized country, the US had recorded a meager US$ 5.2 billion. Whereas, world exports in T&C had touched US$ 385.2 billion in 2008. The

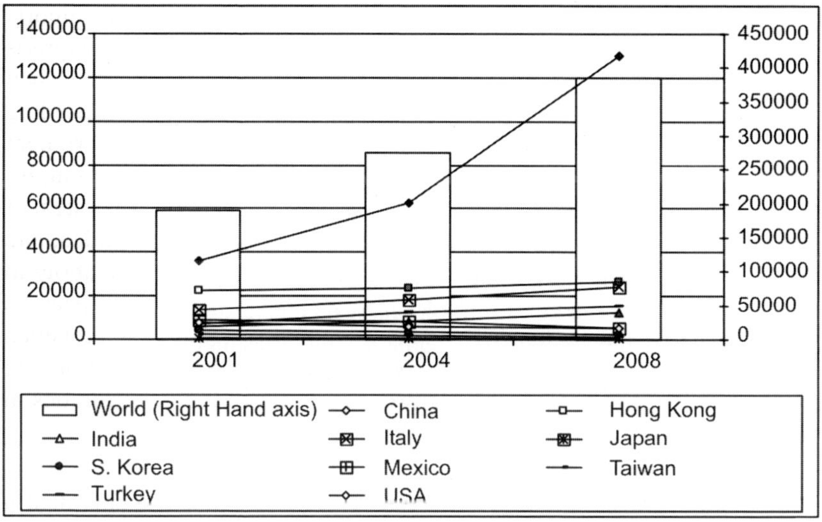

Note: Based on HS Codes 61, 62 and 63.

Source: UN COMTRADE Database 2010, WITS, Accessed on 15 July 2010, URL: http://comtrade.un.org (basic data of all the graphs are in Appendix II).

Figure 4.1: Major Exporters of T&C in Post-Entry Phase (US$ Million)

study has also analyzed China's position in T&C in the world market from another source, i.e. UNCTAD Statistical Hand Book 2007. According to this source (products based on SITC 26+65+84), China maintained a steady rise in its exports to the world by reaching US$ 54.2 billion in 2001 to touch US$ 145.5 billion in 2006. This source further explained that in the post-entry scenario China's exports to the world on T&C has experienced steady growth (Appendix III).

It is observed from the Figure 4.2 above that China's annual export growth rate to its major trading partner, the US had shot up from 2 per cent in 2001 to register 27 per cent in 2004. During 2002-2004 this growth rate has observed a substantial rise touching 18 and 35 per cent in 2002 and 2003 respectively (Appendix II). Such huge growth had occurred as China had joined the WTO. More opportunities for China were created. With this key development in global economy, faith and confidence of the US in China's trade practices were restored. Cotton knit shirts and trousers showed the highest growth with 18 million shirts shipped from 1 million (1,332% growth) and 27 million trousers shipped from 1.9 million January 2004 (1,836% growth). Industry figures show a decline of 45 per cent in prices in cotton trousers and 28 per cent in cotton shirts (China Customs).

Most increases in shipments are fuelled by China's ability to manipulate and control its pricing structure in textile and apparel products. This could affect eight product groups (China Customs) such as brassieres, cotton knit shirts, men's woolen shirts, cotton trousers, dressing gowns, underwear, man made fibre knit shirts, and man made fibre trousers that represent the major employment and production sectors of the US yarn and fabric industry. In 2004, the Chinese exports of apparel in quota-free categories increased by 513 million square meters, or 55 per cent, and brought China's share of the US import market in these categories to a record 70 per cent. Imports from the rest of the world fell by 91 million square meters in 2004 (US Department of Commerce). China's share of 25 apparel categories increased from 10 per cent in 2001 to 34 per cent in 2002; 57 per cent in 2003 and now to 70 per cent in 2004. The study by Nordas (2004) suggested that China could capture 29 and 50 per cent of the EU and US markets. In December 2005, China had a 72 per cent share of the import markets of the US, Hong Kong, and Japan. From Figure 4.2 it is noticed that China had secured an annual export growth rate of 83 per cent share of the US market.

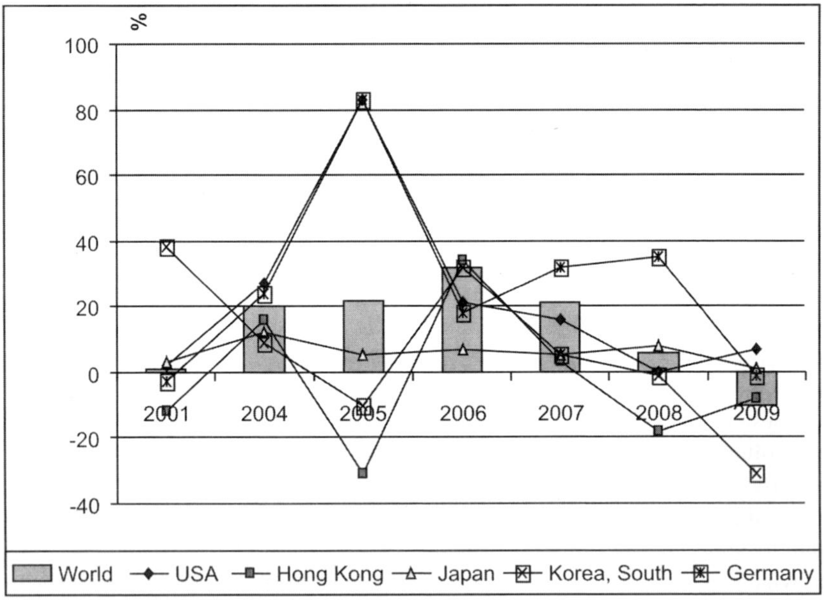

Note: Based on HS Codes 61, 62 and 63.

Source: Calculation based on World Trade Atlas Online Database 2010, Accessed on 16 July 2010.

Figure 4.2: China's Annual Export Growth Rates in T&C in Its Major Markets and the World in Post-Entry Phase

To this development, the US government and textiles association has sharply criticized the Chinese government, by alleging that China has adopted wrong means to boost its exports. The Chinese government employs numerous illegal and unfair trade practices to ensure that the Chinese exporters can under-price their textiles and apparel. Anti-competitive actions by China's government claimed by the US industry include currency manipulation (estimated to provide up to 40% subsidy for the Chinese exporters), illegal direct government subsidies of its money losing state-owned textile and apparel sectors; illegal export tax rebates (13%); and the deliberate extension of billions of dollars in non-performing (free money) loans by China's central banks in order to award a competitive advantage against foreign competition (National Council of Textile Organization: 2004). Import curbs on the Chinese textiles products are sometimes arbitrary. As China entered the WTO and continues to be a non-market economy, it was easy for developed countries to impose dumping measures whenever they see danger for their domestic industry (Guoxing 2009: Personal Interview).

As the Chinese exports had surged, exports from the US free trade and trade preference countries fell sharply, mainly from NAFTA countries. With the removal of quota control, the US imports in apparel products from Mexico fell nearly 50 per cent to 40 million square meters over the last three years and Mexican market share declined from 8 per cent to 2 per cent. The Caribbean and Central American countries also saw sharp decline. The impact on the US industry has been felt most in North Carolina with 126 plants closed since 2000. States like South Carolina, Georgia, Virginia, and Alabama also experienced huge losses by closing down their 70, 34, and 30 plant operations respectively during this period. The National Council of Textile Organization (NCTO) claimed that over 200,000 jobs have been lost in 5 years. It is also argued that apart from open and implicit subsidies given by the Chinese Government to its producers, it is the artificial low rate of exchange between the Chinese currency and the dollar that had resulted in massive surge in Chinese exports to the US. China has been letting its currency fall apace with the dollar over the past few years, thus giving its exports a large cost advantage vis-à-vis exports to the US from most other countries.

Likewise, it is clear from the Figure 4.2 that China's annual export growth rate to South Korea had registered 38 per cent in 2001, which further came down to 9 per cent in 2004, indicating South Korea's decline in imports of the Chinese T&C products. China's export to Germany noticed a negative growth of 3 per cent but had increased to 24 per cent in 2004. This explains the rise in opportunities and demand in Germany after China joined the WTO. China's exports to Germany had seen a positive trend as China registered annual export growth rate of 17 and 47 per cent and 83 per cent in 2002, 2003 and 2005 respectively. (Appendix II). Similarly, Hong Kong has been a favourable destination for export of the Chinese T&C products as China registered an annual export growth rate of 22 per cent in 2002, more than the US in that year. However, Hong Kong imported less compared to Germany in 2004 from China. Such volatility of Chinese T&C exports to Hong Kong had occurred because the demand for such Chinese products was less. Hong Kong and some other Asian countries were focusing less on the low technology products like textiles which China was exporting to these markets (Lall and Albaladejo 2004: 1448). During this period Japan was also another important destination for the Chinese products. It is also noticed from Appendix III that India and Mexico experienced rise in exports. However, in another study it was found that during 2002-2006 Mexico's annual average growth rate dramatically declined registering a negative growth of 3.3 per cent. This largely happened due to China becoming a WTO member (Branstetter and Lardy 2006: 51). From Figure 4.2, it is seen that China's annual export growth rate to the world had also gone up registering 1 per cent in 2001 further rising to 20 per cent in 2004 and 22 per cent in 2005.

Figure 4.3 explains China's top export markets in the world. After it has joined the WTO, its exports to Japan have risen. Touching US$ 12.6 billion worth of exports in 2001, it registered US$ 15 billion in 2004. Similarly exports to the US have gone up from US$ 4.0 billion in 2001 to see a continuous rise till 2004 to touch US$ 8.2 billion. In 2005 its exports to the US in these products experienced a huge increase as China exported US$ 15 billion. This

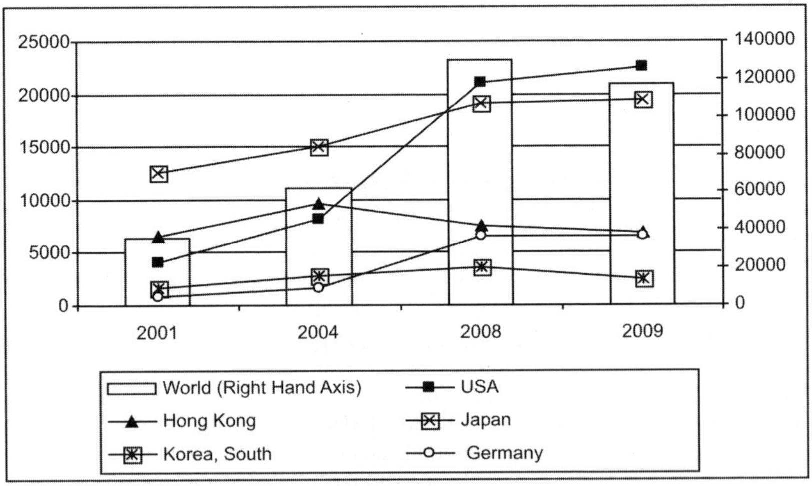

Note: Based on HS Codes 61, 62 and 63.
Source: World Trade Atlas Online Database 2010, Accessed on 16 July 2010.

Figure 4.3: Significant Export Markets of China's T&C in Post-Entry Phase

rise in exports explains about the elimination of quota regime which was in place for more than three decades and came to an end on 1 January 2005. Similarly, South Korea, a key importer of China's T&C products, has increased its imports from China. In 2001 it received US$ 1.6 billion imports of textiles products and went to increase its imports worth US$ 2.8 billion in 2004. However, its imports came down in 2005. In 2006 and 2007 it witnessed an increase in its imports from China (Appendix II). Germany, another major importer of T&C products also witnessed an increase in its import from China from registering US$ 0.8 billion in 2001 to US$ 1.7 billion in 2004.

Figure 4.4 provides share of major exporting countries in the world on T&C. It is noticed that China has a share of 19 per cent of world exports in 2001. It has continuously improved its world share in T&C, registering 23 per cent and 34 per cent in 2004 and 2008 respectively. Hong Kong has been the closest rival in this sector, whereas the US has a small share of 4 per cent in 2001 and then reduced its world share to 2 and 1 per cent in 2004 and 2008.

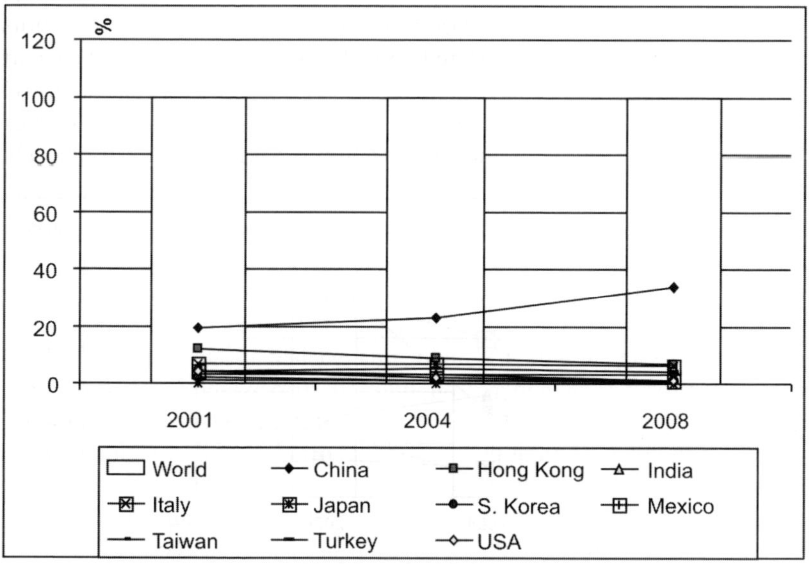

Note: Based on HS Codes 61, 62 and 63.

Source: Calculation based on UN COMTRADE Database 2010, Accessed on 17 July 2010, URL: http://comtrade.un.org

Figure 4.4: Share of Major Exporters of T&C in the World

Post-Multi Fibre Agreement (MFA) Phase

The MFA phase came to an end on 31 December 2004. The post-MFA phase is assumed to be the most dynamic and growth friendly period as the phase out of quota restrictions gave a level playing field to the individual countries to establish their competitiveness in the T&C sector in world market. Looking at the four Figures 4.1, 4.2, 4.3 and 4.4 given above, one gets a detailed picture about China's position vis-à-vis individual countries and the world. The analysis suggests that China has been in a unique position since it has joined the WTO. Its performance in the sector justifies that it has exploited the global opportunities in a competitive manner. Such massive rise is largely due to phasing out of quota restrictions and the end of MFA (*China Daily* 2005: 11). MFA phase out has been a push factor in China's exports of textiles. Exports from China jumped in the first half of the year 2005 registering almost US$ 16 billion (World Trade Atlas Online Database, 2010) to the US, whereas in 2004 it exported textile products worth US$ 10 billion. However, in 2006, one year after the total phase out of quota restriction, China's annual export growth rate to the US which had noticed an upward trend from 2001 to early part of 2005, registered a huge decline bringing it down to 21 per cent from 83 per cent in 2005. Germany too witnessed such significant decline as the annual export growth rate came down from 83 per cent in 2005 to 18 per cent in 2006. China's annual export growth rate to the US and Germany were higher than the world rate of 22 per cent (Figure 4.2).

It is well known that traditionally China has been a great exporter of the knit and woven textile products to the world and especially to the US. Yet this sudden increase in high volume of exports to the US in the earlier half of 2005 had created an alarming situation for the US to re-look at its trade policy towards China. It seriously considered invoking safeguards to restrict garment exports from China. Similarly the EU countries also faced a surge in textiles imports from China. The EU too equally wanted to resort to some mechanism by which it would be able to cut drastically its textiles and garment imports from China. As a result, the EU and China reached an agreement on a three-year "transitional arrangement" on June 10 2005 which limits the annual increase in Chinese garment imports to about 10 per cent until trade is liberalized in 2008. Though the transitional arrangement of China with the EU would allow the Chinese exports to continue to grow, yet at a rate that would allow the EU producers to adjust to new levels of competition. The EU also imposed certain NTBs like SPS, as a result China's exports to Germany had decelerated in 2006 (Figure 4.2). The US and China made a similar agreement in 2005, restricting nearly half of China's garment imports into the US by the end of 2008. These transitional safeguards imposed on China forced her to scout for new markets in other parts of the world. From Figure 4.2 it can be analyzed that in 2006 China's annual export growth rate to Hong Kong, South Korea, Japan, etc. experienced a significant increase. The restrictions in the US and EU market had subsequently pushed China to negotiate and divert its attention towards East and Southeast Asia as a major destination for its T&C exports.

Imposition of textiles safeguard measures by the US and the EU vis-a-vis China had again crippled the natural growth of world trade in T&C. China had felt that it was going back to the restrictive phase of MFA which remained in operation from 1974 to 1994. It was only when the WTO was established in 1995; it was assumed that the MFA system of controlled and restrictive trade regime would be phased out by 31 December 2004, as such an arrangement would be against the fundamental principle of the WTO (Gereffi and Memedovic 2003: 14). These discussions on safeguard measures had formed a part of China's accession process at the WTO.

Safeguards can be negotiated between the countries involved or unilaterally adopted. The Textile Monitoring Body in the WTO (WTO: 2005) monitors the placing of safeguards on a global basis and must approve their use. During 2005 the trade safeguards were placed by the US and the EU in the form of quotas on many textile and apparel products imported from China. Imposition of such safeguards was earlier a part of the accession clause of China to the WTO; hence it came in handy for the developed countries to restrict China's exports. On 23 May 2005 the US imposed restrictions on three categories of imports from China. These were cotton knit shirts and blouses (category 338/339); cotton trousers, slacks and shorts (category 347/348); and cotton and man-made fibre underwear (category 352/652). On 27 May limits were imposed on an additional four products: cotton yarn (category 301); men's and boys' cotton and man-made fibre shirts (non-knit) (category 340/640); man-made fibre knit shirts; blouses (category 638/639); and man-made fibre trousers (category 647/648). The reason given for introducing quantitative limits is a sharp increase in the imports of these items.[10] Restrictions from the US government are imposed from the date of the request for consultations with China until 31 December 2005.

Surge in imports from China has also disrupted the domestic market and has heavily resulted in the loss of jobs for America. As a result, the US and China had many times entered into a row over textiles issues. In 2005, the US administration informed that it has accepted petitions from the US textile industry to launch investigations into whether quotas should be imposed on 21 categories of clothing and textile imports from China in 2004 and 2005. It observes that such petitions are against the fundamental principles of the WTO. It suggests that an amicable settlement can be arrived at by looking at prospects of both the sides (*China Daily*: 2005 http://www.chinadaily.com.cn/english/doc/2005-10/06/content_482840.htm).

However, its exports to the US increased to US$ 18.1 billion in 2006 and US$ 20.9 billion in 2007 (Appendix II). China's exports of T&C in volume terms to the world have gone up to reach US$ 130 billion in 2008 (Figure 4.1).

Its exports to the major industrial markets like the US and Germany have also registered an increase amounting to US$ 21.0 billion in 2008 and US$ 22.5 billion in 2008 and 2009 respectively (Figures 4.2 and 4.3 and Appendix II).

Imposition of transitional safeguards during 2005 had played a critical role in limiting the surge of China's textile exports to the US. First of all, the transitional special safeguard measures introduced by the Agreement on Textiles and Clothing (ATC) were binding on China until 31 December 2008. Secondly, the base for quota expansion for China is much smaller and slower than other WTO Members. For instance, the bilateral textile agreement between the US and China permits an annual average growth rate of less than 1 per cent, one of the lowest among importing countries. Indeed, because of this low annual permissible growth rate and the low quota bases, some keen watchers in China have expressed the view that joining ATC would be detrimental to the Chinese textile and apparel exports. Moreover, according to the Report of the Working Party on the Accession of China which has the same legal status as the WTO agreements, it is not very clear whether China can receive ATC benefits retroactively from January 1995 when ATC took effect or from the date of the Chinese accession to WTO, i.e., 11 December 2001. The wording of the Report is thus: "To these base levels, the increase in growth rates provided for in Articles 2.13 and 2.14 of the ATC should be applied, as appropriate, from the date of China's accession."[11]

During the past seven years of ATC's operation, T&C products were supposed to be progressively integrated into the WTO regime and quotas for the rest of the products were to be increased gradually at specified rates. Though major importing countries have not implemented ATC at the pace indicated by the agreement, there have nevertheless been some benefits. Under the application of the ATC to China, the coverage of its products by quotas is wider and the extent of quota increase will be less than for other WTO members. Under the ATC "growth on growth" provisions, until the end of 2004, the incremental increase for existing quantitative restrictions maintained by the WTO members on the Chinese exports will be no more than 16 per cent while in the same period other members will, in principle, enjoy an expansion of a further 25 per cent, following the first two stages of implementation of the ATC. These conditions constitute a ceiling for the Chinese exports and will make the expansion of quotas insignificant for China in some products. In addition, the Chinese utilization of existing quotas is often 100 per cent or close to 100 per cent, while that of countries such as Indonesia, Thailand, and Bangladesh has been hovering around 80 per cent. This too puts a check on the potential export expansion for China.

Moreover, other WTO members were able to increase their exports without restriction of quotas starting from 1 January 2005 when the ATC came to an end, and their trade in textiles and clothing were integrated into trade liberalization provision of the WTO. For China, however, a special transitional safeguard continued to restrict it from benefiting from the post-ATC free trading regime in T&C. The special safeguards allowed importing countries to impose import restraints if market disruption is deemed to be caused by an import surge while some other countries such as Mexico, Turkey, and some Asian countries will benefit from the preferential provisions of their respective regional trade agreements (RTAs).

Up to 2013 i.e., after 12 years of the Chinese accession, countries importing the Chinese products will be able to use special safeguards to address rapid increases in imports from China that cause or threaten market disruption. Imports could be considered as undergoing rapid increase when measured by volume or value relative to the previous levels so long as evidence is produced to show "material injury, or threat of material injury to the domestic industry." These specific mechanisms permit importing countries to apply restraints unilaterally based on criteria lower than those stipulated in the WTO Safeguards Agreements. Ordinary WTO safeguards apply when imports from all sources "cause or threaten to cause serious injury to the domestic industry that produces like or directly competitive products"[12] but under the transitional product-specific safeguard mechanism, importing countries will be able to evoke safeguard measures that target imports from China. Arguably, a decision to resort to trade defence mechanism could be made much more easily when the exports of only one country are affected.

It was also found that China has increased its exports through other means, i.e. by linking itself to prominent retail chains. Walmart is operating in various provinces of China without adversely impacting country's domestic retailers (ASSOCHAM: 2006). The global MNCs have taken the Chinese products, particularly apparels, to almost all corners that one can identify in the world. Global retailers like Walmart buy about US$ 60 billion worth of goods including textiles from China (Kanungo 2006: 30). Entry of these retailers has expanded the scope of China's exports. They source their goods from inside. Thus, FDI is instumental in building China's productive capacity to become the world's largest producer and exporter of textiles.

It is further analyzed on consulting the World Integrated Trade Solution (WITS) database that China's major global trading partners like the EU and the US experienced a rise in their imports from China in the post MFA phase in the T&C products categories defined under HS codes (61, 62 and 63).[13] China exported more than US$ 6 billion in 2004 to reach US$ 9.4 billion and US$ 10.3 billion in 2005 and 2006 respectively. Its exports to the US in 2004 registered US$ 4.33 billion to touch US$ 6.96 billion and US$ 8.44 billion 2005 and 2006 respectively. An analysis of pre and post MFA phase provides interesting results for both China and the world. It was found that the annual growth rate of garment exports of China to USA was 56.77 per cent in 2005 which was very high compared to the total garments imports of USA from rest of the world which was 5.89 per cent. With the imposition of transitional safeguards by the US, China's exports on textiles shrunk significantly in 2006. The growth rate for China was as high as 18.19 per cent (US Department of Commerce, Bureau of Census by World Trade Atlas).

China's export drive on garments to the EU countries also witnessed a significant rise in 2005. China exported US$ 13, 714 million worth of garments in 2004, while the export totalled reached US$ 20, 361 million in 2005. The growth rate for China up to the third quarter of 2005 was 54.41 per cent. Its growth rate for January-October 2006 was lowered and came to be even lesser than the world average of 10.74 per cent in 2006 (Yamagata and Tatsufumi 2007: 10).

Another market where China's export penetration in textiles and garments has shown upward trend in 2006 is Japan. Japan is one such market, which has always exported garments; hence it has not imposed any quota restrictions on garments in the past (Yamagata 2007:12). China has been a major exporter to Japan in post-MFA period. Japan sourced about 83-84 per cent of its garment imports from China between 2004 and 2006. In spite of the structural changes made in a significant way in other two biggest markets of the world, namely the US and EU, Japan has somewhat experienced insignificant changes even after the MFA phase-out has come into force. China's comparative advantage in textiles is noticed from Revealed Comparative Advantage[14] (RCA) exercise. As of 2003, based on Revealed Comparative Advantage (RCA) Index, China has a high comparative advantage in textiles and electronics, while it lags behind in automobiles and petrochemical sector. In textiles RCA of China was 2.97 whereas Japan's 0.28 and Korea's 1.37 (Development Research Centre of China *et al.* 2004 http://www.nira.or.jp/past/newse/paper/joint4/report.html).

China's strength in T&C, however, was known to the world which is why industrialized countries had negotiated such imposition of safegaurd measures on its textiles products during its accession period. As China had agreed to such accession provisions, it became easy for the developed countries to impose such measures immediately after the MFA phase-out and whenever they experienced surge of textile products from China during 2005, 2006, and 2007. China's signing of Memoranda of Understanding with the US and the EU restricted the rapid growth of Chinese textiles and clothing exports to their markets. It also became a deciding factor for China to scout for export markets in other regions of the world like Southeast Asia and Africa. During this period China increased its world exports by 21 per cent, 25 per cent and 18.9 per cent respectively (WTO, 2008).

Industry Scenario

Though protectionism in apparel industry had a long history in the US, the global shift towards reduction of quota and tariffs had begun more than a decade back, and the ATC being in place the change was noticed. The elimination of restriction on apparel imports was brought into effect on 1 January 2005 which created a shift in the manner sourcing decisions are made. It is suggested that by removing quotas, apparel production in China will surge by 70 per cent and in other Asian countries by 26 per cent [United States International Trade Commission (USITC: 2004)]. The North American production is expected to decline by 19 per cent and European production by 11 per cent (USITC 2004).

Apparel exports from China are expected to increase by 87 per cent and 36 per cent respectively after the removal of quotas (USITC 2004). This is because the Chinese textile products are cost competitive and cater well to the wide variety of global demands. Such dramatic changes signal a fundamental change in the dynamics of buying and sourcing decisions. In specific woolen segment, China's performance during post-MFA phase showed significant progress. In the first 6 months of 2005, the export volumes of scoured wool, tops, wool fabrics, cashmere sweaters, wool woven apparels maintained a high growth rate of 21 per cent, 55 per cent, 22 per cent, 78 per cent and 30 per cent respectively. In contrast, exports of wool yarn and wool knitwear have slowed down with traditional destinations of Hong Kong and Japan taking lower volumes. For the same period, imports of wool totalled 123,200 tons increasing by 3.2 per cent year on year. Growth of major wool exports is also an important factor for industry development. During 2006-07 China's textiles exports looked up registering around US$ 15 billion (UNCTAD Statistical Hand Book 2007).

In 2008 preliminary import figures released by the US Department of Commerce show that the Chinese apparel exports took a record 54 per cent of the US apparel import market in November and Chinese exports in key quota categories were surged by as much as 132 per cent as China approached the end of quotas on January 1 2009. November 2008 was the first month in history that the Chinese share exceeded 50 per cent. Cass Johnson, President of NCTO, said that while Chinese exports dipped earlier in the year, this end of year surge was not a surprise: "When the Chinese government saw textile exports under performing, they did what they have always done—they increased subsidies. China has pumped $ 10 billion in new export subsidies into their textile sector since July and they are having the desired effect."[15] The American textiles industry lobby has expressed its deep concern to the US Government to deal with the issue to save the US domestic industry and its workers from losing their jobs as they expected a huge surge from China during 2009 since the quota imposed in 2005 came to an end on January 1,

2009. The US textile industry is worried that China would use various subsidies such as currency manipulation, land, rent, privatization, financing, energy costs, etc. to surge into the US market.

Challenges and Future Prospects

Multiple studies and analyses done by widely varying groups and institutions have all come to the same conclusion—that China will dominate world trade in textiles and apparel once quotas are removed. These include studies by the WTO, the World Bank (Ianchovichina and Martin 2001: 21), the US International Trade Commission,[16] and the McKinsey Company[17] as well as analyses of China's past trade behaviour in non-quota countries and in apparel categories removed from quota control. In another significant study (Nordas 2004: 34) by the WTO on the phase-out of quotas predicted that China and India would take 71 per cent of the US apparel market with China (including Hong Kong) gathering 56 per cent and India taking the rest. The study's econometric model shows sharp declines for all major suppliers with Mexico and the Caribbean Basin countries taking an especially hard hit.

Challenges

The T&C has a long tradition in China and its development has been central to China's industrialization process. In China's move to a market economy and its integration into the international trading system, the T&C industry has gone through a difficult structural adjustment process in which 1.4 million textile workers (the majority of whom were middle-aged women) lost their jobs during the period from 1995 to 2005 (ILO 2005: 22). In the pre-entry period lack of market competition secured the existence of small and medium enterprises to continue, as a result employment in the sector did not come down dramatically. In the post entry phase competition was set in and non-competitive firms had to wind up their business activity. This led to massive decline in employment opportunities. Through this measure of integration and competition China may have improved its position in international trade; yet the challenge of providing employment opportunities and maintaining social harmony occupies priority.

The opening of China's market entailed by its accession to the WTO led to a shift in resources in response to the forces of comparative advantage. With population increase every year, China has to provide employment for its huge labour force including the millions of migrants from rural areas who have been displaced by increased agricultural imports. Work opportunities had to be found in sectors where China possessed international comparative advantages, and the T&C industry is a key sector in that respect. Today, the T&C industry provides employment for 19 million workers (22% of total employment in manufacturing industry), and another significant proportion of population is estimated to be indirectly dependent on the T&C industry.

Most of the human resources in China can find employment in labour intensive industries as rural mass is not equipped to handle technology-dominated industries. Clothing being a key labour-intensive sector, the pressure on the Government will remain high to absorb people in this sector.

Private capital including foreign capital has played a leading role in the modernization of the T&C sector where adjustment has resulted in a fundamental change in the ownership structure. Currently, only 13 per cent of the industry is held by state-owned capital whereas private ownership accounts for 87 per cent (15% is foreign owned, another 15 per cent is owned by companies from Hong Kong and Macau Special Administrative Regions and Taiwan, China). Such foreign capital is always necessary to upgrade modernization of the industry. Maintaining a regular receipt of large-scale of foreign capital is a big challenge for the government.

The domestic textiles industry has not progressed much in China. It is the FIEs operating in China whose contribution has been quite significant. Rules of the game in this sector have been unfavourable for China for all these years. Restrictive regime in T&C industry combined with imposition of safeguard measures in 2005 had curtailed the growth of textiles sector in the global market. The need of the hour is to develop and promote its own brands and market them internationally. This is a major challenge for the Chinese textiles industry. China is going to face wide ranging demands coming from consumers in its domestic market because the Chinese industry needs to expand (Hong 2009: Personal Interview).

Access to the most competitive inputs is an important factor in the competitiveness of the Chinese clothing industry. China's garment exports depend greatly on the import of fabrics, raw materials and textile machinery from other countries. It is estimated that about 50 per cent of exported clothing is made from imported textiles. In 2004, China's clothing exports reached US$ 61.62 billion in value while its import of fabrics, raw materials and textile machinery from other countries reached US$ 24.02 billion. China is the world's third largest textile importer just behind the EU and the US. The Chinese textile industry is the world's largest importer of raw cotton. China is also among the top importers of wool in the world (220,000 tons in 2004) and the world's largest importer of textiles machinery and parts (importing US$ 4.48 billion worth in 2004, of which 43.1 per cent, or US$ 1.95 billion, came from the EU). Through its imports, the Chinese T&C industry has contributed to the growth of other T&C activities worldwide. Such kind of dependence entails a long and stable relationship with both developed and developing countries. Maintaining a delicate balance between herself and the developed countries will be a key challenge for China itself as more often trade relationships develop into a conflict because of certain unforeseen events like global financial crisis, volatility in the market, and surge in oil prices, etc.

Speedy and timely deliveries are an important element of competitiveness. China faces certain problems in this regard. There is a need to catch up with these supply constraints as world market will demand more and more customized products at faster pace. Besides, power shortages have considerably disrupted T&C production in China in the past. There are also bottlenecks in the transport and distribution infrastructure for locally produced and imported coal and oil. All these problems require immediate solution.

A major concern is China's "non-market economy" status at the WTO for 15 years (or upto 2016). China accepted this provision as a part of its accession. This poses adequate threat to its status of competitiveness as anti-dumping duties on T&C products from China can be higher than those from other market economy members of WTO like the ASEAN and several other developing countries. Again the transitional safeguard mechanism accepted by China as a part of its accession procedure valid until December 2013 will restrict its exports to other countries. Developed countries' imposition of this rule is a big drawback for China's future exports in this sector.

Another challenge China faces is in the area of imported cotton and raw materials. As the global financial crisis has reduced demand for products, imports of such material are curtailed, which in turn proves difficult to produce products for even domestic consumption. The Chinese government and textile producers are depending on the domestic market consumption rather than external demand. During January-October 2008, China bought 826,000 tons of cotton from the US; 570,000 tons from India; and 166,000 tons from Uzbekistan; which have come down by 18.8, 34.4, 15.8 per cent respectively (*Xinhua*: 13 January 2009).

The Chinese textile sector export growth may decline during the present recession. The rising labour cost and decrease in demand will definitely affect its performance in world trade (Zhu 2009: Personal Interview). From 1990s to 2007 end, the growth in textiles has been phenomenal. The Chinese products could capture large part of the world demand. With the onset of global financial crisis and significant rise in labour costs in textiles industrial clusters and in major cities, competitiveness of this sector is fast eroding. Countries like Vietnam, Indonesia, and Bangladesh will take advantage of this situation, because labour cost is still cheap in these countries and the developed countries can enter into better bargain with them in terms of bulk sourcing (Ho 2009: Personal Interview).

Many other trade experts also echoed almost similar views. China might lose its global competitiveness in T&C by 2015 because of the rise in labour costs. It will face sudden fall in FDI as most of the countries have started identifying Vietnam as a cheaper destination for growth of T&C in Asia (Song 2009: Personal Interview). It is a big challenge for China to maintain its dominance in world market. China must adopt the strategy of investing in great measure on R&D. Institutions like the National Innovation Center may upgrade innovation in the T&C sector. Chinese textiles sector has provided critical support to its rise in GDP growth in both the 1980s and 1990s. Even the growth has been significant after the dismantling of quota in 2005. During the first quarter of 2005, China's export growth went up by 35 per cent.

In response to such concerns, the Ministry of Textiles in China has drawn out certain plans to tackle this challenge. China should slow down its currency appreciation and increase export tax rebates to help lift its textile industry. The paper[19] prepared by the Ministry of Information Industry, and based on recommendations from a range of bodies including the Ministry of Commerce, the China National Textile and Apparel Council (CNTAC), and the China Cotton Association (CCA) suggests certain recommendations. These include lifting the export tax rebate on textile products to 13 per cent from the current 11 per cent raising the tax rebate on garment exports to 15 per cent from 11 per cent cancelling of import duties for some textile machinery to help the industry increase efficiency in the face of rapidly rising costs and increasing labour costs by up to 40 per cent in 2008 because of a new labour law. All these challenges pose serious concerns for the Government as it prepares to rejuvenate the industry in the aftermath of the global financial crisis.

Future Prospects

The T&C industry is based in the Eastern coastal region, the most industrialized area of China and the one which contributes significantly to the growth of national GDP. Zhejiang, Guangdong, Jiangsu, Shandong Provinces and Shanghai municipality are the five top exporting regions of China's textiles representing 77 per cent of the total T&C output. These provinces are constantly making efforts to invite more foreign investment which will step up their production activities to capture domestic market. The prospect is high in this sector as China is now concentrating on expanding its domestic base (Zhu 2009: Personal Interview).

Saturation in the traditionally developed market sometimes indicates a country with high potentiality to scout for partners to expand its exports and growth. Of late China has increased its collaboration with the Least Developed Countries (LDCs). It has provided to free market access for many products imported from those LDCs that have diplomatic relations with China. The T&C technical assistance programmes including training courses and technology transfers have been implemented in a number of LDCs. China is supporting international initiatives within the international financial institutions to provide further assistance to the LDCs and other developing countries to adjust to the quota-free trade regime.

China is also collaborating with other developing countries to upgrade their production and strengthen their competitiveness in the T&C sector.

China's foreign investment in the T&C industry has reached US$ 500 million mainly in developing countries. More Chinese enterprises are considering investing in other developing countries that benefit from low cost labour and duty-free access to major importing countries. In May 2005, the Deputy Minister of Commerce led a business delegation to Malawi, where it discussed investing in textiles and cotton industry and developing their industrial base and providing employment to the locals. By 2008, roughly US$ 6.5 billion were set to be invested and more than 1000 locals were to be employed.[19]

The Chinese Government has implemented a number of preferential policies with a view to encouraging its T&C manufacturers to invest more in other developing countries. These measures include preferential loans, simplified administrative procedures, enforcement of legal rights, and enhanced information and intelligence support. China's overseas investment in the T&C sector is expected to grow faster in the coming years as mutually beneficial cooperation between China and other developing countries proceeds rapidly. China also expects that the competition in the sector will get tougher. It is planning to upgrade its products by moving into higher segments, i.e., manufacturing branded products. As most of the manufacturers are gaining experience and know-how through practicing original equipment manufacturing (OEM)[20], stronger enterprises are contemplating of designing and manufacturing branded products. There will be a shift from low and medium end to higher end products. China's strength lies in OEM (Guoxing 2009: Personal Interview).

It is generally argued that the textile and clothing firms in China will benefit from the reduction of import tariffs and the eventual elimination of export quotas (Zhang 2000: 123). The Chinese T&C sector will benefit from the WTO as China can import raw materials and machines at much lower tariffs, which will reduce the production costs and improve their competitiveness.

China's core competence in manufacturing especially in labour intensive products like T&C is well established. As a highly competitive producer and exporter of T&C, it is likely to have a great deal of influence both in expanding market access opportunities for these products and in defending against measures that would reduce developing countries' market access for these products (Martin and Ianchovichina 2001: 1209). However, the data provided by China Customs[21] suggest that China's apparel exports consisting of HS Codes 61 and 62 registered higher exports to the US reaching US$ 1.67 billion in 2007. But, in 2008 the export value has come down marginally to US$ 1.63 billion. This sudden decrease in exports may indicate the effect of the current global financial crisis. Experts believe once the impact of the global crisis is over, China will be able to improve its export prospects as it has competitive advantage in the sector.

Impact of American[22] Financial Crisis

The US sub-prime crisis that broke out in the summer of 2007 had an adverse impact on the global economy after the bankruptcy of Lehman Brothers and General Motors in September 2008. Bankruptcy of these established institutions followed by acute liquidity shortage and credit crunch snowballed into a worldwide economic slowdown. The US, the Euro Zone and Japan all slipped into recession in 2008. The emerging countries have faced not only a dramatic decline of economic growth but also a surge of capital outflows. China's embrace of openness coupled with the inexorable forces of globalization has meant that their economies are now deeply interwoven into the global economy (Naughton 2007; Panagariya 2008).

Given these processes, China's economy remained vulnerable. As external trade in merchandise and services contributes to a significant portion of its economy, a global slump in demand had a negative impact on China. A study conducted by the World Bank (2009) projects that the world GDP growth would 2.5 per cent in 2008 and 0.9 per cent in 2009. Developing countries would likely to grow by 4.5 per cent the following year, down from 7.9 per cent in 2007 whereas growth in high-income countries would turn negative. With world trade volumes projected to contract 2.1 per cent in 2009, countries experienced big drops in their exports. Moreover, sharp declines in consumer spending and unemployment in the US because of the financial crisis may resulted in dramatic reduction in exports from China. The US, the EU and Japan which account for 46 per cent of the external demand for China's exports have all slipped into recession due to the impact of the American financial crisis.

Emerging markets such as Hong Kong, Taiwan, South Korea and the ASEAN countries which are China's major export markets have also slowed down dramatically (Xiangshuo 2009: Personal Interview). As a result of the weakening external demand, China's exports have declined significantly. Both exports and imports have registered a contraction since November 2008. Due to the impact of the American financial crisis a large number of export-led private enterprises in China's coastal provinces, especially in Pearl River Delta dealing with textiles sector have gone bankrupt (Song 2009: Personal Interview). Around 20 million unskilled workers lost their jobs. Furthermore, the slowdown in China's exports along with the decline in real estate investments has led to a decrease in GDP growth from 13 per cent in 2007 to 9 per cent in 2008.

Therefore, the Chinese government has accorded priority to the export growth with the intention that the export sector can accommodate excess labour. The huge number of workers released from bankrupt or poorly operated enterprises has caused a surge in the real unemployment rate which could lead to social unrest. Hence, the Chinese government has continued to provide tax rebates to export goods, increasing its intervention in the foreign exchange market to prevent further appreciation of the RMB against the US dollar and lowering its environmental and energy-consuming criteria even during 2008 (Zhang 2009: Personal Interview).

Despite these measures, exports of textiles have been hit. China's textiles firms' profit declined for the first time in ten years. This sharp fall in profits is due to the decline in overseas demand. The National Bureau of Statistics in China says that the decline is about 1.77 per cent over 2007. The losses for the textile firms added up to 22 billion Yuan from January to November 2008. The causes were sharply noticed during this period when the financial crisis began impacting the world economy.

Cotton, a major component of China's textile production, witnessed a decline in its imports during first ten months of 2008. Global financial woes had depressed the import demand. According to the General Administration of Customs between January and October 2008, China imported 1.866 million tons of cotton at a combined value of US$ 3.11 billion, a decline of 8.3 and 10.1 per cent respectively for the same period of 2007. The imports of SOEs and FIEs stood at 508,000 tons and 369,000 tons respectively down by 14.5 per cent and 18.4 per cent on a yearly basis (*Xinhua*: 13 January 2009).

As the American financial crisis prolonged, China's textile industry is under dual pressure from weakening demand at home and abroad. The growth rate of China's textile exports began to decelerate in 2008. According to statistics provided by the General Administration of Customs, China exported US$ 185.17 billion of T&C in 2008, up 8.2 per cent from the previous year. However, the rate of growth was down by 10.7 percentage points from that in 2007. The Government expected the growth rate of China's overall textile exports in 2009 to continue to slow down as the economy also began to get affected by the rising labour costs, the appreciation of the Renminbi, and reduced demand in major export markets.

In addition, after a period of transition following the textile integration in 2005, the potential of exports of relevant products have already been fully released. As anticipated, no sharp increase is expected in exports of Chinese textile products that had been under bilateral textile agreements with relevant countries. However, the Government and industry sources feel its textile industry and its major trade partners in the world market would find ways to complement each other's advantages and improve their interdependence. China has bounced back previously in such crises. Now it is an opportunity for China to look for other markets as well as create demand at home. The Central Government is paying adequate attention to this problem.[23] Other trade experts also believe that China's textile trade with other countries after 2010 would see a stable and healthy development.

Since the third quarter of 2008, China's textile industry has encountered pressure from declining demand both in the domestic and international markets as the country's real economy began to feel the negative impact of the spreading international financial crisis. During the 104th China Import and Export Fair, the contract value in textiles dropped by 31.5 per cent compared with the previous fair. Enterprises are feeling the pressure. The number of enterprises that stopped production and went bankrupt in the last two years has increased. Large-scale textile enterprises in China experienced negative growth in employment and small and medium-sized enterprises recorded serious downsizing.[24]

This is also reflected in the data provided at Figure 4.2. Though in volume terms China's exports to the world have gone up (Figures 4.1 and 4.3), yet annual export growth rate has witnessed a significant decline. China's annual export growth rate to the world has dramatically come down from 21 per cent in 2007 to 6 per cent in 2008. The year 2009 has witnessed even much lower growth rate as it reached a negative growth rate of 10 per cent (Figure 2 and Appendix II). Similarly China's annual export growth rate to the US has substantially come down from 16 per cent in 2007 to 0 per cent in 2008. China's performance in Hong Kong and South Korea has also been affected significantly. It has witnessed a negative growth of 18 per cent and 8 per cent in 2008 and 2009 respectively in Hong Kong and negative growth of 1 and 31 per cent in 2008 and 2009 in South Korea (Figure 4.2 and Appendix II). This huge decline has taken place due to the impact of global financial crisis on China's trade.

Strategy to Counter the Impact

The global financial crisis was both a challenge and an opportunity for China. Although the crisis was affecting its exports, employment, and foreign exchange reserves, it was also generating external pressure for China to carry out further structural adjustments and provide a window of opportunity to expand overseas investment. The Chinese government tries to utilize this opportunity not only to sustain short-term economic growth but also to achieve long-term strategic objectives. To stimulate short-term economic growth and to speed up structural reforms, China should diversify its domestic demand and increase household consumption as the top priority. The most effective way to boost consumption is to increase household income (Zhu 2009: Personal Interview). Xue Lei is of the opinion that current global financial crisis is an opportunity for China to showcase its strength in the textiles sector. Being a manufacturing hub in T&C products especially in low and medium range, China should move higher up in the production by producing and designing high-end products. It must invest more and develop skills to produce domestic high end products for world market (Lei 2009: Personal Interview).

As unemployment in textiles sector is rising, to mitigate the problem the Central Government should not over-emphasize the policy of export growth. Rather, it is time for the Government to look at the services sector as an immediate alternative to minimize this social crisis. It should devise policies to strengthen services sector by opening it up to the outside world in a regulated manner (Yong 2009: Personal Interview).

However, the government is keen to take immediate measures to provide stability to the sector because it believes that it has enough potentiality to remain as an engine of growth (Ho 2009: Personal Interview). In that direction, China's State Council recently unveiled a detailed three-year support plan for the textile industry. It is of the opinion that the plan is aimed at ensuring stability in the industry and upgrading its structure. The plan is geared at rejuvenating the industry. The annual production of large textile enterprises (with annual revenue of more than 5 million Yuan) is expected to increase by 10 per cent year on year. If the plan is carried out with meticulous implementation strategy, the annual output of such enterprises will rise to 1.2 trillion Yuan by 2011 from 812.6 billion Yuan in 2007 and 850 billion Yuan in 2008.

The Government is also planning to develop state-of-the art technology, reduce energy consumption and increase efficiency in the textile industry. The Government is also determined to provide higher export tax rebate rates for textile products. China has raised the export tax rebate rate for textiles, five times since August 2008, to help textile makers cope with stagnant demand. The most recent increase, announced in April 2009, took the rate from 15 per cent to 16 per cent. The Government will also grant preferential loans to the exporters and enterprises and will exempt import tax on inputs. Since January, China has announced stimulus plans for 10 major industries including textiles vehicles, steel, ship-building, machinery, electronics, and information technology (*Xinhua*: 2009). Major incentives like these are extremely important to raise the morale as well as future prospects of these exporters who have been in this trade for so long (Zhu 2009: Personal Interview).

Summary

The Textiles sector in China has been regarded as one of the pillar industries. Its role in the economy is well recognized in terms of its contribution to GDP and domestic employment. With the opening up of China and onset of globalization, the sector found huge opportunities in terms of its export prospects. Since then the Central Government has accorded priority to this sector as one of the potential sectors for export promotion. Cheap labour cost, attractive FDI policies, developing an industrial cluster approach and meeting the low and medium range global demand of products have been the hallmarks of China's rise in world's T&C market.

Though the world trade in T&C remained restrictive in nature, under the MFA regime, China performed significantly better compared to other developing countries. Due to the abundant supply of cheap labour with regular infusion of technology, China could register high export growth in the world market in the 1990s. After joining the WTO it continued to increase its share until the transitional safeguards were imposed in 2005 by the US and EU. This provision was targeted at China specifically to curtail its prospects in textiles trade as developed countries were convinced about the comparative advantage China has in the sector. Only during 2005 and beginning of 2006, China's exports received a temporary jolt but soon they picked up. It continued to accelerate its exports and share in global market during 2007 until the global market in textiles experienced the slump caused by the global financial crisis in the third quarter of 2008.

China's textile firms' profits declined for the first time due to reduction in overseas demand. The growth rate of China's overall textile exports in 2009 continued to slide as the economy also began to be affected by rising labour costs, the appreciation of the Renminbi, and reduced global demand in major export markets. Moreover, sharp decline in consumer spending and growing unemployment in the US will further result in the deceleration of exports from China.

To minimize the sudden impact of the crisis the Chinese Government has taken a series of measures such as stimulus package, widening of domestic demand base, creation of own brands, locating new markets, and automation of the textiles industry which are also the immediate priority for securing the revival of the industry. China believes that such crisis can always be treated as opportunities. China would be able to retain its global competitiveness as it is a huge country and its labour costs vary greatly from region to region. This would mean that textile and clothing exports will remain competitive and important for some time to come in the future as long as production is able to move to lower-cost areas or labour can freely move to the coastal areas.

Sectoral analysis of textiles sector has provided a broad overview of how China has taken necessary steps to integrate its sector globally and prepared itself domestically. This sectoral approach is also employed in the telecommunications sector to locate its position in the world and analyze how it has evolved after China has joined the WTO in the following chapter.

Notes

1. Textiles sector analyzed in the chapter includes textiles and clothing (T&C).
2. Such huge employment figures are because of the displacement taking place in the agricultural sector as part of growing imports available at http://eu2.mofcom.gov.cn/aarticle/chinanews/200509/20050900352110.html

3. Standard International Trade Classification (SITC) is a classification of goods used to classify the exports and imports of a country to enable comparing different countries and years. The classification system is maintained by the United Nations.
4. The Harmonized Commodity Description and Coding System, generally referred to as Harmonized System or simply HS, is a multipurpose international product nomenclature developed by the World Customs Organization (WCO).
5. Many demonstrations were made by textile workers at Nanchong, Sichuan province, Shanxi, and Hefei despite tight restrictions on such activities. In January 1999, hundreds of workers from the Chngde textile plant in Hunan province protested against lay off of 30 percent of mill workers (China News Digest, No. 408, 22 January 1999).
6. Calculated from UNCTAD Statistical Handbook 2007 based on (SITC 26+65+84)
7. World Trade Online Database, 2008 based on (HS codes 61+62+63)
8. http://www.chinadaily.com.cn/bizchina/2006-04/18/content_570634_2.htm, 18 April 2006. Accessed on 17 November 2009.
9. Profits made by companies that are allocated the rights to import goods, that are subject to quotas and are therefore artificially scarce.
10. Announcement of Request for Bilateral Textile Consultations with the Government of the PRC and the Establishment of Import Limits for certain cotton and manmade fibre textiles and textile products in categories 301, 340/640, 638/639 and 647/648, produced or manufactured in the PRC *Federal Register/Vol. 70, No. 99/ Tuesday, May 24, 2005/Notices*, Committee for the Implementation of Textile Agreements, 26 May 2005.
11. For more see (Doha Ministerial Declaration: http://www.wto.org/english/thewto_e/ minist_e/min01_e/mindecl_e.htm). Accessed on 7 August 2009.
12. Article 2, Agreement on Safeguards.
13. Knit and woven garments are defined as commodities with HS codes of 61, 62 and 63.
14. The Revealed Comparative Advantage is a macroeconomic concept for calculating a relative advantage or disadvantage of a certain country in a certain technological field.
15. NCTO 2008: http://www.fibre2fashion.com/news/fashion-news/newsdetails.aspx?newsid=67080).
16. Textiles and Apparel: Assessment of the Competitiveness of Certain Foreign Suppliers to the U.S. Market (Investigation No. 332-448, sent to USTR in June 2003), Pub. 3671, January 2004.
17. "DHL-McKinsey Apparel and Textile Trade Report" AFX News Limited, 3/28/04.
18. Policy Paper 2008 prepared by the Ministry of Information Industry, Beijing, China.
19. http://www.malawi-invest.net/chinese.html, Accessed on July 11, 2008.
20. OEMs are manufacturers who resell another company's product under their own name and branding. It refers specifically to the act of a company rebranding a product to its own name and offering its own warranty, support and licensing of the product. The term is really a misnomer because OEMs are not the original manufacturers; they are the customizers.

21. Calculated from the World Trade Atlas Online Database (Data provided by the Governments of different countries; in the case of China it is done by the China Customs.
22. Though popular parlance suggests it to be global financial crisis, in the thesis we emphasize it to be American, because it originated there as the real American sub-prime mortgage realty crisis. The crisis of course later became global in nature and took the shape of global financial crisis. It also came to be known as global economic crisis as global economic and trade activities were intricately related to global finance.
23. From the discussion held at a business meet organized by CII and Embassy of India, Beijing at Marriot hotel in Beijing on April 15 2009
24. *People's Daily* Online 2009 http://english.people.com.cn/90001/90776/90884/6579775.html

5

China's Telecommunications Sector and Its Implications

China's telecom is one of the fast growing sectors in the world. Constant upgradation of technology and monitoring of communication have put up several challenges for the Government to constantly restructure the sector. There is pressure to develop telecom infrastructure in the country as China made commitments to open up the sector. Free and fair competition in the market needs to be carried out in a transparent and efficient manner. While doing so, the Government faces the key challenge of monitoring the flow of communication with the entry of foreign players for safeguarding its own national security. China has already made certain commitments in the GATS under the WTO to open up its telecommunications sector further after joining the WTO. These are geographic restrictions on paging and value-added services which will be phased out two years after the WTO accession while the phasing-out period for mobile and domestic fixed line services will be five and six years respectively. Such commitments are important to measure the future growth of the sector.

This chapter makes an attempt to analyze the telecommunications sector in detail in China especially after it has joined the WTO. Though the chapter aims to take into account the historical perspective of the sector, it devotes adequate analysis to the post-WTO regime. The chapter is organized as follows. First, it provides an overview of the structural and policy changes and framework starting with the reform process in 1978 to its accession to the WTO. Second, it deals with the telecom market situation in China after acceding to the WTO. It describes the domestic component of China's telecommunication reforms and also as to how domestic industry has performed during this period. It also provides an analysis of telecommunications services growth while exploring as to how liberalization of services has contributed to the growth of China's economy, and assesses dimension of regional employment in the sector. Third, it analyzes the implications of the WTO's services commitments on China and its relations with major powers. The issues of foreign direct investment, sovereignty and national security have also been addressed. Fourth, it summarizes main findings of the chapter.

Overview of Structural and Institutional Policy Changes in the Telecommunications Sector in Its Accession to the WTO

China's telecommunications sector witnessed a series of fundamental institutional changes and strong centrally planned initiatives during the eighties and the nineties. These initiatives radically changed the incentive structure of telecommunications enterprises and their business environment. When China began modernizing its economy in the late seventies through structural reforms, the telecommunications sector appeared as a visible bottleneck in the economy. The inaccessibility of the infrastructure hindered the advancement of reform programme. This hindrance had raised serious concerns among the policy makers. By then China was fully aware that the sector was significantly backward and there existed remarkable gap between supply and demand.

Moreover, the Chinese telecommunications sector remained a strong state monopoly since the early eighties when several government circulars were issued to protect it. It was one of the most centrally planned and controlled sectors where market entry, pricing, and business organizations completely remained under the regulation of the state through the Ministry of Posts and Telecommunications (MPT) (Bhalla and Qiu 2004:120). To correct the system and make it useful for the running of the economy, the State Council intervened and took an active part to reform the telecommunication system. Its earlier realization of telecommunications sector along with transport and energy as the big bottleneck for economic growth pushed the leadership further to designate telecommunications as the area for priority development (Yu *et al.* 1999: 479). This resulted in the telecommunications industry witnessing four phases of development—featuring four significant reforms. These processes were carried out in anticipation of promoting healthy competition in the industry. A number of reforms were introduced to make the telecom sector grow from a bottleneck to an expanding strategic sector.

Since 1990s the telecommunications sector has been undergoing profound changes across the world. Technological advancement coupled with ever increasing business activity has necessitated the evolution of this sector on a continuous basis. More and more opportunities coming in the wake of globalization influenced many developing countries to re-look into the specificity of this sector, so as to benefit optimally from the ever expanding global markets. Following this general pattern, China had developed a sophisticated telecommunication network since the 1990s.

Thereafter the telecommunications sector in China has undergone a sea change. From a completely state controlled, regulated, and operated sector, it has moved towards liberalization and privatization of the sector by introducing structural adjustment and institutional changes. These include: revamping of the Ministry of Posts and Telecommunications (MPT); creating the Ministry of Information Industry (MII) for regulation of the industry; and introducing private capital and competition in the industry. This experience of competition and liberalization of the industry allowed the economy to benefit immensely from the overall application of the sector in the conduct of the economic activities of the country. With the onset of liberalization, a number of players have been allowed to operate in the domestic market. It has helped the sector in many ways; allowing the telecommunication industry to experience significant growth and providing better service facilities to the consumers.

Initial Development During 1978-1993

In the first phase a major initiative was taken to restructure the earlier semi-military administration in the Ministry of Posts and Telecommunications (MPT) system. The MPT is the functional organ of the State Council responsible for providing country-wide postal and telecommunications services. In 1979, the State Council took interest in reorganizing the MPT. It wanted to make the MPT as the central planner of the entire country-wide postal and telecommunications development. It issued a directive to reorganize the entire setting of telecommunication network in the country. All the local postal and telecommunications enterprises came under the dual control of provincial governments and the MPT, the latter becoming the main decision maker. As stipulated by the directive, the government administration and business management remained separated. The postal and telecom administration had to function separately. The enterprises were to have their own account and were made financially independent.

As decentralization slowly gained acceptance in the country, the local postal and telecommunications administrations (PTAs) were set up at the provincial level under the dual leadership of the MPT and the provincial governments. From 1983 to 1985, the MPT introduced a new accounting system known as "Enterprise Own Revenue;" an exhaustive methodology mainly created to calculate the revenue of an individual postal and telecommunications enterprise. Thereafter all the Post and Telegraph Enterprises (PTEs) had established their independent accounts and started to operate on a system of contractual responsibility in which their earnings were linked to their business performance (Jain *et al.*, 2000:16). Since then, the administrative structure of China's telecommunications sector has evolved as a vertically organized hierarchical structure. The national ministry at the top is responsible for overseeing the planning and management of the industry. It controls international and inter-provincial communications and was in charge of setting and enforcing various technical standards and formulating key policies. The PTAs performed similar role at the provincial level. Hundreds of municipal and prefecture bureaux were created and remained under its rule.

By mid-1980s, Li Peng, the then Vice Premier had taken keen interest in revitalizing the telecommunications sector. He had mobilized the interests of the Government to indicate the huge importance the sector was assuming, as China was trying hard to integrate itself with the world economy. The framework of long term policies of the sector was laid down during mid-1980s, in line with the renewed emphasis Deng had placed on science and technology. A leading group for the revitalization of electronics industry under the stewardship of Li Peng took the responsibility of propelling the growth of this sector as part of the drive to electronic age. Like in South Korea, Singapore and Taiwan their respective governments took the full advantage of electronic age to promote their telecom manufacturing. China began to approach telecommunications as a crucial sector; a vehicle to stimulate domestic equipment and component manufacturing. Indigenous enterprises like Huawei Technologies and Zhong Xing Telecommunication Equipment Company Limited (ZTE) were supported by the Government to produce quality products. In the mid-eighties, although they were in their early stages of growth, they were encouraged to adopt a "Go Out" (Li 2006: 1) strategy to upscale their products and compete with major multinational firms like Motorola and Nokia. Though China was trying hard to promote its domestic companies, yet it knew it had to develop advanced telecommunication networking and the role of foreign players in the sector was inevitable. This role of active participation of foreign players grew during this period as it insisted upon foreign suppliers of telecommunications equipment entering into technology transfer agreements through joint ventures to China. In 1985 under this stimulus, the MPT submitted a fifteen-year plan for telecommunications development to the State Planning Commission. The MPT had set up a highly ambitious plan. By the year 2000, the country was expecting to have a teledensity (lines for 100 people) of 2.8 (Ure 1997: 16). In fact, the targets were achieved far ahead of schedule.

The Government further initiated some major reforms in 1988 when the MPT underwent a deeper revamping. Beijing announced the so called "sixteen character policy" for telecommunications infrastructure development. The policy was summarized by four principles (Wong and Lu, 2002: 334-335):

1. Overall planning of industrial development should be unified under the MPT.
2. Ministerial administration should be coordinated with regional authorities.
3. Responsibilities should be defined and shared among different administrative levels.

4. Construction of infrastructure should mobilize resources from all concerned.

Following these principles, postal and telecommunications investments were largely decentralized in the late eighties. The Seventh Five-Year Plan (1986-90) stipulated that the intra-province telecommunications projects to rely mainly on local financing. Institutions and individuals were also encouraged to invest in infrastructure proposals. During this time the MPT established the Directorate General of Telecommunications (DGT) and the Directorate General of Posts (DGP) to incorporate business enterprise functions.

This came to be known as China Telecom with 29 provincial postal and telecommunications authorities (PTAs), all of which offer local and long distance services. The PTAs located in the advanced cities like Beijing, Shanghai, and Guangdong also provide international services. The MPT also handled the regulatory matters through its Department of Policy and Regulation and other governmental functions were looked after by the Telecommunications Administration Department, the Department of Science and Technology and the Department of Finance. Thus these set of reforms provided financial administrative autonomy to the PTAs. Given the policies, technological improvement and supporting factors, sources were further mobilized to promote the rapid development of the telecom industry. After consistent efforts the sector made progress in terms of network size, level of technology and service. By the end of 1993, telephone penetration had reached 2.2 per cent across the country (Baark 2009: Personal Interview). China established an extensive communication network with the application of technologies and equipment like programme-controlled exchanges, mobile communications, data communications, optical fibres, digital microwaves, etc.

Another set of policies implemented in China during the late eighties also held the key to liberalized policy changes of telecommunications sector. This includes economic assistance to the MPT in the form of the 'three 90 per cents': 90 per cent of Central government's loans may not be repaid, PTA could keep 90 per cent of its taxable profits, and the MPT could retain 90 per cent of its foreign currency earnings from incoming international traffic (Ure 1997: 16). The policy was a great success as some of the results are seen in Table 5.1.

Tougher Competition Due to Industrial Restructuring During 1994-2001

Till mid-1994 China's telecommunications industry was not competitive. China Telecom, one of the biggest state-owned enterprises (SOEs), was managing the communication services and distribution network as the only single service provider in the country till 1994. Till this period it remained under the control of the Government. The Chinese people were not satisfied with the poor service

Table 5.1: Growth of China's Telecommunications Sector, 1978-1994

	1978	*1994*	*Avg. Yearly Growth (1949-1978)*	*Avg. Yearly Growth (1978-1994)*
Telephone Switching Lines	1.7 million	48.8 million	6%	23.1%
No. of Long-Distance Calls	186 million	7,777 million	11%	26.2%
Revenue (RMB)	6,039 million	53,900 million	6.6%	14.6%
Investment (RMB)	266 million	61,500 million	6.8%	40.5%
No. of Phone Subscribers	1.9 million	28.8 million	6.6%	18.4%

Sources: *China Posts and Telecommunications Annual Report,* 1995 (Beijing: "China Posts and Telecommunications", Editorial Group of MPT, 1996), p. 33; Ante Xu and Phillip Armstrong, *Chinese Telecom Market* (New York: Northern Business Information, 1995), p. 2.

and high fees charged by the SOE. In addition, the weak telecom infrastructural facilities faced by the domestic as well as export oriented enterprises also put pressure on the Government to introduce competition in the domestic market. Process of accession to the WTO had also necessitated this urgency. The Central leadership thought that competition was necessary for two purposes. First, the domestic industry needed to provide better and more telecom services to the Chinese customers. Second, local service providers needed to improve their competitiveness against foreign rivals when China would open its domestic market to the world.

As the telecom sector began to witness competition in China, changes in the telecom services were noticed. Propelled by the global demand and situation, China initiated the process of liberalization and privatization of the sector. Several small steps were taken starting in 1994. China Telecom was split in 1994 to two as China Telecom and China Unicom, another government backed company. China Telecom was separated from the MPT. Further, a set of organizations were created to provide value added services to the wide ranging demands of the consumers. Soon China Telecom faced competition from China Unicom. This was another state sponsored organization supported by the Ministry of Electronics Industry, the Ministry of Railways, the Ministry of Electric Power, and a few more state run enterprises which had shown interest in entering China's telecom services market (MII, Annual Report, 2000).

In 1994, China for the first time witnessed movement of privatization in the telecom market. The move was made to introduce competition in the industry to improve service quality and production efficiency. As China witnessed competition in the market in the mid-nineties, overall service facilities and infrastructural support were improved. Competition could set in lower tariffs and installation fees, shorter time for waiting and better service. Competition also forced companies to adopt more advanced technologies.

With this change in the market it is observed from the Table 5.2 that the numbers of long-distance calls during the year 1994 were 7777 million. It increased to 21, 998 million by 2001, almost a three-fold increase.

Table 5.2: Growth of China's Telecommunications Sector, 1994-2001

Item	*1994*	*1995*	*1996*	*1997*	*1998*	*1999*	*2000*	*2001*
Number of Long-distance Calls (million)	7,777	10,139	12,739	15,540	18,259	17,825	21,075	21,998

Source: Statistical Yearbook of China 2003, p. 603.

Through this policy and the central direction of surpluses from the wealthier provinces such as Guangdong and municipalities of Beijing and Shanghai to the poorer central and western provinces, the Ministry wanted to narrow the gap between them (Ure 2007: 9). By 1997 the Government realized that the policy was no more required to lure the MPT and the PTAs to expand the network. The initial advantage of striking a better rate of growth of telecommunications was achieved within couple of years of its implementation. As years went by, the policy failed to maintain the expansion of network at the provincial level because it could never provide business license or legal sanction to local and postal telecommunication bureaux in the mould of an enterprise. Enterprise was still not a very familiar term in the Chinese business and administration, especially the functional definition of an enterprise was not very clear in the Post and Telegraph Ministry of Chinese establishment. As the policy failed to infuse enterprising venture into the Chinese society, the Government repealed the 'three 90 per cents' policy in 1995 (Harwit 1998: 187).

In 1996, there were already about 93 million telephone lines and 78 million telephones (Harwit 1998:184). Such ambitious results were far ahead of the Government's schedule of establishing a vast network of telecommunications in China by 2000. This ambitious task became achievable because the Chinese government took adequate measures in the policies to expand the network. Rapid expansion of telecommunication network in the late nineties in the country only justified the significance the Central Government had attached to it by declaring it as one of the seven priority areas in 1986 (*Telecommunications Development Asia Pacific* 1994: 67-70).

By the end of 1996, telecommunications sector was fairly well developed in the Chinese market. The MPT formally announced that the telecommunications infrastructure in China was finally equipped to satisfy the basic demand of the economy and the public. This was an important turning point where the Chinese telecommunications market had turned into a buyer market rather than a seller market (Kan 1999: 9). Looking at the success rate, the Chinese Government pushed the telecommunications industry to adopt the policies and mechanism of the market economy. Operational efficiency became more important as the Government realized that the high growth rate of telecommunications had mainly resulted from the preferential policy that it adopted in the early nineties.

Besides the influence of policy change as a direct cause of telecom growth, changing life style pattern and rise in savings since 1990s were attributed to the growth of telecom sector. Since the early nineties, there has been a marked rise in the living standards of the Chinese people. The yearly growth of consumption per capita has been about 15 per cent, and annual average growth in the savings deposit balances of residents have been over 50 per cent since 1978. The four cities with the highest per capita consumption are Shanghai, Beijing, Tianjin and Chongqing, while the five provinces with the highest total personal consumption are Sichuan, Guangdong, Shandong, Jiangsu, and Liaoning. Since the Chinese government readjusted the allocation of resources, stimulating more consumption, and less capital accumulation, the savings of the people had accumulated rapidly and steadily. New pattern of standard of living coupled with glamorous lifestyles, desire for value added services and personal savings had resulted in the explosion of telecom devices and services. Many local as well as foreign manufacturing companies had developed their businesses in China because of growing demand emanating from personal life style and savings (Zhu 2009: Personal Interview). It can be observed from the Figure 5.1 how the number of urban and rural telecom subscribers has gone up in China during the nineties.

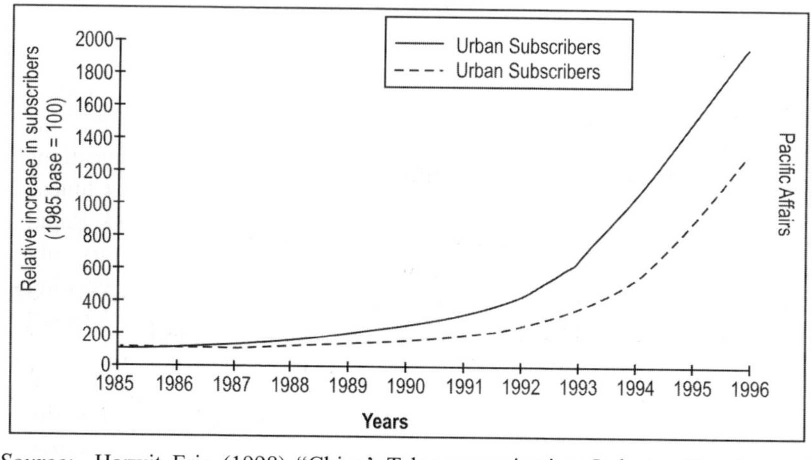

Source: Harwit, Eric, (1998), "China's Telecommunications Industry: Development Patterns and Policies", *Pacific Affairs*, Vol. 71 (2): 186.

Figure 5.1: Development of Telecommunications in Urban and Rural Areas, 1985-1996

Till 1994 and even 1995, China followed the traditional model of a government-owned-and government managed post and telecom authority, with the MPT administering the nation's postal and telephone systems. This ministry was devoted to the entire regulation and operation mechanism in the country. It functioned both as a regulator and an operator. The telecommunications service providers operated as a national monopoly through a hierarchical structure with the Ministry in Beijing at the top followed by the provincial offices, and then the country offices and municipal and local offices (Figure 5.2).

Enterprise offices those were formed as a part of the competition drive were also segregated from government functions; separate directorate-generals were established for post and telecom operations, and a wide range of decision-making responsibilities were shifted from the central ministry to provincial and municipal operating entities. A degree of local autonomy was introduced, allowing the local PTAs greater management flexibility in planning, investment, and tariff setting policies. Provincial and municipal operators were permitted to purchase network equipment, from a variety of competing MPT approved suppliers and the terminal equipment market, and the paging services sector were opened to competition by the late nineties.

China Telecom's long affiliation with the MPT in securing a monopoly in the country had developed a unified interest group until 1998. In the absence of any legal framework and transparent policy guidelines, such a situation meant that it was inevitable that new entrants would be treated unfavourably. Friction between China Telecom and China Unicom continued till the Government finally set up a regulatory body by merging certain departments called the Ministry of Information Industry (MII) to streamline the path of telecommunications liberalization. Though the Chinese telecommunications policy experiment during 1994-1998 was seen as a significant development in the entire process of structural and institutional changes, yet the task of creating a climate of healthy competition could not be achieved.

What really hindered the competitiveness of telecommunications market in China till 1998 was the lack of a proper legal framework. It is essential to establish an impartial legal framework to ensure an orderly development of the sector and to adopt an appropriate mechanism by which the entire sector is to be regulated. This is very much amplified in the Basic Telecommunications Agreement of the WTO which suggests that member countries should be committed to establishing an independent regulatory body that "is separate from, and not accountable to, any supplier of basic telecommunications services. The decisions of, and the procedures used by regulators, shall be impartial with respect to all market participants."[1] It is normally argued that independent regulatory agency should also remain at a distance from the government because when a regulatory body is also simultaneously a

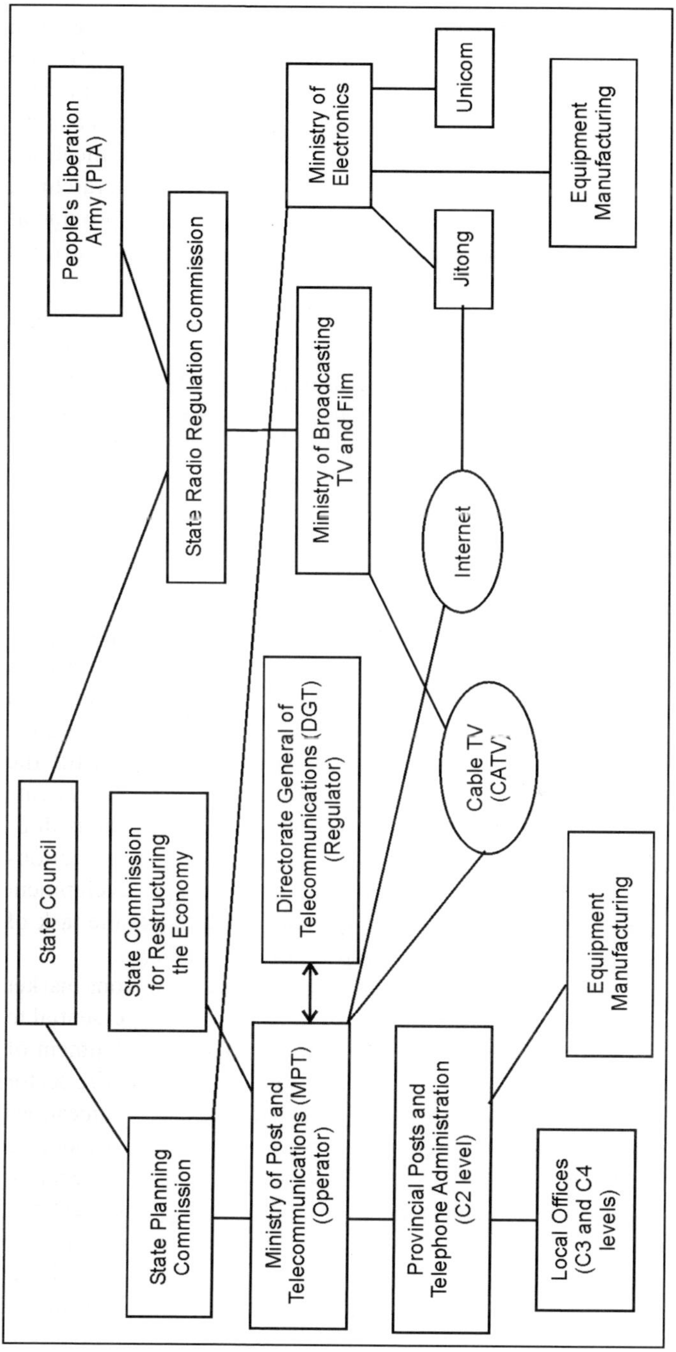

Figure 5.2: Major Players in the Telecommunications

Source: Harwit, Eric, (1998), "China's Telecommunications Industry: Development Patterns and Policies", *Pacific Affairs*, Vol. 71(2): 188.

government department since chances of it getting influenced or remaining vulnerable to political intervention are high (Selvarajah: 1999).

Experience in many countries, however, has demonstrated that transition from a traditional regulatory framework with the government having regulatory and operatory functions to a single independent regulatory agency can be slow and contentious process. Many late comers have learnt it the hard way (Yan and Pitt 2002: 91). The friction over interconnection issue between China Telecom and China Unicom only indicates that ineffective regulatory framework was unfavourable to the new entrant and patronized only the incumbent. China, therefore, suffered in fostering competitive telecommunications industry early on.

Nevertheless China was keen to integrate with the world economy and wanted to join the WTO, it understood the significance of having a domestic competitive sector sooner by putting in place an independent regulatory framework with a sound legal regime. Besides, the principles of good regulatory system are well known. They include transparency, objectivity, efficiency, professionalism, and independence (Intven and Oliver 2000: 19).

Thus in March 1998, the Ninth National People's Congress, the supreme legislative body, approved an institutional restructuring scheme proposed by the State Council. On 1 April 1998, the MII was officially established as a result of amalgamation of the MPT and the MEI (Ministry of Electronic Industry). The aim of this restructuring was to consolidate the government's regulatory role and create an environment for effective competition. As an example, since the restructuring, China Telecom and Unicom were to be treated in the same fashion under the guidance of MII and were to compete on a more equitable basis. Under the new administrative system, the MII is the sole regulator responsible for price setting, licensing, and other regulatory matters. The MII became the sole watchdog for the IT sector. In addition to establishing telecommunications-related policies, laws and regulations, the ministry was entrusted with the responsibility of negotiating with foreign enterprises. The MII had broad discretionary powers to formulate regulations and apply them. Only important strategic policy decisions were approved by the State Council. Such restructuring was brought about with the hope that it would make the sector efficient and effective.

An overhaul of this bureaucratic system was accompanied by reform of the structure of telecommunications enterprises. In a major move, China Telecom was broken into four separately operated companies responsible for fixed line, mobile, paging, and satellite communication services (*People's Daily*: May 17 2000). The rationale behind this was to break the dominance of China Telecom and to allow new independent service providers to operate in a regulated market to promote effective competition in the telecommunications industry.

The passing of the legislation of regulation in 2000 came to be recognized as the first major state instrument in handing telecommunications in China in a transparent manner. Many scholars and industry experts noted the importance attached to such legislation. According to DeWoskin: "The document is an extremely important step towards clarifying the roles of all the players in the sector…and it has created a fixed set reference points for further regulatory work" (DeWoskin 2001: 641).

Table 5.3: China's Commitment under its WTO Service Schedule, 2001-2007

Percentage and Geographic Coverage of Foreign Investment Permitted						
Type of Service	*12/01-12/02*	*12/02-12/03*	*12/03-12/04*	*12/04-12/05*	*12/05-12/06*	*12/06-12/07*
Basic telecom services fixed	0%	0%	0%	25% in Beijing, Shanghai, and Guangzhou	35% in 17 cities	49% with no geographic restrictions
Basic telecom services-mobile	25% in Beijing, Shanghai, and Guangzhou	35% in 17 cities	No change	49% with no geographic restrictions	No change	No change
Value-added services and paging service	30% in Beijing, Shanghai, and Guangzhou	49% in17 cities	50% with no geographic restrictions	No change	No change	No change

Source: WTO-http://docsonline.wto.org/DDFDocuments/t/WT/ACC/CHN49A2.doc Accessed on 17 March 2009.

China's commitment on telecommunications in the WTO, after initiating structural and institutional changes on home front, gave a signal to the outside world that its market was well regulated, stable, and provided enormous opportunities. By early 2000 and 2001, China's commitment to the WTO had thrown the administration of telecommunication services into a market mode. This included several measures. Important among them were change in sourcing investment from different quarters, reorienting resource-planning managements in the event of restructuring of industry and tariff making policies based on cost-based pricing.

Telecommunications Sector in China Since 2001

China becoming a member of the WTO was seen as a significant development for world economy. Thus, a new chapter opened in China's telecommunications services. The Chinese Government's WTO commitments allowed the foreign direct investment to come into the indigenous telecom operating entities. According to the commitments, a foreign investment cap on basic telecommunications services operators was set at 25 per cent in major cities and at 49 per cent in semi-urban areas allowing the Chinese government to retain control by securing more than 50 per cent of ownership.

In mobile telecommunications, foreign investment allowed upto 25 per cent share immediately upon accession. This share was to be allowed to rise to 49 per cent after a 3-year period. For fixed network services, it was to take 5 years to reach the investment cap. The arrangement further calls for the cap to be raised to 50 per cent after 2 years for value added services and paging services. The foreign investment cap also applied to the internet service providers. Detailed Chinese commitments under its schedule of the GATS are given in Table 5.3. By the time China became a member of the WTO, its telecom sector had opened up domestically in a significant way and many major service providers like China Telecom, China Unicom, China Mobile, China Netcom, and China Jitong were competing with each other.

Concern for national security had resulted in delaying of complete restructuring of telecommunications sector in China. It was kept under the tight state control and remained protected from foreign competition. National security and national sovereignty were of vital importance to the Chinese Government as articulated in the "Five Principles of Peaceful Co-existence." In order to ensure that these principles were abided by the Chinese domestic laws and rules in the telecommunications sector remained non-transparent and obscure (Kobayashi 2007: 146). However, the approach to the sector began to change when China joined the WTO. The WTO commitments came into effect throwing the sector open to foreign competition.

China witnessed a virtual explosion in the sector as both fixed and mobile users shot up significantly in its post accession period. By 2002, China's telecommunications exchange capacity had reached 201 million lines and mobile switching capacity amounted to 235 million lines. The total number of telephone subscribers had gone upto 388 million— with 188 million fixed users and 162 million mobile users—making China's telecommunications network the largest in the world in terms of size and subscribers.[2] The number of wireless phone users in China had also reached 250 million by the end of 2003 (*Statistical Year Book of China*, 2005).

China was not only regarded as a market for service providers but also as a manufacturing base for telecommunications equipment. Increase in subscribers had resulted in the expansion of domestic manufacturing industry. Demand for value added services by consumers led to constant upgradation in industry, which had forced China to look for state-of the-art technology. As telecommunications is a technology and capital intensive sector opening up the sector to foreign investment became a necessary condition for achieving constant improvement in the industry.

Up-Gradation of Industry

Major expansion in telecommunications industry called for up-gradation. With the competition setting in especially after the accession to the WTO, the market segments for all the players were geared up aggressively. The local competitors had emerged to dominate the low-end market segment and were stepping up their efforts to compete in the medium-end market. Foreign companies were permitted to sell telecom equipment in the domestic market and were allowed to set up joint ventures with local manufactures, for production of equipment in China. Large foreign companies such as AT&T, Motorola, Siemens, and NEC had taken advantage of this policy, and some of their products for example, Motorola mobile phones, dominate the domestic market.

Since the demand for domestic equipment market was continuously rising, the establishment of sophisticated technology telecommunications equipment enterprises was urgently required. Against this background, the increasing demand for telecom equipment ranging from telephone handsets to infrastructure construction was supported through the inflow of foreign capital and the increasing level of international co-operation. These measures led to the development of a domestic communications equipment industry. After its accession to the WTO, China witnessed the growth of a number of telecommunication enterprises of a considerable level of technological competence, which could match up to the international level in terms of competition. China Putian Information Industry Group Co. was ranked as the twentieth in the top fifty giants of telecommunications manufactures in the world (*People's Daily*: 23 June, 2000).

As the domestic market grew more technology-driven and sophisticated, China decided to focus on high technology related equipment, for which it substantially had to depend on imports of such technology. The development path of telecom industry took a different turn and to fit these requirements, the MII took a policy decision of allowing significant imports in this area. The policy decision sent out by the Chinese government was to adequately strengthen the domestic manufacturing industry by importing latest technological inputs from outside world. Around mid-2002 China saw an impressive growth of 38 per cent of the information technology manufactures and an increase of exports of 46 per cent within the same period (*People's Daily*: June 26, 2002).

The development of the domestic mobile phones manufacturers[3] had a similar dynamic. After its entry into the WTO, telecom industry has become open. Demand for cheap handsets has increased. Since 2002, the domestic industry has developed very fast due to substantial initiatives taken in the stream of research and development. By the mid-2003 a share of 16 per cent was occupied by the local manufactures. The demand for domestic mobile phones had exceeded the supply around this period. However, technological level of domestic mobile phones varied: most manufacturers produced handsets which compete on a low or mid-tech level, but only some offered high-end products like WAP mobile phones for internet access as well.

Chinese domestic telecom companies had established themselves in their production facilities by the time China joined the WTO. Domestic companies like Huawei, ZTE, Julong, and Datang had become competitive enough to compete in the international market like China. To promote the brand value of domestic industry, professionals in telecommunications used the title 'Ju Da Zhong Hua' (the combination of the first character of the above corporations' names) which in Chinese connotes 'Giant China.' This was adopted to showcase the indigenous telecommunications industry as something big, of giant size to attract foreign investment and to compete internationally (Yan and Pitt 2002: 147).

Looking at the performance of these domestic companies, the Government was motivated to enter into the mobile communication market. It wanted to spur the quality production of mobile phone market. The Government allocated 5 per cent of the telephone installation fees during the period 1999-2003 as a special grant to develop R&D centres for mobile communication technology (Yan and Pitt 2002: 124). Initiative to upgrade the industry has also come from the Central Government when the Ministry of Information Industry (MII) planned out an investment proposal of 198.6 million Yuan to build a third-generation mobile technology (3G) testing lab. The move promises to help promote the development of TD-SCDMA, China's homegrown 3G standard, and support the commercialization of 3G in general. Construction of the 3G lab is undertaken by the China Academy of Telecommunications Research under the MII.

After its entry into the WTO, telecom industry has expanded and China is catching up with most advanced form of mobile business. Foreign mobile players have entered the Chinese market with cutting-edge technologies and the Chinese market place has boomed with wide range of products in demand. China has become R&D hub for multinational companies and a test laboratory for large-scale telecom operations (*Beijing Review,* 23 February. 2006: 36). Innovation of products also became a key selling point in the telecom industry. Latest technology was built into the mobile phones to work as a camera for consumers as consumers wanted to use mobile phones for multifarious activities (*Beijing Review* 9 June, 2005: 39). Mobile phones are multitasking in nature. Consumers want to possess one good quality to take care of many aspects of life (Guoxing, 2009: Personal Interview).

According to Nokia's multimedia chief Anssi Vanjoki, the Chinese market is constantly looking for value added service, hence the industry demands upgradation in its product range. Facilities like data communication, mobile internet, messaging, and mobile television are some of the upgraded facilities provided through Nokia mobile sets to cater to the demands of the consumers (*Beijing Review* 29 September, 2005: 28). Many Nokia's R & D centres have been opened up in China.

China also experienced advanced technological upgradation in telecom industry when Motorola came forward to provide state-of-the-art technology. Motorola provided China Telecom with network infrastructure for the upgradation of a portion of its nationwide CDMA 2000 1X network in 2009. Motorola has expressed its desire to install CDMA radio access infrastructure in 42 cities in nine provinces across China in 2009. The entire infrastructure was installed in early 2009 and is part of an overall project to upgrade China Telecom's nationwide CDMA network to next-generation capability. It will also offer the latest versions of its CDMA2000 1X and next-generation CDMA equipment. Ruey-Bin Kao, president of Motorola China, said: "China is a major market for Motorola. The deployment of next-generation CDMA technology for China Telecom is another milestone in Motorola's long history of supporting major telecom operators in China. Motorola has a very significant install base of CDMA 1X equipment that will be expanded and upgraded reinforcing our position as a leading wireless infrastructure supplier in China" (*People's Daily*: 24 December 2008).

China is already caught up with the 3G era. Local manufactures have sufficiently invested in building up a strong base for providing reliable equipment to the consumers. Analysts have pointed out that 3G cell phones can provide users with diversified services and a whole range of functions which offers a new platform as well as opportunities for other growing industries like entertainment (*Beijing Review* 3 march 2005: 38). The Ministry of Industry and Information Technology estimates that China will have 150 million 3G subscribers by the end of 2011. Telecom manufactures have started figuring out entirely new ways to use the combination of power and connectivity (*People's Daily*: 2 July 2010: http://english.peopledaily.com.cn/90001/90778/90860/7049479.html).

Investment Measures to Promote Industry

Continuous expansion of telecom industry has resulted in profit sharing for the Government and companies. Entry into the WTO has augmented the need for further expansion of the industry. As the sector was profitable, the Government never hesitated to invest in the sector. In fact, the investment pattern was by and large self-generated. MII had encouraged the private players in the market to come forward to invest in the sector. As the competition had become after China has joined the WTO, market players like China Telecom, China Unicom and China Mobile had invested in the business.

China Telecom's failure to provide mobile connection to the consumers had encouraged China Unicom to enter the mobile network. In such a scenario, as a weaker player compared to China Telecom, it could not mobilize offshore investment for its own expansion, rather it devised a unique formula of entering into a joint venture scheme called CCF (China-China-Foreign) whereby a separate Sino-Foreign joint venture teamed up with Unicom to establish a third entity which was allowed in 1999 prior to its entry. China's telecom sector had witnessed large amount of FDI in its manufacturing base in China much before the accession. On account of revenue sharing, however, that scheme was later abolished (Aldrich and Rooth 1999: 174).

The Government toyed with many ideas to make the domestic sector more competitive. This obviously required huge amount of investment. Looking at that angle, it adopted the policy of listing the telecommunications sector in major stock exchanges of the world such as the New York Stock Exchange and Hong Kong Stock Exchange since 2002. The listing process heralded a new beginning in the telecommunications sector where financing was sought through initial public offering (IPOs).

The new model is peculiarly Chinese or telecommunications 'with Chinese characteristics'. All state-owned assets in China ultimately came under the supervision of the State-owned Assets Supervision and Administration Commission (SASAC). In the case of telecom sector, when they were incorporated for their IPOs the assets of four operating companies—China Telecom, China Netcom, China Mobile, and China Unicom were vested in their respective state-owned enterprises. A portion of the fund generated by the IPOs was used to buy further assets from the corporations on a province-by-province basis. Over the years operating profits of the companies were utilized to buy all network assets, which was the situation till the end of 2006. Under the commitments of the WTO, foreign ownership or equity today is allowed up to 49 per cent and there is no provision to liberalize the telecommunications market (Ure 1997:18), which is part of China's commitment in the WTO.

With the new round of restructuring and China's entry into the WTO, foreign investment came in a significant way to upgrade and innovate the telecom industry. Foreign investment inflows to China came into the areas of high tech industries like deep processing, telecom and IT from labour intensive sectors like textiles, rubber, etc. The telecom sector received investment in a continuous manner from 2003-04 onwards. These investments were put into developing R&D centres where new design and upgrading of industry were worked out on a continuous basis to suit to the specificity of the industry (*Beijing Review* 1 September 2005: 30).

According to the MII, telecommunications service providers of China such as China Telecom, China Netcom, China Mobile, China Unicom, China Tietong, and China Satellite invested some US$ 28.7 billion in telecom infrastructure in 2006. As a result of this investment, Chinese telecom service providers added 86.2 million additional new subscribers (19.6 fixed line users and 66.6 mobile phone users) to bring the total number of telephone users in China to 830 million. Fixed line telephone penetration rate reached 28.3 per cent and mobile communications penetration rate reached 35.2 per cent. In 2007, the MII had projected that the Chinese telecom carriers would invest US$ 25 billion to capture 70 million fixed line telephone subscribers and mobile phone users. The number of telephone users in China reached more than 900 million by the end of 2007. By the end of 2007, the MII projected the fixed line penetration rate to reach 29 per cent and mobile communications to reach 39.4 per cent. China's total number of telephone users were 986 million towards the end of Decmber 2008. The number of mobile users was to the tune of 660 million and landline users were around 350 million (*Beijing Review* 22 December 2008: 16).

Entry of Foreign Companies

The entry of foreign companies to the Chinese market has not been easy as the Chinese Government pursued a policy of indigenous development model considering the issues of security and sovereignty. However, China needed the involvement of multinational corporations (MNCs) to leverage its growth. As MNCs were well equipped with capital, technology, and management skills, it sought their help and MNCs were particularly interested to come in as they visualized China as a big market, having low cost labour for production, political stability, and certain advantage in terms of R&D facilities.

The MNCs had intensified their operations in a big way after China had entered the WTO. Motorola, Nokia, Siemens invested heavily into their R&D facilities and produced equipments catering to the 3G requirements. Such activities in turn could help in strengthening China's local manufacturing and R&D capacities. This in a way also helped China to develop its global competitiveness. Therefore, a large part of market competition in China's telecommunications sector has centred on the strategies of MNCs and practices of local manufactures, together with leveraging by the Chinese government.

Strategies drawn up by the MNCs from the beginning were very clear as they aimed at increasing their profits by a wide margin. However, they were forced to transfer the technology directly or indirectly, due to the Government's policies and market competition from their global and local rivals.

While product sale, technology transfer and local technology capability upgrading work together in a complex Chinese environment, MNCs' operations in the Chinese market can be characterized as an adding-and-dropping model.

This is a model which has worked in many developing countries. All products are divided into three categories based on their technological sophistication—high (H), medium (M), and low (L). At any point of time all the three categories remain. What have seen actual change are the actual products in the three categories. The MNCs have added new products to their 'H' category. Market competition and local capacity keep downgrading products from H to M and from M to L. This model can be applied to the telecommunications market in China in the 1990s.

A significant aspect of entry of foreign companies to China is that foreign telecom equipment manufacturing companies like Motorola, Nokia, Siemens, etc. were allowed to come to China before its entry, whereas the foreign service providers like Vodafone and others were allowed after entry.

Local Manufacturing Companies

Evidence shows that local telecommunication companies have successfully enhanced their market share over the years. Local manufactures got a boost only when they tasted success with the Central Official Switches. It has been extended to optical fibre transmission systems, wireless, mobile base stations and switches, and most recently mobile handsets. In mobile handsets emphasis has been given to produce advanced technology so that consumers are satisfied with 3G connection. Local companies are engaged in manufacturing three mainstream standardized technologies such as WCDMA, CDMA2000 and TD-SCDMA for 3G mobile (*Beijing Review* 3 March 2005: 36). These standardized technologies are approved by International Telecommunication Union (ITU). Many indigenous manufacturers have recently emerged as successful corporations. Since use of internet has gone up, many indigenous telecom manufacturing companies have come out with latest modem to support the fast pace network of internet usage (*Beijing Review* 20 January 2005: 30).

Table 5.4 above provides a list of successful indigenous telecom manufacturing companies. These companies share certain interesting features. They were products of reform era that began in 1978 which marked the beginning of transition of China's economy from one of a central planning to a market oriented model. Many of them spent substantial amount of revenue on their R&D over 10 per cent, which drives the technology development in China's telecommunications industry. Many of them emanated from China's research institutes.

Market size and rapidly growing demand have spurred the growth of the indigenous manufacturing companies. This is facilitated by the significant upgrading of technological capacity. Different strategies have contributed to the upgrading of local firms' technology capacity, including imitation and internal R&D. The importance of R&D expansion has been regarded as a major policy decision in China's upgrading technology. National and global

Table 5.4: Top Indigenous Telecom Manufacturers in China

Company	*Revenue (Million RMB)*	*Profit (Million RMB)*	*R&D (Million RMB)*	*Export (Million RMB)*	*Background*
China Putian	64,248	2,644	613	14,533	Founded in 1980, it was originally called China Posts and Telecommunications industry Corporation and affiliated to the former MPT and current MII. It ranked No. 1 in the Top 100 Chinese Electronic & Information Enterprises in 2001 and 2002 and ranks 10th in the overall listing of China's largest enterprise groups.
Huawei Technologies	16,229	2,654	3,050	999	A private corporation established in 1988 by several enterprises.
ZTE Telecomm-unications	10,926	797	1,130	353	A joint corporation sponsored by No. 691 Factory under former Ministry of Aerospace Industry (MAI), Changcheng Industrial Co. Ltd. (Shenzhen office), and Yunxing Electronic Trading Co., Ltd. In February 1985.
Xi'an Datang Telephone Corp.	3,163	90	390	5	A joint venture established in 1993 by China Academy of Telecom Technology (CATT), the tenth Research Institute of former MPT and International Telephone and Teledata Incorporation (ITT).
Wuhan P&T Institute	2,744	241	116	178	Wuhan Research Institute of the former Ministry of Posts and Telecommunications (MPT).
Jinpeng Telecom	2,262	15	23	0	Sponsored by the 54th Research Institute of the former Ministry of Electronics Industry (MEI).

Source: MII's List of Top 100 IT and Telecom Enterprises in China (2002).

expansion of R&D has therefore been recognized as one of the effective competitive strategies by many large Chinese firms including Huawei (Chen Jin 2003). Based in the Guangdong province China has R&D centres in Beijing, Shanghai, and Chengdu. These R&D centres are adequately connected to local centres to take full advantage of the big market. They provide access to local talent, information and connection to local markets. At the international level,

Huawei has R&D centres in India to have an access to the might of Indian software engineers.

Huawei, the major telecommunications equipment maker in China, also had opened up R&D centres at various locations including the Silicon Valley in the US to gain access to cutting edge technology and talent. This kind of expansion in global R&D helps companies like Huawei and ZTE to update themselves with state of the art technology capability and produce their own advanced products. Through such measures, Huawei witnessed its overseas sales rising from US$ 50 million in 1999 to US$ 2.24 billion in 2004, accounting for 41 per cent of its total sales (Huawei Technologies, 2005). Its overseas revenue in 2005 crossed the domestic sales for the first time, accounting for more than half of the company's total revenue.

Huawei's competitive prices have been a major reason for its expansion in sales. A price of 30 per cent lower than other suppliers has been possible because the company relies heavily on a pool of local engineers whose salaries are meager compared to their counterparts in developed markets. It is believed that Huawei capitalized so much on its price factor that initially when it launched its products in markets, Laos and Cambodia "its prices were below walk-away prices" for any developed country member (Harney 2005:15).

Another successful strategy which worked in the case of China was the reversed "partial technology outsourcing" from developed countries. As China always wanted to modernize its economy, it had understood the significance of technology. Knowing fully well that it has to look up to developed countries like the US to have latest technology; it followed the policy of partial outsourcing of technology, which it combined with aggressive in-house R&D innovation to produce updated products and sharpened its own competitive advantage. Through such innovations and access to latest technology indigenous manufactures could retain their market share. The success of these indigenous manufacturing companies came as a big lesson for the fledgling Chinese telecom vendors. Therefore an analysis of their globalization drive or strategy is of significance to this study.

The Chinese telecommunications equipment industry has been on an expansive mood since it has joined the WTO. Companies like Huawei and ZTE are entering into global markets like the US, EU, Southeast Asia, Africa and other places. It had developed high ambition of cutting into the markets of other telecommunication industry giants by focusing on a well thought out strategy. Many customers from Middle East, Africa and Southeast Asia found the Chinese products to be more stable and cheaper compared to Cisco (CSCO), Nortel (NT), and Alcatel-Lucent (ALU). Both Huawei and ZTE have signed deals to intensify their production and sales in the US markets.[4] In August 2009, the U.S. wireless carrier Clearwire added Huawei to its supplier list of base stations and other key infrastructure parts under a three-year contract.

This exemplifies how Huawei is moving beyond China and other emerging markets to tap into established markets in Europe and North America. In November 2009, Huawei surpassed Ericsson and Nokia Siemens to strike a deal with Norway's largest telecom operator, Telenor ASA. Under the six-year contract, which includes services and maintenance, Huawei will provide the Norwegian carrier with telecom equipment based on fourth-generation standard, known as Long Term Evolution (LTE), which offers cheaper operating costs and supports faster data uploads and downloads for mobile devices. (*Beijing Review*: Accessed on 14 January 2010: http://www.bjreview.com/business/txt/2010-01/09/content_238773.htm). Both companies emerged as globally competitive serious contenders for international market. Similarly, the ZTE increased its revenue by 25 times during 1997-2004 (Ji: 2005). Huawei also had experienced similar kind of revenue growth till 2005. An interesting aspect of this growth factor was that, they were never affected by the collapse of dot com or IT bubble in late 1990s. An analysis of strategy adopted by these two companies suggests that they have too many similarities in their approach. A set of unique characteristics emerges when their globalization drive was assessed. The strategy has been a mixture of technology intensive involvement of telecom business and country origin.

The People's Republic of China is the home country as well as the market for these two companies. China being a huge market, the sales and turnovers of these two companies soared high within a short period of time as their major market operations took place within the country itself. Essentially, the growing number of fixed lines and the wireless connections helped these companies to register high sales and revenue. The revenue of these companies also went up high outside China's border because of the initial globalization push that they received through joint ventures and favourable government policies.

The Chinese centric approach was not only visible in sales and revenue but also in the human resource or work force of these firms. In ZTE's R&D centres and overseas offices more than half of the members of staff were recruited locally and the rest were sourced from China only and in Huawei's R&D centres across the world except Bangalore, most of the staff were the Chinese (Huawei Annual Report: 2005).

The focus on R&D has been a priority in their globalization drive. A high degree of Huawei and ZTE employees are well qualified personnel. About 30 to 40 per cent of employees are working on research and development of products and technologies. This is directly related to the technology intensive nature of telecommunications industries where large telecom giants invest more than 10 per cent of their annual revenue on R&D activities. In order to attract well-trained personnel especially from developed countries as well as developing countries, these Chinese companies have set up their R& D centres outside China in key regions and areas such as already mentioned—the Silicon Valley, Canada, and Bangalore in India. Followed by this were the sales and representations offices in various parts of the world. This approach minimizes the poor local adaptation and knowledge. The partnership with foreign companies has paid rich dividends to these companies. At one level, they could produce advanced products with the available technology and finance. At other level, the assistance and influence provided by foreign companies with distinctive and rich experience of globalization have inevitably sped up the globalization process of these companies. Besides, partnership with foreign firms provides credibility and legitimacy to products of these two companies.

The backing and support of the Government plays a key role in China as it has a strong influence in any business operation in the country. The guiding macroeconomic policies have enabled and facilitated the founding and continuous growth of Huawei and ZTE. It is not a coincidence that both these companies are headquartered in Shenzhen, economically the most open city in China. A ZTE in Shanghai and Huawei in Beijing would not have been possible because of different political and economic conditions prevailing in these cities.

China was able to register a big technological success because the current global political and economic environment favours the free flow of technology between China and many other nations. The political and economic change brought forward through the reform programme somewhat loosened many previous restrictions on technology import and export, which made technology outsourcing possible. Secondly, many of the Chinese have abandoned the strict ideological belief in nationalism and self reliance as far as importance of technology is concerned. They argue, the idea is to produce 100 per cent China based technology through collaborations or joint ventures. In the case of China it looked apparent that the theory of globalization and advantage of low labour which view China as an emerging global economy argue that China could rely more on foreign suppliers for access to foreign technology and this would provide a competitive edge over other emerging economies. This view slowly began to be accepted among the Government circles.

China's telecommunications industry has become an extremely sophisticated and dynamic industry. Constant engagement of MNCs and the indigenous manufacturers has made the sector extremely competitive.

Consolidation of Mobile Phone Industry

Industry experts believed that China's mobile phone industry would take advantage of the country's WTO entry to grab more market share. This is because the tariffs on raw materials for mobile phones—especially CMOS (Complementary Metal Oxide Semiconductor) chips—will be lowered as a result of the WTO entry. This could benefit domestic mobile phone companies, who traditionally imported CMOS chips. In fact, China's mobile phone market has been open to overseas companies for so many years, that the domestic companies had never been fully protected by state preferential policies. Therefore, the WTO entry did negatively affect domestic mobile phone companies.

However, there are few technological differences between domestic mobile phones and those made overseas. In terms of function and price, the domestic mobile phones have the upper hand said the head of China's TCL Mobile Telecommunications Co. Ltd (*Xinhua*: 27 November 2001). Foreign mobile phone giants including Nokia, Motorola, and Siemens claim over 70 per cent of the market share in China. But domestic mobile phone companies have developed rapidly in recent years occupying the remaining 30-plus per cent of the market. Since 2002, more and more dealers and customers have started to buy domestic mobile phones. Sales of TCL mobile phones exceeded one billion Yuan (US$ 125 million) during the first eight months of 2001, nearly six-fold over the same period of the year 2000 (*Xinhua*: 27 November 2001). Sales of TCL mobile phones were expected to have reached 16 billion Yuan in 2009. In 2008 sales were supposed to be around 14.2 billion Yuan.

From this analysis, it is evident that China's industrial policy in the telecommunications sector experienced success and demonstrates the global technology leveling strategies of China's indigenous manufacturers. The policies adopted by the Central Government and strategies evolved under the normal pressure of market openness have created a situation where time and market space for indigenous players existed for them to grow and compete.

Table 5.5 clearly indicates that the manufacturing trend in China's mobile phone industry witnessed a continuous and significant rise in the post-entry phase. Producing more than 52 million mobile phones in 2000, the volume of production reached 121 million in 2002 immediately after its accession to the WTO, which signifies that opening up has resulted in greater demand for boosting China's indigenous telecommunications equipment industry. The same industry went on to produce 303 million mobile phones in 2005, almost six times more than the production it achieved in 2000. China's mobile phone industry has maintained a high speed growth in subsequent years. In 2006, 480 million mobile phones were produced in the country, increasing 58.2 per cent over 2005 and the number increased by 14.3 per cent to 549 million in 2007. However, the growth slowed down in 2008 with an annual growth rate of 2 per cent to 560 million. Similarly, landline instruments witnessed a rise in output from 95 million in 2000 to reach 103 million in 2001. Production output registered a continuous increase from 2001 onwards till 2005 in respect of the landline sets. Landline production declined marginally in 2006 and came further down to reach 165 million in 2007 (Table 5.5).

Table 5.5: Output of Mobile and Telephone Sets, 2000-2008

Year	*Mobile Telephones (10,000 Units)*	*Telephone Sets (10,000 Units)*
2000	5248	9598
2001	8032	10303
2002	12146	11892
2003	18231	12936
2004	23751	13967
2005	30354	18862
2006	48013	18648
2007	54857	16516
2008	56000	16687

Source: http://www.stats.gov.cn/english/statisticaldata/yearlydata/, Accessed on 17 October 2010, National Bureau of Statistics of China: 2009.

This explains the continuous rise in mobile users which has consequentially led to the decline in production of landline sets. According to an Assocham Study, almost half of global electronics and telecommunication manufacturing occurs in Asia. Out of which China's share is about 23 per cent.

Exports of Mobile Phones and Other Telecom Equipment

China is considered a significant player in telecom equipments in world market. It exports products to a wide range of countries. Table 5.6 below indicates that in relation to China's other telecom equipments especially in the HS Code: 8517 (which includes equipments line telegraph, etc. and electrical apparatus), China's exports to the world have witnessed a continuous rise. It is also observed that China's exports to the world in this product category have witnessed a quantum jump in 2007 from 2006 almost registering a jump of seven fold.

It is found that China's share of exports in the field of telecommunications equipments (HS Code: 8517) to the United States in 2001 was highest in the post-entry phase, registering 34.2 per cent of its total manufacturing exports. The share thereafter till 2008 end saw a continuous decline falling to 14.38 per cent. Similarly, Japan and the UK have experienced a decline in imports from China from 2001 to 2008. Gainers have been India, Russia, Hong Kong, and Thailand—all these countries have been continuous and huge importers from China over these years. China's exports to France particularly have remained almost the same.

China's major domestic telecom manufacturing company, Huawei, is an important global payer in world market. In 2009, it exported around 110 million units of telecom equipment to different parts of the world. It continues to dominate this segment in the world market after the Swedish major, Ericsson (http://www.isuppli.com/Abstract/P11020_20091014140826.pdf). Its exports amounted to US$ 2.2 billion or 40 per cent of sales in 2004, a significant rise compared to the exports of US$ 1.05 billion or 27 per cent of sales in 2003.

Table 5.6: China's Exports in Telecommunications Equipments to Major Trading Partners and Countries in HS Code 8517, 2001-2008

(in million US$)

Country	*2001*	*2002*	*2003*	*2004*	*2005*	*2006*	*2007*	*2008*
Hong Kong	652.9	862.2	1143.7	1462	1792	2463	19124.2	23032.9
United States	1206	1302	1453.1	1632	1912	2488.4	14766.8	12926.1
South Korea	44.9	84.3	74.5	100	135.2	167.6	3202.9	6591.5
India	19.1	83.4	119.2	288.6	249.8	297.8	3810.2	3941.3
Japan	368	480.3	444.8	660.2	569.3	391.8	2082.2	2444.3
Singapore	43.9	36.1	116.7	140	175.7	193.4	3359.3	2239.5
Germany	98.2	104.3	134	206.2	258	366.6	3364.0	2146.3
Netherlands	92.5	89.5	114.2	150.1	306.2	496.4	1757.2	1931.0
UK	138.2	111.5	174.3	268.3	296.1	366	1723.8	1837.5
Brazil	29.2	17.7	24	64.1	144.5	127.5	1002.3	1642.8
France	74.5	54.6	98	189.5	200.6	254.7	1500.3	1487.6
Russia	14.5	29.3	37.1	119.4	209.6	230.3	960.2	1465.9
Mexico	1.5	10.7	12.2	37.9	60.4	180.4	960.4	1448.2
Taiwan	53.1	81	109.5	106.5	115.2	130.7	1033.2	1369.8
Italy	23.4	36.5	69.6	189.1	184.5	146.9	619.9	790.3
Spain	10.1	14.8	23	58.7	118	159	831.5	749.2
Thailand	47.9	33.7	50.6	129.8	160.8	231.7	673.1	745.8
Sweden	121.2	19.9	55.9	103.4	103.4	134.5	708.5	702.3
Pakistan	6.1	22.5	33.9	68	148.2	152.7	537.3	518.2
Belgium	7.9	13.9	84.3	163.5	231.1	227.5	313.6	327.7
World	3527.5	3953.4	5174.0	7672.5	9433.9	11805.4	78648.5	89886.3

Source: China Customs, World Trade Online Database 2009, accessed on 16 May 2009.

Table 5.7 gives an indication as to how foreign and domestic telecom manufacturing companies operating in China have performed in terms of their exports. Nokia has topped the list in its exports from China followed by Motorola, Samsung, Sony Ericsson, etc. Huawei and ZTE the leading domestic manufacturing companies of China have comparatively exported much less to the world market. More than 60 per cent of telecom instrument exports from 2000 onwards are shipped by foreign companies (Guoxing 2009: Personal Interview). Every year since 1996, FIEs have accounted for more than 40 per cent of China's total exports (Moore, 2002: 3).

Data provided in Table 5.8 suggest that China's world exports have risen significantly in a span of seven years especially after its accession to the WTO. Between 2001 and 2008, the value of total exports has gone up more than five times. In relation to HS Code 8517, China's share in world exports has reached 26.28 per cent in 2008 from 5.19 per cent in 2006 indicating that the share in 2008 was more than five times of the share in 2006. Looking at China's world

Table 5.7: Export Volume of Key Mobile Phone Manufacturers 2007-2008 (1st Half)

Companies	(10,000 Units)	(10,000 Units)
Nokia	4202	5482
Motorola	2798	1460
Samsung	1920	3201
Sony Ericsson	1611	1351
LG	717	1761
Foxconn	636	2369
Flextronics	1861	972
Compal	1626	1022
ZTE	709	1159
Huawei	305	1101

Source: General Administration of Customs and the Ministry of Industry and Information Technology, 2009.

Table 5.8: China's Share in World Exports, 2001-2008

(in million US$)

	2001	2002	2003	2004	2005	2006	2007	2008
China's total exports to World	266403	325642	438473	593647	762327	969324	1218155	1428869
8517 Electric Apparatus for Line Telephony etc., and Parts	6.88	6.07	5.81	5.91	5.47	5.19	26.19	26.28
851711 Line Telephone Sets with Cordless Handsets	29.57	26.21	24.59	19.18	16.99	15.05	2.72	2.17

Source: China Customs, World trade Online Database 2009, accessed on 4 July 2009.

imports in the same product category—HS Code 8517—it was found that the imports have seen a continuous rise from 2006 onwards till 2008. In 2006, imports amounted to US$ 3.6 billion and the same reached US$ 18.8 billion in 2008 (China Customs World Trade Online Database). Consistent rise in imports speaks volumes of the significance that is attached to the joint venture initiative between China and MNCs. This surge in activities has helped China to increase its exports in this product group category by innovating products through such value added imports.

Analysis of Telecommunications Services Growth

China operates one of the largest telecommunications networks in the world. With 215 million telephone lines in the world compared to 186 million in the US and around 42 million telephone lines in India in 2002 at the time of its accession to the WTO, it has seen a big jump in expanding its network over the last few years. Within a span of seven to eight years the expansion of the industry has gone up by almost four times (*China Statistical Year Book*: 2009).

Recent trends showed that the mobile phone industry in China has also experienced a substantial rise in its sales. Driven by a growing number of handset users, increasing component prices for handsets, and a wider range of services bringing more value to customers, the market touched 4.7 billion Yuan in 2008 and 5.56 billion Yuan in 2009, according to the CCID Consulting[5] blue paper. The paper suggested, "The key driver is value-added services," (*Xinhua* 27 June 2007). Special services like accessories, music downloads or mobile TV represented only 2.5 per cent of China's after-sales service market in 2004, but rose to 18.2 per cent in 2006. The blue paper showed that more than 40 per cent of handset users wanted to watch handset TVs and a similar percentage were keen to download music into their handsets. "In half of our authorized maintenance stores, the income from value-added services has already surpassed the fees earned for repairing handsets," said Li Jianquan, Executive Director of Quality, Service and Administration of Lenovo Mobile. "In some stores, the ratio reaches 67 per cent," he said. "When customers come in to get their handset repaired, they might opt for a sophisticated new handset component like a high-definition coloured screen," Jiang observed (http://english.cri.cn/3130/2007/06/27/262 @242972.htm). There are now 487 million handset users in China with six million new users being added every month, according to the MII. According to the Ministry, the number is expected to reach 600 million by the end of 2010.

Though telecommunications growth was hit by the global financial crisis since 2008, current statistics provided by MII suggest that growth has witnessed a rise. According to latest statistics provided by MII in 2009, China's telecom industry achieved accumulated revenue of 2.5 trillion Yuan, a year-on-year increase of 14.4 per cent; and it reached operating revenue of 870.7 billion Yuan, a year-on-year increase of 4.1 per cent. For various telecom sectors in China, revenue from the mobile communications network business increased by 13.2 per cent year-on-year to 509.09 billion Yuan, accounting for 60.4 per cent of total revenue from main businesses; revenue from fixed line local network business declined by 14.4 per cent to 135.68 billion Yuan, accounting for 16.1 per cent; revenue from long-distance call network business decreased by 5.3 per cent to 98.26 billion Yuan, accounting for 11.7 per cent; and revenue from data communications network business increased by 0.3 per cent year-on-year to 99.4 billion Yuan, accounting for 11.8 per cent. In 2009, the number of China's total landline and mobile phone users increased by 79.467 million to 1.061 billion from 2008. The number of fixed line users decreased by 26.671 million to 314 million in 2009; and in the same year the number of mobile phone users increased by 106.138 million to 747 million. In addition, the number of broadband users in China increased by 20.347 million to 103.226 million in 2009 (*China Statistical Year Book* 2010).

According to Prof. Andong Zhu, Tsinghua University, Beijing "prospects for telecom exports (equipments) during this global financial crisis look more promising than other manufacturing products. As China is a manufacturing engine for world economy, it will be able to produce quality telecom products at a cheaper price in the world with new innovations required for value added service. Major winner has been the Huawei Technology. It has exported many telecom equipments like modems to India and other developing countries. FIEs in China have also contributed nearly 60 per cent to this growth and it is estimated that their contribution would rise further in future."

It is also analyzed from that the number of Urban Household Telephone Subscribers during the year 2005 was 172 million. In the year 2006, the number rose and had reached the 176 million mark. In the year 2007, the number decreased to 169 million. The number of rural fixed telephone subscribers during the year 2005 was 110 million. It increased in the year 2006 and had reached at 116 million, showing an increasing trend to the tune of 6 million, and it further went up by 1 million to reach 117 in 2007. The number of rural household telephone subscribers during the year 2005 was 100 million. It further increased in the year 2006 and had reached the 105 million mark. There was, however, no increase in this category in 2007 (*Statistical Yearbook of China* 2008).

The growing number of subscribers during the year 2006 created more business, and the ministry's projection of the telecom business income in 2006 reached more than 700 billion Yuan (US$ 86 billion). During the 10th Five-Year Plan period between 2001 and 2005, China's telecom business income grew by an average 13.4 per cent annually, with 100 million new subscribers every year. China has the world's largest number of phone subscribers, both for fixed-line and cell phones.[6]

In 2001, at the time of accession, China had more than 180 million landline telephone users which reached to 367.7 million in 2006 showing a compound annual growth rate (CAGR) of 15.3 per cent. Similarly in 2006, landline phone users per 100 inhabitants were 27.79 per cent compared to 14.06 per cent in 2001, registering a CAGR of 14.6 in 2006 over 2001 (Table 5.9). It can be also observed from the Table 5.9 that the percentage of CAGR registered at 15.3 per cent during the period 2001-2006. However, calculation based on sourcing data from the International Telecommunication Union (2007), it was observed the percentage of CAGR during 2000-2005 stood at 19.3 percent which suggests a decline in the growth of mainline telephone in China. There has been a significant decline in terms of mainline telephone services in China possibly due to growth in mobile services. China also experienced like the other countries in the world, a mobile revolution making its telecom sector to grow as one of the fastest in the world.

Table 5.9: China's Main Telephone Lines (CAGR %) (2001-2006)

Year	*Main Telephone lines (in 000')*	*CAGR % (2001-2006)*		*Main Telephone lines per 100 inhabitants*	*CAGR % (2001-2006)*
2001	180368	15.31	2001	14.06	14.6
2006	367786		2006	27.79	

Source: International Telecommunication Union 2007, accessed on 9 July 2009, URL: www.itu.int/

Table 5.10: China's Mobile Cellular Subscribers (CAGR)

Cellular Mobile Subscribers (in 000')

Year	*Subscribers (million)*	*CAGR % (2001-2006)*	*Year 2006*		
			Per 100 inhabitants	% Digital	As % of total telephone subscribers
2001	144820	26.1			
2006	461058		34.83	85.3	55.6

Source: International Telecommunication Union 2007, Accessed on 9 July 2009, URL: www.itu.int/

Table 5.10 indicates that the growth of cellular mobile subscribers in China witnessed an upward swing after its accession. China registered 144 million mobile users in 2001 and 461 million in 2006. It had about 55.6 per cent of mobile users out of total telephone subscribers in 2006. It can also be observed from the Table 5.10 that a CAGR of 26.1 per cent was noticed in 2006 (*World Telecommunications Development Report*, 2006, International Telecommunication Union).

From the available data in Table 5.11, it is clear that the telecommunication services sector over the next seven years especially after its accession to the WTO in 2001 performed better. The total business volume of Post and Telecommunications in 2001 amounted to 4.55 billion Yuan, and reached to 5.69 billion Yuan in 2002. The volume further increased to 9.71 billion Yuan in 2004 and showed a continuous increase, registering 23.6 billion Yuan in 2008 (International Telecommunication Union). The Number of mobile subscribers went up gradually. In 2001 at the time of accession,

China had 145 million mobile users, one of the highest in the world. It experienced a significant rise in the year 2003, when it registered 269 million mobile users compared to 206 million in 2002. Between 2003 and 2004 and between 2004 and 2005, the rise is also significant as in 2004 it touched to get 334 million in 2004 and recorded 393 million in 2005. In 2008, it further increased to register 641 million. Similarly, local landline telephone subscribers also witnessed a rising trend. It registered 180 million in 2001 and rose significantly to reach 214 million in 2002. The number further increased to

Table 5.11: Basic Conditions of Post and Telecommunication Services during 2001-2008

Item	*2001*	*2002*	*2003*	*2004*	*2005*	*2006*	*2007*	*2008*
Business Volume of Post and Telecommunication Service (100 million Yuan)	4556.26	5695.80	7019.79	9712.29	12028.54	15325.87	19805.06	23649.52
Number of Mobile Telephone Subscribers at Year-end (10000 subscribers)	14522.2	20600.5	26995.3	33482.4	39340.6	46105.8	54730.6	64124.5
Local Telephone Subscribers of at Year-end (10000 subscribers)	18036.8	21422.2	26274.7	31175.6	35044.5	36778.6	36563.7	34035.9
Local (Urban) Telephone Subscribers at Year-end (10000 subscribers)	11193.7	13579.1	17109.7	21025.1	23975.3	25132.9	24859.8	23155.9
Rural Telephones Subscribers at Year-end (10 000 subscribers)	6843.1	7843.1	9165.0	10150.5	11069.2	11645.6	11704.0	10880.0
Number of Post & Telecommunications Offices (unit)	57136	76358	63555	66393	65917	62799	70655	69146
Length of Postal Routes and Rural Delivery Routes (10000 km)	659.53	659.22	680.20	686.70	697.15	693.64	717.05	735.00

a) The business volume of postal and telecommunication services before 2000 was calculated at 1990 constant prices and that in 2001 was calculated at 2000 constant prices. The rate of increase at constant prices was 27.6% in 2001. The same applies to the table following.

b) Statistical coverage's of business volume of postal and telecommunication services and pieces of express mail services are China Post Group before 2006, and postal enterprises above designated size (with annual business revenue above 2 million yuan). The same applies to the table following.

c) The indicator of number of postal offices referred to postal and communication offices before 1998, and referred to postal offices from 1999 to 2006; It included postal offices and postal sub-stations since 2002, and was postal enterprises above designated size since 2007. The same applies to the table following.

Source: Stats.gov.cn, accessed on 11 September 2009.

311 million in 2004 and 350 million were finally registered by 2005 end. In 2008 the number of local landline subscriber came down, registering 340 million. This has happened due to consumers shifting to mobile phones. Local (urban) telephone subscriber numbers experienced an upward trend consistently from 111 million in 2001, and went up to register 239 million in 2005. It witnessed an increase in 2006 reaching 251 million, but in 2007 and 2008 the number has come down to touch 248 and 231 million respectively (Table 5.11). Likewise from the table, it is evident that other indicators like rural telephone subscribers, and number of post and telecommunications offices (PTO) witnessed some fluctuation in growth.

Telecom Industry During 2008-09

During this period most of the restrictions on the entry of foreign players to domestic market were supposed to be withdrawn. Around 2007-08, the telecom industry witnessed new dynamics in relation to resource distribution and development trends. On one hand, the mobile businesses grew fast while on the other, the landline businesses rapidly declined. Decrease in landline venture resulted in low economic benefits for the economy. As a result, the gap between enterprises at different levels increased and the competition dynamics in the market lost their balance. During May 2008, MII, the National Development and Reform Commission and Ministry of Finance decided to further restructure the telecom industry. The six major telecom operators were reshuffled to three, to improve the performance of the industry. The three major players were China Telecom, China Unicom, and China Mobile, and each one of them is involved with mobile, landline and broadband (*China Daily*: May 25, 2008).

The current telecom industry in China looks quite promising as most of the restrictions have been withdrawn. The foreign telecom players, who have been waiting for a long time to serve the Chinese telecom market were now considering giving shape to their plans of entering the world's largest and highly lucrative telecom industry. Various foreign players such as SK Telecom of South Korea and Telefonica (the second largest phone company of Europe) already enjoyed substantial stakes in China's fixed-line operations, China Telecom and China Netcom. "Restructuring of the Chinese telecom industry would give these players an opportunity to bring their mobile business to the country as the domestic partners now have access to the country's wireless market," says a telecom analyst.[7] This sentiment was also expressed by other Chinese experts (Zhu and Guoxing 2009: Personal Interview). For instance, SK telecom, which held 6.61 per cent of China Unicom's total equity before the telecom industry reorganization sought suitable opportunities to raise its stake in the company.

As if to reward these moves, the Chinese government announced in September 2008 that it would relax access to its telecom industry for foreign investors by cutting minimum investment criteria by as much as 50 per cent. It is expected that deregulation by the government may trigger an influx of foreign investment in the Chinese telecom sector. The Chinese Government took up the initiative to finalize issuance of 3G licenses in January 2009, which had opened up new avenues for foreign players, to venture into the market as the market which was expected to create huge demand for capital among the Chinese telecom operators. These companies are actively expanding and upgrading their existing networks in order to gain a favourable position in the country's most promising 3G environment.

Employment and Its Role in Economy

In the telecommunications sector which is capital and technology intensive, the pattern of employment had focused on having skilled workers. Both the equipment industry and the services sector require skilled workers to operate the system. During the 1990s and even till 2001, SOEs had remained the most important employers in telecommunications, as the state had a complete monopoly in the sector. Compared to other sectors in services such as retail and construction, telecommunications did not see much of a decline in employment because it remained protected. In the 1990s and early period of 2000 and 2001, employment in SOEs of posts and telecommunications remained quite high, i.e., almost 91 per cent (Bhalla and Qiu, 2004: 125).

From the data provided by Statistical Yearbook of China, 2007, it can be observed that before the accession, the total number of employees in the telecommunications and other transmission services was around 1.3 million, which noticed a slight decline towards the end of 2001 to 1.1 million. In 2003, the number had further come down to little over 0.8 million, which meant that there had been a significant decline in terms of employment in this sector during the post accession period. As has been argued earlier, that during the accession time when China was undergoing serious restructuring and competition had already set in the telecommunications sector—being overwhelmingly protected and SOEs driven—it is largely agreed that SOEs had to lay off many workers as it was unable to sustain themselves in the face of fierce competition. However by 2004, employment scenario had marginally improved as the total number of employees had gone up from 812511 to 858992. That was the time when the private sector or the non-state sector had gained much and the employment scenario had started looking bright. The year 2005 also saw a marginal increase in the employment. The number of staff and workers continued to increase in telecommunications sector in China. There has been a substantial rise in employment in this sector, as national total increased to 955771 in 2006 and to 980431 in 2007 (*China Statistical Year Book* 2000:http//www.stats.gov.cn/tjsj/ndsj/2007 /indexeh. htm).

Currently China's services sector may not be contributing as much to its economy as India does, but a significant part i.e., around 32 per cent of its

GDP comes from its services sector. As most of the services require an effective telecommunications system to perform, this sector directly or indirectly contributes to its economy.

The possibility of a rapid growth of telecom sector in China was well visualized as it began experiencing a lot of activity in the ITeS (Information Technology enabled Services) and Business Process Outsourcing (BPO). Over the last few years, the worldwide BPO sector has undergone rapid transformation. Low cost, skill based workers, and good communications skills were proving to be key components of global competitiveness of this sector. Many companies were looking at offshore outsourcing as a strategic alterative. China seemed to have realized this and therefore it was making efforts in terms of developing English language skills and computer software to emerge as an attractive destination for future BPO activities.

The BPO, insurance, banking and financial sectors were, and continue to be the key users of telecom infrastructure. China's opening up to the outside world and foreign companies coming into China will require world class telecom infrastructural facilities and this is a big opportunity for China to capitalize on those gains.

Implications of Services Commitments on China

Unlike GATT, the mandate of the WTO included the services sector. With the introduction of General Agreement on Trade in Services (GATS)[8] in 1995, the growing importance of services sector has assumed significance. As data and literature on post-accession are quite sparse on China's services sector, the component of analysis becomes limited on the issue. A significant work done by Ianchovichina and Martin in 2001 (Mattoo 2003: 303) taking into account the market access and national treatment commitments, says that the coverage of market access commitments (the unweighted average count) was 57.4 per cent. Table 5.12 gives an idea about the analysis done in this study.

Accession commitments in China are much higher than the commitments offered by any other group of countries including high income countries in the Uruguay Round. The 'average coverage' a measure of coverage that better reflects the extent of liberalization of services was 38 per cent for China, which shows more openness about the sector compared to other high income group countries. The share of completely liberal commitments (no restrictions) in the maximum possible commitments was 23 per cent for China, much higher than that of any other group of developing countries but somewhat lower than that of high income countries. From this, one can easily observe that China's commitments towards national treatment are wider and deeper than many other groups of countries.

Table 5.12: Coverage of Specific Commitments During Late 1990s (%)

	High-income countries	*Low and middle-income countries*	*Large developing nations*	*China*
Market access				
Unweighted average count (sectors-modes listed as a share of maximum possible)	47.3	16.2	38.6	57.4
Average coverage (sectors-modes listed as a share of maximum possible, weighted by openness or binding factors)	35.9	10.3	22.9	38.1
Coverage/count (average coverage as a share of the average count)	75.9	63.6	59.3	66.4
No restrictions as a share of total offer (unweighted count)	57.3	45.5	38.7	40.2
No restrictions as a share of maximum possible	27.1	7.3	14.9	23.1
National treatment				
Unweighted average count (sectors-modes listed as a share of maximum possible)	47.3	16.2	38.8	57.4
Average coverage (sectors-modes listed as a share of maximum possible, weighted by openness or binding factors)	37.2	11.2	25.5	45.0
Coverage/count (average coverage as a share of the average count)	78.6	69.1	66.1	78.4
No restrictions as a share of total offer (unweighted count)	65.1	58.0	52.3	63.5
No restrictions as a share of maximum possible	30.8	9.4	20.2	36.5
Memo item				
No restrictions on market access and national treatment as a share of maximum possible	24.8	6.9	14.3	29.8
Number of sectors committed	293.0	100.0	239.0	356.0

Source: Mattoo, A. 2003: 303.

The schedule of commitments towards market access and national treatment that China made while entering into the WTO are very significant. A closer look at those commitments sector by sector reveals that for most sectors modes 1 and 2 are either fully open or unbound and not subject to specific restrictions. Commitments on mode 4 specified horizontally rather than sector by sector are also standard. Entry is guaranteed to managers, corporate executives, and specialists defined as senior employees of a corporation of the WTO members being engaged in the foreign invested enterprises in the territory of the People's Republic of China for conducting business. They may be granted a long-term stay permit as stipulated in the terms of contracts concerned or an initial stay of three years, whichever is shorter (Report of the Working Party, 2001). No commitments are made regarding other categories of movement of natural persons, for example unskilled personnel or movement not linked to commercial presence. With regard to mode 3, dealing with commercial presence, the official policy of China today even puts into effect a lot of restrictive measures. These are as follows:

Form of Establishment: Foreign enterprise can make an entry to China on specific sectors in two ways. The typical restriction is the requirement to form a joint venture; which is either an equity joint venture (EJV) or contractual joint venture (CJV). Foreign ownership in EJVs is frequently restricted to specified levels ranging from minority ownership (49% or less) or majority ownership (50%) or full membership.

Geographic scope: Commercial activity may be allowed only in specified cities, for example in Shanghai or Shenzhen or in special economic zones.

Business scope: Transactions may be permitted only with a subset of consumers or restricted in some other way.

Regulatory requirements: Foreign firms may be required to have certain amount of assets and be established as a representative office for a certain period of time before commencing full business operations.

According to this specific schedule of commitments, FDI in joint ventures will not exceed 30 per cent in specific cities such as Beijing, Shanghai, and Guangzhou. Within one year after accession, this geographical area will be extended to Chengdu, Dalian, Fuzhou, Nanjing, and others. One year after accession, foreign investment up to 49 per cent will be allowed and within two years up to, but not more than, 50 per cent. The above geographical restriction will be lifted within five years from the date of accession.[9] The telecom services will include value added services such as voice mail, electronic mail, online information and data base retrieval, internet content, etc. These were the commitments made by China when it entered the WTO. While the five-year "roadmap" for implementation of its scheduled market opening ended in December 2006 with most of the commitments met, some key commitments in sectors important to the US economy still have not been fulfilled (US-China Business Council).

Similarly, on the issue of national treatment it had not committed any limitation which signifies that the foreign invested enterprises and domestic players will have no discrimination in terms of treatment in the country. That also amply demonstrates that it wanted to encourage foreign players to come in, but in a gradual and geographically restricted manner.[10]

In the services negotiations under the GATS framework countries make offers and request to achieve their specific schedule of commitments. These commitments are made at the time of accession to the WTO. The idea is this that when the negotiations at multilateral level were proving to be difficult to reach its desirable end, countries resorted to offer-and-request mechanism. China did the same thing in 2005 when it revised its offers[11] in a range of services in anticipation that this process or initiative would ease the negotiations to reach its final end. The revised offers in China's telecom services suggested that the foreign service suppliers will be permitted to establish joint venture in value added telecommunications enterprises without confining to 30 per cent equity and restricting to cities like Shanghai, Guangzhou and Beijing. Similarly, in other services such as on-line information and/or data processing, foreign investment in the joint ventures shall be no more than 50 per cent. This is to suggest that with three to four years of accession China proceeded with its liberalization commitments in telecom services. This in a way was expected of China to do it because it had promised to remove such kind of restrictions and also became keen to liberalize the sector.

Implications During Restrictive Phase (2002-2007)

China's opening up of the telecommunications sector in a gradual and phased manner to foreign players was seen both as an opportunity as well as a threat. The Central Government was extremely cautious in allowing market access to foreign players. After joining the WTO, China, as a matter of principle, had to open its sector. For a long time restrictions in the form of commercial establishment have been prevalent in China and being justified as a source of acquiring technology or obtaining a share of monopoly rents. All such restrictions slowly apply to the forms of establishment. Restrictions of these kinds mentioned in the WTO agreement which confine foreign ventures to five cities for five years as in the case of insurance, will encourage agglomeration of these activities in the favoured cities, which will be difficult to reverse when the restrictions are subsequently lifted (Mattoo, A. 2002). Such kind of restrictions will have a rather adverse impact on the rural areas of the country even if they have the potential or the comparative advantage of the designated urban areas. Policies of liberalization towards telecom services pursued geographically was at one level a conscious decision of the Central Government because it knew in such pockets the rising purchasing power and developed infrastructure will be able to sustain such telecom growth and consumers' demands will also be met (Xiangshuo 2009: Personal Interview). It is also the pressure of the domestic telecom lobby, which exerted immense pressure on the Government not to liberalize the telecom policy and allow the foreign players to come in. Though consumers complained because of poor service and high tariff structure, the Government had imposed during this period hardly addressed such concerns. The Government benefited from such policies as it obtained hefty revenue directly from the telecom sector (Xiangshuo 2009: Personal Interview).

China's telecom liberalization is delayed due to vested interests of various interest groups. These groups are domestic telecom operators like the China Mobile, China Telecom and China Unicom who never wanted an early opening up of the sector. Though the commitments made by China in the WTO were regarded, yet the Government took five to six years to phase out most of the restrictions for foreign players to enter the Chinese market. This kind of market restrictions which remained after the accession till 2007 were supported by the Government as it provided lead time to the Government to gauge the impact of telecom liberalization in the country (Lei 2009: Personal Interview).

Positive Impact

China's late entry of telecommunications in world trade is justified as it is a developing country and its domestic industry is not strong enough to face the global competition. Being a strategic sector, the Government may retain its control over the sector. Implications of late opening might not have been profitable for the Government, but the issue of security has never been compromised (Sang Ho 2009: Personal Interview). According to Prof. Hong Song: "Chinese domestic firms were not very strong in terms of their infrastructure, innovation and service. As a result there was intense pressure from the industry lobby not to open up the sector. The Chinese Government respected their concerns" (Song 2000).

According to Prof. Andong Zhu, Tsinghua University, Beijing, China: "When pressure on China mounted as China was negotiating for its entry into the WTO, it decided to open up its telecommunications sector in a phased manner confined to a few cities initially as it wanted to realize the impact of such liberalization policies. Telecom remained a closed sector for political reasons. It is also argued that the Chinese Government wanted to experiment the system of opening up on a selective geographical pattern. The Government was fully aware that such pockets had the purchasing power and initial development of telecom infrastructure will generate revenue for the Government." Implications of this opening up in a phased manner have not put the Government in any jeopardy as far as social and political security is concerned. As a part of the overall WTO's accession commitments, China had to open up and remove its restrictions on foreign players' entry. With the liberalization and FDI coming into the sector, the employment prospects have naturally gone up. In fact, the telecom sector is providing more employment currently than textiles. During this current financial crisis, the prospects for performing better lay more with the telecom compared to textiles (Zhu 2009: Personal Interview).

The overall accession commitments led to some amount of dilution of discretionary power of the Chinese Government as it fulfilled most of its commitments over a period of five to six years from the date of its accession.

It has eliminated all its restrictions relating to foreign entry and foreign ownership. It will observe strictly national treatment, which basically means it will stop discriminating between trading partners and not even favour its own domestic firms. In totality, it vows to follow a free and fair rule-based trading system. What China is going to lose most importantly in the wake of all these developments is its freedom to exercise its own policies at any point of time. The commitments are all desirable but how far the continuous restrictions on foreign entry and ownership will help China to have full benefits of foreign investment is an issue that needs to be debated. The commitments try to eliminate discretion existing in the system. It is a matter of fact that liberalization in many areas is taking place in China slowly because the Chinese government is reluctant to liberalize certain areas. Socio-economic factors and political pressures from various quarters hold them back and as a result protection still continues. The government even feels certain incumbent domestic enterprises or suppliers are unable to cope up or face the challenges of liberalization as the reforms in these may take longer for them to fight back. All these may lead to some form of protection and once protection is given will be difficult to lift it.

In addition, entry through joint venture looks to be a positive step for the foreign firms. Initially they can collaborate with a local firm as the firm will have the minimum assets and they will find an access to operate in China. However, binding ownership restrictions will affect the firm's performance because the firm will not be in a position to obtain new technology and better manpower to raise its performance.

Negative Impact

Though China has agreed to remove all restrictions on foreign entry, the Government feels somehow ambivalent about the nature and scope of foreign entry. What is uppermost in the Chinese Government's mind is whether unrestricted regime will be good for China and to what extent, it is going to devalue the total control of the Chinese government on this issue. One reason could be that unrestricted entry of foreign companies may just completely swallow the Chinese market, as the domestic firms are not so well developed or well equipped in terms of providing better services at such a lower cost. Another reason is the issue of economies of scale. For example, in a vibrant services sector like telecommunications, if one domestic firm has worked out substantial fixed costs of networks, competitive bidding by foreign entry could lead to some kind of an inefficient network duplication (Armstrong, M.; Cowan, S. and J. Vickers, 1994).

In a technologically driven world, technology can even minimize the cost at some level. Openness in the system allows a country to have better technological leverage as to how a country can stop all these and go ahead with its old sterile and obsolete technology. The power and spirit of competition is yielding much better results.

Besides, entry restrictions do not develop a sense of competition among the local firms or incumbents; rather it creates an atmosphere of complacency or sometimes leads to collision, which ultimately results in unproductivity and inefficiency. More importantly, sometimes even the regulator is not adequately placed than the competitive system to derive the number of firms operating in the market and as to how they are being priced to produce or provide the best possible services. All this suggests that China may not worry to open up its sector or restrict foreign entry.

Excessive capitalization requirements to the tune of RMB 2 billion in the telecommunication sector as a part of the China's regulations for foreign invested telecommunications enterprises proved an entry barrier for foreign telecom investors. As a result to develop an economically viable and efficient telecommunications services market in China had become difficult. This kind of restriction inhibited investor to turn to the Chinese market for future investment.

For many successful foreign enterprises such huge capital requirements for commercial purposes were never a practice and to invest so much in developing infrastructure in a different country initially did not look a very profitable proposition. Such policy doesn't make positive contribution to a domestic infrastructural service like telecommunications especially at a time when the global telecom sector is facing huge capital resource crunch.

China's huge capitalization requirements were also inconsistent with the licensing practices of other liberalizing economies. A global review of the start up capital requirement for a basic service provider found no amount of capitalization fee in the US, the EU, Canada, Japan, Australia, Brazil, Chile, Argentina. Hong Kong requires a performance bond; India requires a bank guarantee from US$ 5 million to US$ 80 million depending on geographic scope. It is only Taiwan which maintains a rigid policy like China (Brilliant, M. and Waterman, J.). This high capitalization policy had restricted the movement of foreign service providers entering China. The policy also discouraged the foreign companies to engage in any joint venture with a Chinese partner. China's high capitalization requirement for basic telecommunications services has limited its market access.

This policy adopted by China dissuaded many foreign enterprises to enter the market. As a result, China suffered from developing its telecom sector as a modern, productive, and sophisticated sector. It lost the opportunity of getting sophisticated technological services and other managerial expertise into the sector, which in turn would have helped China in the diffusion of knowledge and make the economy more efficient. Lack of access to better services remained a bottleneck for the whole industrial sector. Such restrictive policy did not help the consumers. This policy remained active for the first three years of accession and slowly such restrictions were lifted in the interest of the economy.

Such restrictions proved to be disadvantageous for the country as well as for the consumers and were also not in conformity with the commitments of the accession process. Restriction on foreign ownership was proving to be a major hindrance in the liberalization of trade services in China. There was only one way in which foreign presence in China can be administered, i.e., entry through a joint venture with varied degree of limits on the extent of foreign ownership. China has undertaken a series of reforms in gradually phasing out those restrictions but still in the areas of life insurance and telecommunications, such restrictions persist.

Besides, the policy of geographical limitation followed after China joined the WTO in terms of opening up of certain major cities like Shanghai and others to foreign players and limiting to rest of the country, greatly impeded China's uniform growth in the telecom sector. As a part of China's own commitments to the WTO, this policy of geographical limitations may have widened the intra-regional disparities. Though China was committed to phasing out of geographical restrictions, sequential approach to this kind of liberalization may prove even more damaging in the long run. The existing pockets of development are going to witness even more progress as more economic activities are going to be concentrated in these areas. This would even widen the scope of intra-regional inequality. With due course of liberalization occurring in the hinterland at a later stage, there is a doubt whether hinterland economy will be able to adjust to the pace of progress that had occurred in the coastal belt. Inequality may thus continue to persist. These lacunae should be able to strengthen its case for lifting the geographical restrictions simultaneously rather than sequentially.

Economic and Political Hurdles for Opening Up

China's policy relating to restrictions on foreign ownership continues to be dominated essentially for two reasons—economic and political. Economic reason can be attributed to the fact of extending limited ownership by which foreign companies will be able to ensure efficiency-cum enhancing cost and services factor, whereas political reason implies that there is a huge adjustment cost involved that an immediate transfer of an ownership would lose control of the firm, which ultimately could lead to layoffs. This picture is well known to the Chinese Government and they visualize a major social backlash. But the liberalization on the other hand promises to provide better service by not developing a monopolistic scenario rather than bringing in a competitive system by introducing competing firms to provide quality service.

The above analysis gives an idea about the fact that accession commitments and its fulfillment are beneficial for a country like China. With its size, and a huge burgeoning middle class having a strong purchasing power, with great amount of infrastructural development and an earnest drive towards modernization, China can achieve spectacular success from this on-going liberalization process. If it is to make the most of liberalization that it had committed to after becoming a WTO member, then it has to put its independent regulatory network in place. China has not so far implemented its WTO Reference Paper commitment to establish an independent regulator.

The Chinese Government still owns and controls all major operators in the telecommunications industry, and the MII still regulates the sector. To create an independent regulator, China requires a series of reforms to be undertaken in the immediate future like establishment of a professional body that is separate from, and not accountable to, any basic telecom supplier. The body should be capable of issuing impartial telecom decisions and rules. Specifically, it is important that the regulatory body adopts transparent procedures for drafting, finalizing, implementing and applying regulations and decisions. It must take appropriate measures consistent with the WTO Reference Paper, to prevent dominant suppliers from engaging in, or continuing with anti-competitive practices. It must set up an independent and objective process for administrative reconsideration of its decisions and appropriate procedures and authority to enforce China's WTO telecom commitments such as the ability to impose fines, order injunctive relief, and modify, suspend, or revoke a license. As the services sector is dynamic and rapidly growing, a strong, flexible domestic regulatory body is very much essential to tackle certain key issues like destabilization in the market, asymmetrical and inadequate consumer information, developing monopolistic tendencies, and guarantee fair and equitable access (Kanungo 2005: 344).

The first regulatory reform should come in the area of physical infrastructure like roads and railways for land transport and other specialized distribution networks, like cable and satellite telecommunications (UNCTAD) and World Bank, 1994). Unless a thorough regulatory mechanism is created, the market is going to witness some disturbance as the incumbent may not allow competition to set in and deny the competitors access to essential facilities.

Second, as services markets in China are being opened up, due importance must be given to providing consumers with the quality information in intermediate and knowledge based services. Normally in a large market, consumers may not find the appropriate information about the kind of services they are buying. For example, a consumer may not easily assess the competence of a professional such as a doctor or a lawyer or the effectiveness of a hospital or services of a transport system. Further obtaining that information from anywhere in the first place is difficult; secondly that information will prove to be expensive. In such a situation, an effective regulatory body having more autonomy and flexibility if in place can take care of increasing demand of social welfare.

Implications During 2008-2009

With the beginning of the global financial crisis, China's telecom manufacturing companies initially experienced a setback. Export of telecom instruments came down from US$ 89 billion in 2008 to US$ 86 billion in 2009 [World Trade Atlas Online Database, 2010 (HS Code 8517-miscellaneous telecom products)]. Domestic telecom manufacturing giants like Huawei and ZTE faced serious slump in the world market during 2008 and early parts of 2009. Their exports witnessed a decline. As their share of profit significantly depended on world demand, decrease in import demand from the world, posed a serious threat to their future expansion. As the wage factor is a determinant in the global competitiveness of these domestic firms, an increase by 15 per cent in wage in rural China will affect the sustainability of these firms. Domestic telecom manufacturing companies may find it too hard to sustain in this current crisis (Lei 2009: Personal Interview).

According to the statistics from China's Ministry of Industry and Information Technology (MIIT)[12], China's mobile phone output decreased by 11.2 per cent year-on-year in the first two months of 2009 and its mobile phone exports decreased by 17.2 per cent during the same period; the largest decline over the past few years. The statistics from MIIT show that in January and February 2009, a total number of 79.672 million mobile phones were produced in China, a decrease of 11.2 per cent compared with the same period of last year.

The statistics from the customs departments show that the exports of China's mobile phones and mobile phone parts were to the tune of US$ 3.598 billion in February 2009, an increase of 25.3 per cent compared with the previous month, but a decrease of 3 per cent compared with the same period in 2008. In the first two months of 2009, the accumulated value of exported mobile phones and mobile phone parts was US$ 6.47 billion, a year-on-year decrease of 17.2 per cent, and the value accounted for 14.8 per cent of the total export value of China's high-tech products during the same period.

The competition of telecom industry is going to get tougher. Its growth will not be affected so much during this global financial crisis compared to financial services, as this sector plays an important intermediary role in business activity. Foreign service providers will find it hard to compete because Chinese consumers are culturally more sensitive and attached to their traditions. They would demand services in the Chinese language, which may prove difficult for foreign providers to adopt. Huge amount of investment has to come in from foreign service providers and to implement such services they have to hire many Chinese skilled workers. This will increase the employment prospects for the local people in this sector (Yong 2009: Personal Interview).

Though the sector experienced the slump due to decrease in world demand, yet in early part of 2010 it started recovering from that temporary slump. Huawei Technologies, the fast-growing Chinese telecom manufacturer reached global contract sales of over US$ 30 billion in the last quarter of 2009, marking a rise of nearly 30 per cent from the year before. It is expected that this domestic company will increase its contract sales to US$ 36 billion by end of 2010. It is fast expanding to big markets (*Beijing Review* 9 January 2010:http://www.bjreview.com.cn/business/txt/2010-01/09/content_238773.htm). Besides, the sector provides key inputs in terms of information and IT enabled services to industry from time to time. Its prospect for growth can be envisaged. The government needs to prioritize the sector as a potential area of investment, which would help in raising its productivity and increasing its economic growth. This sector did not experience any major decline in growth during this global financial meltdown because this is a growing sector and its role is important to the growth of a nation as well as to world trade, as the telecom sector provides critical infrastructural inputs to the proliferation of world trade. Its expansion is inevitable and global financial meltdown requires more and better services from China's telecom sector because it is currently one of the fastest growing economies in the world (Guoxing 2009: Personal Interview).

Issue of FDI in Telecommunications Services

The issue of Foreign Direct Investment (FDI) in China's telecommunications services sector occupies a critical place in China's post-WTO accession period. The FDI in services virtually remained banned or extremely restrictive prior to its accession (Nolan and Wang 1999: 182). The scenario changed when the establishment of MII as the regulatory body came into existence and took measures to put in place an effective regulatory mechanism to monitor the foreign investment.

However, one of the significant reasons for China not allowing FDI in telecom services has been its deep concern towards national security and sovereignty. State control of communications network and services has long been viewed as one of the important aspects of security and sovereignty. Ideological reasons also played a role in restricting FDI in telecom services and allowed the sector to move quite cautiously (Xiangshuo 2009: Personal Interview). As Wu Jichuan explained: "The rules prevented foreigners from owning telecom; there was worry that China's security could be jeopardized" (Kuhn 2010: 322). It has often been observed in Asia particularly the linkage between national security and telecommunication services has been invoked as one of the main reasons for restricting the foreign ownership of operators

(Janda 1999: 23). At the same time, the demand and ability of a country's economic growth is fully dependent on such network of services, which is also equally recognized by the country. The countries, therefore, are trying hard to balance these contradictory and functional imperatives (Drake 2001: 27-28).

Countries in the 1960s and 1970s and during Uruguay Round shared the view that Western technology played a key role in enhancing their economic growth. Based on pragmatic assessment, countries realized giving up a degree of national sovereignty would result in ample dividends in terms of consumers' welfare and deployment of equipment and efficient services (Frieden 2001:149). In a centrally planned economy like China, telecommunications were part of national security network and part of country's requirement to stay in touch with the country side. As a result, sovereignty and national security since 1978 till its accession to the WTO have considerably influenced China's policy on FDI in services and the broader direction of reform agenda in telecommunications.[13]

With the accession to the WTO, the policy debate shifted from a ban to how and to what degree the foreign ownership of operators and network services should be allowed without affecting the country's national interest. Joining the WTO the Government automatically opened up the sector though the deeper issue of national security and sovereignty remained a primary concern. Recent regulations explicitly incorporate the notion of sovereignty. For example, rules governing the administration of telecommunications provide that "when managing telecommunications construction, it is necessary to safeguard the state sovereignty in telecommunications."[14]

With the accession to the WTO, several foreign enterprises have made inroads to China. Flag Telecom from Europe is the first and the only private operator, that landed a submarine telecommunication cable in China. In addition to this, in 2003 South Korea's SK telecom joined hands with China Unicom to develop the first Sino-foreign joint value added mobile service provider in China.

In compliance with the WTO agreements, China till 2004 had allowed foreign operators an equity of 25 per cent in basic services joint ventures. Although 18 foreign firms are reported to have applied for investment in joint ventures, the scope of investment still remained narrow (Laperrouza 2006: 161). High capitalization requirements have acted as a huge disincentive for all these international carriers.

Besides the issue of security and sovereignty, certain other factors also attributed to the formation of restrictive policies. First, it wanted to give a free run to the MPT and thereby closed the gates of entry of FDI into China. Second, the Chinese government, like its counterparts in developing and transitional economies, wanted to protect the interests of the national domestic industry. This view is amply reflected in the work of Mueller and Tan that services market in telecommunication would remain restricted to foreign investors as long as national industrial policy and political considerations define the agenda of reforms. Third, it is believed that the sector did not provide a clear, predictable, and transparent environment for the foreign enterprises. Fourth, immediately after the accession, foreign investors were not clear about the timeline of the liberalization of different services. Fifth, the MII acts as a conservative regulator which limits the scope of expansion in an era of openness. *Sixth*, they were not sure of their profit margins as the post accession period does not liberalize the sector in a speedy manner, rather it does it in a phased manner over a period of six-years.

Summary

China's telecommunications sector has undergone a sea-change since its accession process began. Fundamental changes took place in its structural as well as functional areas. From functioning as a wing of the Government, it went on to introduce market reforms thus institutionalizing the distinct identity and functioning of regulators and service providers. The sector has remained a strategic sector as it contributed both to the manufacturing as well as service segments of the economy. With the joining of the WTO its strategic importance has increased because of the global connectivity and the issues of national security and sovereignty.

China's GATS commitments symbolize a major initiative towards telecommunications liberalization. Within a period of six years from the date of accession, i.e., by the end of 2007, it promised to lift all forms of restrictions as far as market access to its territory is concerned. This is an encouraging sign for the trading partners who are all waiting and genuinely interested in establishing and nurturing a continuous trading relationship with China. By and large the commitments have allowed China to accrue gains in terms of providing employment, improving the service base, satisfying a wide range of consumers' needs and helping in registering high economic growth. Signs of improvement have begun to show as it opened up the sector with some restrictions.

In the post-entry phase growth of the sector has been significant. Its exports in the field of telecom equipment have gone up and it has widened its network of world trading partners. It has increased its domestic consumer base by providing connectivity to many regions of the country and also remaining connected to the outside world. The industry also witnessed a sustained growth in its size since reforms began in the sector. The total value of telecom business services had soared from RMB 1.9 billion in 1978 to around 1.85 trillion in 2007 (*China Statistical Yearbook*, 2008).

The ongoing global financial crisis and global economic meltdown have not affected the sector in a major way. As a strategic and futuristic sector, it has the potential to grow. The telecommunications sector in China is set to prosper as more and more businesses are expected to employ more sophisticated telecom services.

In the long run, China's telecom industry will develop into an information service industry. It will constantly endeavour to improve its quality which can compete with service providers in developed countries. It will aim to provide quality, reliable, safe and diverse information services to the Government and to all sections of the society. As restrictions have been withdrawn, international players are allowed to operate in China. Vodafone is currently entering into an arrangement with China Mobile to provide services. This would infuse a sense of competition among the Chinese service providers. Such competition will lead to form an industrial chain for the coordinated development of all market players. This will help promote economic growth. Many experts believe that with an efficient regulatory system in place, many business brands with indigenous intellectual property rights (IPR) will enter the market. The Chinese telecom service providers will become more competitive in the overseas markets and will create a secure market for themselves as China has done in other sectors like hardware, electrical machinery, textiles, toys, etc. (Yong 2009: Personal Interview).

The telecommunications sector in China is on an expansive mode. Its mobile and internet sectors are the largest and second fastest growing in the world. For China to have an edge over the others, it must focus on innovation and technological upgradation. These requirements will pose a big challenge for the telecom manufacturers as well as for the service providers. To a large extent, the Government's role and involvement will be a major determinant in shaping future growth of China's telecommunications sector.

Notes

1. WTO, "Reference Paper on Regulatory Principles," [Online web], Accessed 16 June, 2007 URL:http://www.wto.org
2. MII statistics as of April 2002. Available online: www. mii.gov.cn/mii/hyzw/tongjiziliao200203.htm.
3. The first domestic manufacturers were Kejian (Shenzhen) and Eastcom (Hangzhou), both collaborating with foreign partners.
4. http://wwwen.zte.com.cn/en/press_center/press_clipping/200708/t20070803_156927.html.
5. A joint stock limited company incorporated in the People's Republic of China with limited liability
6. MII, 2006.

7. From the discussion held at a business meet organized by the CII and Embassy of India, Beijing at the Marriot hotel in Beijing on April 15 2009.
8. Detailed provision relating to GATS can be accessed from http://www.wto.org/english/docs_e/legal_e/26-gats_01_e.htm
9. WT/MIN(01)/3/Add.2 WTO Ministerial Conference Fourth Session Doha, 9-13 November 2001, p. 17.
10. *Ibid*, p. 17.
11. TN/S/O/CHN/Rev.1, 29 July 2005, WTO.
12. MIIT, established in March 2008, is the state agency of the People's Republic of China responsible for regulation and development of the postal service, internet, wireless, broadcasting, communications, production of electronic and information goods, software industry, and the promotion of the national knowledge economy.
13. Several studies have directly attributed to the conservative stance of China on FDI to the issue of sovereignty and national security. See Zhang and Peng (2000:14) and Xu (2002: 25-26).
14. Decree No. 20, jointly issued by MII and SDPC in February 2002.

6
Conclusion

China joined the WTO with the clear objective of consolidating and deepening its integration with the world economy. It was fully convinced that integration with the world economy was a viable strategy to progress further. It formally applied to the GATT in 1986 to fulfil that quest. Earlier, the success of Open Door Policy of 1978 had vindicated the fact that interaction with the outside world was a key factor in China's gradual and continuous economic growth. As a result, external dependence came to be recognized as an important instrument in the rise of its economy.

As the world was moving towards a global village, interdependence had become a rallying point for the world community. Since the Deng era, China has gone through remarkable changes that have intertwined its economy with the rest of the world. Interdependence based on this perception found increasing acceptance among policy makers, government departments, and trade and industry experts in China. China's adherence to interdependence helped China to consider multilateralism as a more meaningful platform for resolving differences than pursuing bilateral arrangement.

Thus China had adopted an interdependent approach to economic prosperity since 1979, much before it initiated its process of accession to the WTO. For instance, its close economic and trade relationship with Hong Kong is a good example of this strategy. Hong Kong has been a gateway for China and both shared close alliance to foster entrepreneurship and business to maximize their individual gains and benefit from the world economic system. The notion that theory of interdependence helps to promote better understanding and relationship in international relations by reducing tensions and promoting economic growth is an established fact. At the same time, it also develops an asymmetrical relationship between two countries. That asymmetrical relationship gives rise to social tensions, strategic imbalances, and unequal trade benefits. In case of China such dimensions were noticed and were resolved through mutual understanding, cooperation, and looking at future prospects.

It is commonly perceived that a single country cannot be globally competitive in all products but can specialize in certain products to register global competitiveness. China adopted sectoral strategy to reap such gains from globalization. As part of the strategy, some sectors were given the much needed support by the Central and provincial governments in terms of liberalizing policies such as easy access to foreign capital, favourable taxation policies, creating a conducive legal regime and favourable labour laws etc. to develop globally competitive industries.

Textiles and telecommunications are the two key sectors in which this approach was adopted. China adopted the sectoral approach to integrate itself with the world economy. Significance of sectoral approach gained currency in the eighties in China. It is the strength and the global competitiveness of a particular industry that became the driving force behind adopting the sectoral approach in China. The key inputs for an industry based sectoral approach are the price, technology, capital, complementary trade policies, and global demand and supply. China could factor these inputs to make individual sectors like textiles and telecommunications globally competitive and boost its exports.

The accession process that began in the late 1980s had greatly accelerated China's domestic reforms and external alignment with the global trading regime. Successive reforms and structural and institutional changes that followed thereafter facilitated the necessary conditions for entry into the WTO.

China's accession to the WTO was a product of the most intense negotiations between China and other major powers which dragged on for fifteen long years. During the process of negotiations, China had to concede to most of the demands of other countries and make significant trade concessions to get an entry as it did not want to slow down its process of economic modernization by remaining outside the ambit of global trading regime for long. As explained in the thesis, these included the granting of trading rights to foreign companies; ensuring that China's economic decision conforms to the most fundamental principle of non-discrimination; and avoidance of unfair trade practices such as export subsidization or dumping. It had to undergo a number of structural as well as institutional changes at the domestic level to match international standards as per the requirements of the WTO.

There has been a gradual yet steady progress towards the establishment of a 'rule of law' to provide a clear-cut signal to foreign investors that a free and fair dispute settlement mechanism exists. To curb any trade violation, China has also introduced laws on trademarks, copyrights, patents, technology transfer, and unfair competition. Many new departments and institutions have been created at the government level to ensure that the WTO related laws and regulations are uniformly implemented in the entire country. China being a member of the WTO has to adhere to universally accepted norms of free and fair trade and ensure unhindered flow of goods and services across the countries. The WTO accession negotiations have been tougher and more cumbersome than those in the GATT.

However, China's accession to the WTO was not completely based on economic considerations. Political relations had also equally determined the course of negotiations. Bilateral relations between China and the US during the period of negotiations witnessed tumultuous ups and downs. After the collapse of the Soviet Union, the notion of a unipolar world had gathered momentum signifying the dominance of the US in world politics. It was clear by then that the anti-Soviet rationale for the US-China ties had disappeared. Both the countries were trying to define the new foundation and intrinsic value of their long-term relationship in the post-Cold War era. Although human rights, trade, and nuclear weapons proliferation issues were major obstacles to the improvement of bilateral relations, constant interactions and dialogues had eased their level of irritation and shown that by making mutual concessions and showing good will, China and the US could avert confrontation and build a constructive relationship.

While China was striving for integration with world economy, it realized the significance of regional trade agreements (RTAs). It believed that under the current state of Doha negotiations where hardly any movement was noticed, formation of RTAs is a viable medium to integrate with different regions. The ASEAN-China Free Trade Agreements (ACFTA) is a crucial component of the East Asian regional economic integration. It covers a market of 1.90 billion consumers and a combined gross domestic product of almost US$ 2.5 trillion. Trade has immensely increased between the two reaching about US$ 100 billion in 2004 and further increased to US$ 130.3 billion in 2005. China's rise as a hub for entire business activity of the Southeast Asian region is being argued that China is proving to be commanding dominance in the region. It is held that such a strategic move could be geared to undermine continuous influence of the US in the region. China's coming closer to this region is analyzed as an attempt to curtail the hegemony and pre eminent status of the US. It could be that China is doing this to reshape the regional politics to serve its interests. Such a strategy for China is meant to gain more political and economic influence in the region to rise further.

Since its entry into the WTO in December 2001, China has developed a proactive strategy to participate in the world economy. The past eight years witnessed China's phenomenal growth and integration into the world economy. By the end of 2007, China was ranked as the second biggest exporter and third largest trader in the world after its exports grew at over 20 per cent per year for the sixth year in a row. The increasing competitiveness of China has been driving the efficiency of production, innovation, and growth of global exports to new heights. China has emerged as a centre of business activity in the East and South East Asia. Regional production networks in East Asia grew substantially in the past few years and were largely centered on China. From China's perspective, accession to the WTO meant more than the secure and non-discriminatory market access to the world economy and gains in export. The accession provides China the platform and incentives to make more decisive strides in its already progressive reform. It lays a multilateral platform for the country to develop trade relationships with its partners where openness can be explored further. It also puts the country at an international level to fulfil its legal and regulatory commitments, among others, in a transparent and rule-based global trading system.

With this goal in mind China had engaged itself with the policies of further opening up to the external world and laid down policies that are conducive for its exports and economic modernization. China's successful economic development has rested on expanding external trade. After nearly 30 years of economic reform, China's external trade grew rapidly and accelerated following its accession to the WTO in 2001. By 2008, China's annual merchandise exports and imports had reached US$ 1429 billion and US$ 1133 billion respectively, making China the second largest exporter and the third largest importer in the world. China's total trade volume in 2008 is sixty-seven times that of 1980 and the trade surplus amounted to US$ 295.5 billion in 2008. The liberalization brought about by the WTO accession was substantial. The average tariff rate dropped from 40.6 per cent in 1992 to around 9.6 per cent in 2008. Trade openness, as measured by the ratio of goods trade to GDP, is nearly 60 per cent. China also made unprecedented commitments in service trade liberalization in the WTO's General Agreement on Trade in Services (GATS).

The study, while highlighting the political economy angle of China's entry into the WTO through the framework of interdependence, focused in detail on two important sectors of manufacturing and services, namely textiles and telecommunications. In the course of analysis, it also significantly reflects this trend of interdependence in the growth of the Chinese economy and trade in the post-entry phase.

Textiles being an important sector in terms of contribution to trade and employment generation has played a key role in China's economy over the years. It is considered as a pillar industry employing more than 20 million people and representing 22 per cent of total employment in the manufacturing industry. Besides, another 80 million workers are estimated to be indirectly dependent on this sector. China's adoption of industrial cluster approach during initial years of reform contributed to the growth of textiles sector. The SEZs in textiles became a growth engine for the domestic economy as well as for its exports in the world.

China began to experience a rising market share around the time it completed its accession to the WTO. During this period it increased its market share in the EU, Canada, and the US, but the surge that many countries had expected did not take place. This was evident because higher tariffs as well as quota restrictions were still restraining China's trade with them. Beginning January 1 2002, China felt the pressure of reducing the tariffs imposed by developed countries. It started bearing the liabilities of cutting tariffs for joining the WTO. According to the commitment, the average duty of textiles and clothing (T&C) was gradually reduced from 17.8 per cent in 2002 to 9.8 per cent in 2008. That is why sometimes it is argued that the terms of agreement proved too costly for China vis-à-vis other countries to enter into the WTO.

China's entry into the WTO had demanded certain fundamental changes in the functioning of the Government relating to the textiles sector. Structural changes and the abolition of Ministry of Textile Industry diluted the power of the government. Reduction of control over the industry since the 1990s led to reduction in number of employees working in the ministry. Planning, production as well as policy-making for the national textile industry was decentralized. The Government was mainly responsible for setting guidelines for the industry's development, exercising macro control and making structural adjustments in the industry. Presently, the State Development and Reform Commission (SDRC) is responsible for monitoring and adjusting the economic operations of the industry as well as establishing industry development plans. As a result, state-owned economic component has a diminished role in China's textile industry. In 2002, state-owned enterprises in the whole textile industry were 2,723 in total, accounting for 11.5 per cent, whereas non-state-owned enterprises are numbered at 20,877, occupying 88.5 per cent.

The performance of textile enterprises varied geographically and across sub-sectors. Profits earned in western and central China were much lower than those earned in the eastern China. Non-state-owned enterprises began to perform better than state-owned enterprises. Another significant finding is that employment has declined in the Chinese textiles sector following restructuring of the sector, while it had managed to level off in clothing sector in spite of high export growth. It is indicative that employment in the T&C sector is expected to grow by about 12 and 30 per cent respectively over and above what it otherwise would from 2005 to 2018 as a result of quota phase-out. It was found that till 2007 employment in the T&C sector after joining the WTO has expanded by 50 per cent.

As world trade in the T&C remained under a restrictive regime for considerable period of time, dominance of the EU and the US were well noticed. However, during this period the study highlights that China performed significantly better compared to other developing countries. The abundant supply of cheap labour with regular infusion of technology allowed it to register high export growth in the world market in the 1990s. After joining the WTO it continued to increase its share until the transitional safeguards were imposed in 2005 by the US and EU. This provision was targeted at China specifically to curtail its prospects in textiles trade as developed countries were convinced about the comparative advantage China has in the sector. Only during 2005 and the beginning of 2006, China's exports received a temporary jolt but soon they picked up. It continued to accelerate its exports and increase its share in global market during 2007 until the global market in the textiles experienced the slump caused by the global financial crisis in the third quarter of 2008.

With the unfolding of global financial crisis, the textiles sector had been hit. China's textiles firms' profit declined for the first time due to decline in overseas demand. The growth rate of China's overall textile exports in 2009 shows the trend of sliding down as the economy had also begun to get affected by rising labour costs, the appreciation of the Renminbi, and reduced global demand in major export markets. To minimize the immediate impact, the Government is engaged in serious planning and implementation process. Some of the measures such as stimulus package, widening of domestic demand base, creation of own brands, locating new markets, and automation of the textiles industry are the immediate priorities for revival of the industry.

Similarly, telecommunications sector also noticed high export growth. As a strategic sector, this sector occupies a significant place in China's economy. It plays a dual role of not only directly contributing to the economy as an important and growing sector like financial, insurance, IT, etc. but also plays a supporting role in the conduct of other economic and business activities of the country by virtue of being a communicative medium. Telecommunications sector is visualized as a key infrastructure sector in China. The Government, therefore, is constantly making endeavour along with the private players to keep the sector technologically progressive, innovative and economically viable.

China's telecommunications sector has undergone a sea-change ever since accession process began. The negotiations at the WTO brought about fundamental changes in its structural as well as functional areas. From strictly functioning as a wing of the Government, it went on to introduce market reforms thus institutionalizing the distinct identity and functioning of regulators and service providers. The sector has remained a strategic sector as it contributed both to the manufacturing as well as service segments of the economy. With the joining of the WTO, its strategic importance has increased because of the global connectivity and issue of national security and sovereignty.

The Telecommunications sector till the mid-1990s remained a monopoly of the government. Since 1994, China Telecom, the sole service provider until then with the gradual introduction of reforms had to face competition from China Unicom, another state sponsored organization supported by the

Ministry of Electronics Industry, the Ministry of Railways, the Ministry of Electric Power and a few more state run enterprises who had shown interest in entering China's telecom services market. Competition set in the market with the fresh entry of China Unicom that had resulted in intra departmental conflict. Policies adopted to create free and fair competition had in fact, followed some asymmetrical policies. As a result, the earlier incumbent was favoured and not the new entrants. The nature and pace of the liberalization process of telecommunications and the objective of market contestability were influenced by political, social, and cultural considerations. This system met with uneasiness and difficulties in terms of laying down the rules and regulations for free competition. A major restructuring came into force with the establishment of MII. Under the new administrative system, the MII is the sole regulator responsible for price setting, licensing, and other regulatory matters.

The preparation to join the WTO needed certain urgent reforms. The structural changes on home front gave a signal to the outside world that its market was well regulated, stable and provides enormous opportunities. By the early 2000 and 2001, China's commitment to the WTO has thrown the administration of telecommunication services into a market mode. Sources of investment changed, resource-planning management had undergone radical changes as the industry had restructured and tariff making policies were shifted away from transfer pricing and brought closer to cost-based pricing.

China's GATS commitments further led to telecommunications liberalization. Within a period of five to six years from the date of accession, i.e., by the end of 2007, it promised to lift all forms of restrictions as far as market access to its territory is concerned. Till 2009 China has honoured most of its commitments and gradually opened up its telecom market by regions, proportion and categories of services. Currently, the geographical limitation for value-added and paging services has been eliminated with the cap of foreign investment in these services reaching 50 per cent. Mobile voice and data service market has been opened up to cover 17 cities including Chengdu, Chongqing, and Dalian as well as the intercity communication with the cap of foreign investment at 49 per cent.

Basic telecom (namely the fixed communication) service has been opened to the foreign investment in Shanghai, Guangzhou and Beijing as well as between the cities, with a foreign investment of no more than 25 per cent. This is an encouraging sign for the trading partners who were genuinely interested in establishing a continuous trading relationship with China. Based on the Closer Economic Partnership Arrangement (CEPA) with Hong Kong and Macao SAR governments, China has opened nation-wide markets to service providers of Hong Kong and Macao to provide value added services.

Foreign service providers are scouting for local partners to enter into joint venture to deliver services.

China witnessed a virtual explosion in the sector as both fixed and mobile users shot up significantly in its post-accession period. By 2002, China's telecommunications exchange capacity had reached 201 million lines and mobile switching capacity amounted to 235 million lines. The total number of telephone subscribers had gone upto 388 million with 188 million fixed users and 162 million mobile users making China's telecommunications network the largest in the world in terms of size and subscribers.

China was not only regarded as a market for service providers but also as a manufacturing base for telecommunications equipment. Increase in subscribers had resulted in the expansion of domestic manufacturing industry. Demand for value added services by consumers led to constant upgradation in industry which had forced China to look for state-of the-art technology. Such expansion in telecommunications industry called for huge foreign investment. Foreign companies were permitted to sell telecom equipments in the domestic market and were allowed to set up joint ventures with local manufactures for production of equipment in China.

The size of China's market was a major attraction for industry expansion. It was not only the foreign companies who succeeded in enticing the consumers and expanding their businesses but it was also the domestic enterprises who also could succeed in developing and expanding their businesses. Domestic enterprises like Huawei, ZTE, Julong, and Datang had become competitive enough to compete in China. This group of local manufactures dominated the equipment market significantly in the 1990s.

The importance of R&D expansion has been regarded as a major policy decision in China's upgradation of technology. National and global expansion of R&D has therefore been recognized as one of the effective and competitive strategies by many large Chinese firms. Huawei is a pioneer in such ventures. These R&D centres are adequately connected to local centres to take full advantage of the big market. They provide access to local talent, information and connection to local markets. At the international level, Huawei has R&D centres in India and has an access to the strength of Indian software engineers. Huawei also had opened up R&D centres at various locations including the Silicon Valley in USA to have access to cutting edge technology and talent. China's industrial policy in telecommunications sector experienced success and demonstrates the catching up strategies of China's indigenous manufacturers. The policies adopted by the Central Government and strategies evolved under the normal pressure of market openness have created a situation where time and market space for indigenous players existed for them to grow and compete.

The growth of mobile subscribers in China is noticing an upward swing. In 2000, before its accession to the WTO, China registered about 85 million mobile users and in 2005 it went up to 393 million mobile users. The growth has been enormous and between 2000-2005 the Compound Annual Growth Rate (CAGR) has been almost 36 per cent and about 30 subscribers per 100 inhabitants in 2005. The total numbers of mobile subscribers were 52.9 per cent of total telephone subscribers in 2005, which was less than Hong Kong and also India in the same year. From the available data, it is understood that the telecommunication services sector after its accession to the WTO has performed gradually better.

In a sector like telecommunications which is capital and technology intensive, the pattern of employment has focused on having skilled workers. Both the equipment industry and the services sector require skilled workers to operate the system. Before the accession total number of employment in the telecommunications and other transmission services was around 1.3 million which came down to 1.1 million in 2001 just after the accession. In 2003, the number further slid to about 0.8 million. This shows that there has been a decline in employment in the post-accession period. This decline is attributed to the factor of market competition which became inevitable as China prepared to join the WTO. All the SOEs underwent restructuring to remain financially competitive and this led to laying off excessive and unproductive workforce in the system. Again by 2004, due to opening up and competition, many private players came into the market, consumers' demands grew and this led to increase in productivity. Finally, the sector expanded and resulted in the rise in employment. The sector noticed marginal rise in 2004 but by the end of 2007 there was a substantial increase in employment from 0.8 million to 0.98 million.

The pressure of the domestic telecom lobby exerted immense pressure on the Government not to liberalize the telecom policy and allow the foreign players to come in. Though consumers complained about poor service and high tariffs, the Government during this period hardly addressed such concerns. The Government benefited from such policies as it obtained hefty revenue directly from the telecom sector. These groups are domestic telecom operators like China Mobile, China Telecom, and China Unicom, who never wanted the opening up of the sector soon. Following the WTO provision, yet the Government took five to six years to phase out most of the restrictions for foreign players to enter the Chinese market. A critical interpretation of this restrictive policy is that reform measures taken by the Chinese Government were designed to protect domestic firms by speedily boosting their growth in order to meet foreign competition. This kind of market restriction, which remained after the accession till 2007, was supported by the Government as it provided the lead time to the Government to gauge the impact of telecom liberalization in the country.

The role of FDI has also been extremely crucial for China's telecom growth. FDI from different regions and countries like Hong Kong, Macao, Finland, and the US helped to make the telecom equipment industry as one that is globalized, productive, innovative, advanced, and consumer friendly. China's labour competitive advantage coupled with capital, technology and skills produced a resurgent telecom sector. The interest of the foreign service providers are also multiplying as they visualize China to be a growing market with huge opportunities. It looks apparent that absence of any pressure to join the WTO would have resulted in less inflow of FDIs into this sector and telecommunications would have remained a partially closed sector.

Given the potential of growth, the current financial meltdown will not adversely affect the sector. As a strategic sector, the telecommunications sector in China is set to prosper as more and more businesses are expected to employ more sophisticated telecom services. According to the Eleventh Five-Year Programme on information industry, total revenue of the industry will reach RMB 886 billion by 2010, i.e., at an average annual growth of 7.6 per cent. In the long run, China's telecom industry will develop into an information service industry. It will constantly make endeavour to improve its quality, which can compete with service providers in developed countries. As most of the restrictions have been withdrawn, international players are allowed to operate in China. This would infuse a sense of competition among the Chinese service providers. Such competition will lead to form an industrial chain for the coordinated development of all market players. This will help promote economic growth in China.

It can also be observed from the study that though the two key constituents of the Chinese economy i.e., the textiles and telecommunications played a remarkable role in China's growth, both the sectors nonetheless followed slightly different approach of opening up and trade liberalization. The textiles sector was pursued aggressively while telecommunications was slowly and gradually opened up. China's T&C sector integrated with the world textiles trade faster than the telecommunications sector. This is because the issue of national security and sovereignty remained critical factors which hindered the progressive liberalization of the telecommunication sector. Though China's GATS commitments are very strong on paper, in practice China remains more protective in services sector than it is in goods trade.

The ambition of China's trade liberalization programme manifests in its resilience and adaptability to global trading regime. The pro-active approach demonstrated recently by the Chinese leaders in response to global financial crisis to shift its focus from export-led growth to widening of the domestic consumption model is a sufficient indicator of the extent to which China is ready to face the future challenges. China's export-growth model has produced positive results but such policies have also exposed China to high risks. It is observed that the Chinese leaders are currently contemplating the process of adopting domestic demand model, in addition to export growth model, to be a more viable alternative for China's sustainable growth. China is exploring ways and means to diversify its domestic economic base.

Clearly, external trade has contributed to China's economic development by enhancing the efficiency of resource allocation, expanding the supply of some natural resources needed for production, transferring technological know-how via imports of capital goods, and factoring in its competitive advantage to promote exports. As a result, China was able to maintain a record-high average GDP growth rate of 9.5 per cent during 1980-2006 and continued to register around 7.5 to 8 per cent in 2007 and 2008. The growth in trade has contributed strongly to the creation of non-farm jobs and rural economic development. China's experience amply demonstrates the importance of trade liberalization in facilitating the change in economic structure towards more competitive sectors. It also validates the significance of trade for the overall growth and development of the economy. Behind this growth and performance, political leadership has also played a key role. It is the combination of political will matched with gradual and sequential economic reforms that catapulted China's position in the world economy. In essence, political economy has been a key driver of China's sustained growth in general and textiles and telecommunications in particular.

In future the role of China in the WTO will be significant. Because, it promises to play a proactive role in the WTO negotiations till the time its developmental concerns are fulfilled. It will assert its viewpoint on benefiting from trade gains which were promised to her at the time of entry. Based on those gains it had convinced its people that why joining the WTO is better than remaining outside the multilateral system. It will play a leadership role in G-20 and G-33 as important issues like providing food security, livelihood and rural employment will be the central concerns of these groupings. It will try to influence the policy decisions of major powers like the US and the EU to accommodate interests of the developing countries who form two-third majority in the WTO. Its influence in the WTO will be more because China is no longer marginal rather a dominant player in the world economy.

In terms of T&C, this sector is equipped to perform better because its advantage in labour cost and economy of scale will continue to have an edge over other developing countries. World demand for the Chinese textiles and clothing are still large. Chinese cotton sector will feed adequately to the rising demand of raw material. Supply chain management facilities are well developed and are constantly monitored to provide advantage to the enterprises. Big retail chain like Walmart and others will continue to source bulk of their demand from China.

China will continue to witness fast growth in the telecommunications sector. Constant innovation and upgradation of technology will help domestic manufacturing companies to produce new products at a cheaper price. FDI will come into the sector as China is visualized to be the global hub for telecom equipment industry. Incentives from the Government will continue to attract more investment to keep the sector globally competitive. China will have to open up the telecom sector to allow foreign service providers to come in. It cannot restrict them for long as it has made commitments in the WTO. National security and sovereignty will remain major concerns. How China will handle this sensitive issue in future will remain a major challenge for the Government.

Economic common interests and economic frictions are like a double edged sword. On the one hand, common gains can promote win-win cooperation. On the other hand, increased economic interaction does lead to more friction. On the whole it is reasonable to argue that economic interdependence has become a dynamic driving force for multilateral cooperation and global integration.

China faces a daunting task in moving through the transition from plan to market and seeks to catch up with the developed countries while the global economy grapples with the rise of the knowledge economy.

China's aspiration to play an increasingly important role in the world economy was visible from the time it applied for joining the GATT in 1986. Its continuous higher economic growth in the 1990s raised its expectations to benefit from an expanding world economy. It no longer wanted to remain on the margins of a system where opportunities were largely available to others. In addition, a transparent, rule-based, free and fair multilateral trading regime, having an extraordinary provision of a dispute settlement mechanism, convinced the Chinese leadership that joining the WTO would be in the interest of China. It was also convinced that economic engagement with the world economy would also help in accomplishing its political and strategic objectives vis-à-vis world community thus paving the way for its rise as a major power. Thus China joined the WTO to fulfill such expectations.

Once in the WTO China has been proactive in various negotiations pertaining to agriculture, industry and service sectors. As a key member of the G-20, it has played an important role by advocating the Doha development agenda. It has brought the issue of developmental concerns of the developing countries into the centre stage of the WTO negotiations in different WTO ministerial meetings like Cancun, Hong Kong, and Geneva. It continued to defend the aspirations of the developing countries in the recently concluded G-20 meeting at Seoul during 11-12 November 2010. It also emphasized on creating a transparent world financial architecture to safeguard the interests of weaker developing countries and avoid such global economic imbalances.

China has gained substantially in garnering a larger share of world trade by joining the WTO. Sectors like textiles and telecommunications have experienced better export growth and domestic expansion. Having a traditional strength in textiles sector, China after joining the WTO has made inroads into world trade in T&C. Advantage of low labour cost, favourable FDI policies and cutting-edge technology have helped the sector to register a significant export share in world trade. With the advantages of labour, capital and technology China could expand its domestic consumer base keeping competitive price as a key factor. Similarly, telecommunications manufacturing industry witnessed a significant growth. Its exports of telecom equipment saw a dramatic rise after its entry into the WTO. Foreign telecom manufacturing companies found China a big market with huge opportunities. In telecommunications services, China is also witnessing a revolution as foreign services providers are slowly entering China.

Given its track record so far, China is likely to abide by its commitments to the WTO in the immediate future. Whether or not it will continue on this path is an issue that one will have to wait and see in the long term.

Bibliography

Acharya, A. and G.P. Deshpande (2000), "Season of Opportunities: China's Impending Entry to the WTO", *China Report*, 36(2): 167-190.

Adiga, A. (2004), "Hanging by a Thread: Textile Factories throughout Asia Face Extinction as a Long-standing Global Trade Pact is Set to Expire" *Time*, 1 November: 36-38.

"Agriculture Discussions Open WTO Meeting", *China Daily*, Beijing, 13 July 2005: 5.

"Agriculture Discussions Open WTO Meeting" [Online: web] Accessed on 25 January 2009, URL: http://china.org.cn/english/2005/Jul/134846.htm.

"Al Gore Supports China's WTO entry" (2000), *Beijing Review*, 43 (13): 7.

Aldrich, M. and A. Rooth (1999), "Market Opportunity: An Investment Threat", *Telecommunications*, 33(10): 168-170.

Armstrong, M. *et al.* (1994), *Regulatory Reform: Economic Analysis and the British Experience*, Cambridge, Ma, USA: MIT Press.

Ash, R.F. and Y.Y. Kueh (1993), "Economic Integration within Greater China: Trade and Investment Flows between China, Hong Kong and Taiwan", *The China Quarterly*, 136: 711-745.

Baark, Eirk (2009), Personal Interview, School of Humanities and Social Science, The Hong Kong University of Science & Technology (HKUS&T), Hong Kong, 9 April 2009.

Baer, Werner (1972), "Import Substitution and Industrialization in Latin Amercia: Experiences and Interpretations", Latin American Research Review, 7(1): 95-122.

Bell, Daniel (1976), *The Coming of Post-Industrial Society*, New York: Basic Books.

Bergsten, C. Fred (1996), "Competitive Liberalization and Global Free Trade: A Vision for the Early 21st Century", *Asia Pacific Working Paper Series*, No. 16, Peterson Institute for International Economics, Washington DC.

Bhagwati, J. (1993), "Regionalism and Multilateralism: An Overview," in Jaime de Melo and Arvind Panagariya (eds.) *New Dimensions in Regional Integration*, Cambridge: Cambridge University Press.

Bhalla, A.S. and Shufang Qiu (2004), *The Employment Impact of China's WTO Accession*, London: Routledge Curzon.

Bhattasali, D., Shantong Li and W. Martin (2004), "WTO Accession, Policy Reform and Poverty Reduction: An Overview", in D. Bhattasali, Li, Shantong and W. Martin (eds.) *China and the WTO: Accession, Policy Reform and Poverty Reduction Strategies*, Washington DC: World Bank.

Brilliant, M. and Waterman, J. (2004), *China's WTO Implementation: A Three Year Assessment Report*.

British Broadcasting Corporation, Summary of World Broad Casts, Part 3: The Far East (Weekly Economic Report), FE/W0244, 19 August 1992, p. A/1.

Cao (2010), "Chinese Government Expects More Trade with India", *China Radio International* [Online: web] Accessed 1 September 2010: URL: http://english.cri.cn/6826/2010/01/20/1721s543813.htm.

Caporaso, James (1978), "Dependence, Dependency and Power in the Global System: A Structural and Behavioural Analysis", *International Organization*, 32(1): 13-43.

Chai, Trong R. (1986), "The Future of Taiwan" *Asian Survey*, 26(12): 1309-1323.

Changhong, Pei (2004), "Improving China's Competitiveness in the International Labour Division System", *China & World Economy*, 12(2): 83-92.

Cheow, Eric Teo Chu (2004), "China as the Center of Asian Economic Integration", The Jamestown Foundation, *China Brief*, 4(15): 3-4.

"China: US textile move against WTO rules" (2005), *Chinadaily* [Online web] Accessed 5 May 2008, URL: http://www.chinadaily.com.cn/english/doc/2005-10/06/content_482840.htm

"China, EU Progress on WTO Entry" (2000), *Beijing Review*, 43(6-7): 6.

"China Prepares for WTO Membership" (2000), *Beijing Review*, 43(9): 4.

"China, EU Talks" (2000), *Beijing Review*, 43 (15): 6.

"China, EU to Resume Talks" (2000), *Beijing Review,* 43(19): 6.

"China Focus: Dalian Meeting Encouraging for WTO Members" (2005), *Xinhua*, 14 July.

China's Ministry of Commerce (2003) *Foreign Investment* Report [Online: web] Accessed on 16 July 2009, URL: www.mofcom.gov.cn

"China's Cotton Imports Down Upon Weak Demand" (2009) *Xinhua*, Beijing, January 13 2009: 1-5.

"China Announces Stimulus Plan for Textile Sector" (2009), *Xinhua*, Beijing, 24 April 2009 [Online: web] Accessed 25 May 2009, URL: http://english.cri.cn/6826/2009/04/24/1461s478449.htm.

Chong, F. (1995), "APEC, WTO, 301: The United States Team Forging Access to Regional Markets", *Asia Today* 13(10) October.

Chongwei, Ji (1981), "China's Utilization of Foreign Funds and Relevant Policies", *Beijing Review*, 24(6): 11.

Clarke, P. (2007), "Interdependence Theory, China and American Security Interest", Paper Prepared for the 48th Annual Convention for the International Studies Association held during 28 February—3 March 2007: Chicago.

"Clinton Supports China's WTO entry" (2000), *Beijing* Review, 43(4): 5.

Copeland, Dale C. (1996), "Economic Interdependence and War: A Theory of Trade Expectations", *International Security*, 20(4): 5-41.

Dahlman, Carl and Anuja Utz (2005), *India and the Knowledge Economy: Leveraging Strength and Opportunities*, Washington DC, USA: The World Bank.

Dahlman, Carl., *et al.* (2005), *Finland as a Knowledge Economy*: *Elements of Success and Lessons Learned*, Washington DC, USA: The World Bank.

de Jonquières, Guy (2004), "Clothes on the Line: The Garment Industry Faces a Global Shake-up as Quotas End," *Financial Times*, London, 19, July 2004, p. 9.

______ (2001b), "Fragmentation in Simple Trade Models," *North American Journal of Economics and Finance*, 12 (2): 121-137.

Deardroff, A.V. (2001), 'International Provision of Trade Services, Trade and Fragmentation', *Review of International Economics*, 9(2): 233-48.

Deardorff, A.V. (2001a), "Fragmentation across Cones," in S.W. Arndt and H. Kierzkowski (Eds.), *Fragmentation: New Production Patterns in the World Economy*, New York: Oxford University Press.

Deng, Yong (1998), "The Chinese Conception of National Interests in International Relations", *The China Quarterly,* 154: 308-329.

Deng Xiaoping (1983), *Selected Works of Deng Xiaoping*, Volume 3, Beijing: People's Press.

Deng, Xiaoping (1993), Deng Xioaping's Collectanea, Volume 3, Beijing: People's Publishing House.

Dernberger, Robert F. (1999), "The People's Republic of China at 50: The Economy", *The China Quarterly*, 159: 606-615.

Development Research Center of China *et al.* (2004) "Joint Report and Policy Recommendations on Sectoral Implications of a China-Japan-Korea FTA" [Online: web] Accessed 2 June 2009, URL: http://www.nira.or.jp/past/newse/paper/joint4/report.html

DeWoskin, K.J. (2001), "The WTO and Telecommunications Sector in China", *The China Quarterly*, 167: 630-654.

Dixit, A.K. and J. Stiglitz (1977), "Monopolistic Competition and Optimum Product Diversity", *The American Economic Review*, 67(3): 297-308.

"Doha Ministerial Declaration" (2001) [Online: web] Accessed 16 February 2010, URL: http:/ /www.wto.org/english/thewto_e/minist_e/min01_e/mindecl_e.htm).

Dommen, E. and P. Hein (1985), *States, Microstates and Islands*, London: Croom Helm.

Drake, W.J. (2001), "Telecommunications Revolution" in P.J. Simmons and C. de Jonge Oudrat (eds.), *Managing Global Issues: Lessons Learned*, Washington, D.C.: Carnegie.

Eckstein, Alexander (1997), *China's Economic Revolution*, London: Cambridge University Press.

Edwards, Sebastian (1993), "Openness, Trade Liberalization, and Growth in Developing Countries", *Journal of Economic Literature*, 31 (3): 1358-1393.

Elegant, Robert (1998), "Clinton's Visit to China Can Do More Good than Harm" *The International Herald Tribune*, New York, 24 June 1998.

Ergas, Henry (1997), "International Trade in Telecommunications Services: An Economic Perspective" in G.C. Haufbauer and Erika Wada (eds.). *Unfinished Telecommunications Business: Telecommunications after the Uruguay Round*, Washington: Institute for International Economics.

Evans, Peter C. (2002), *Liberalizing Global Trade in Energy Services*, Washington DC, USA, The AEI Press.

Falvey, R. (1981), "Commercial Policy and Intra-Industry Trade", *Journal of International Economics*, 11(3): 495-511.

"FDI in Retail Hiked China's Textile Exports 700%" (2006), *Assocham*, New Delhi.

Findlay, R. (1995), *Proportions and Growth Factors*, Cambridge, MA, USA: MIT Press.

Flam H. and E. Helpman (1987), "Vertical Product Differentiation and North-South Trade" *The American Economic Review*, 77 (5): 810-822.

Forge, Simon (1995), *The Consequences of Current Telecommunications: Trends for the Competitiveness of Developing Countries*, Washington DC: The World Bank.

Frank, Andre Gunder (1972), "The Development of Underdevelopment," in James D. Cockcroft, Andre Gunder Frank, and Dale Johnson, (eds.), *Dependence and Underdevelopment*, Garden City, New York: Anchor Books.

Frieden, R. (2001), *Management Internet-Driven Change in International Telecommunications*, Boston: Artech House.

Fung, K.C. (1991), "Collusive Intra-Industry Trade", *The Canadian Journal of Economics*, 24 (2): 391-404.

Fung, *et al.* (2002), "Foreign Direct Investment in China: Policy, Trend and Impact" Preliminary Draft [Online: web] Accessed 9 February 2009 URL: http://www.hiebs.hku.hk/ working_paper_updates/wp.1049.pdf.

Fung, *et al.* (2002), "Japanese Direct Investment in China and Other Asian Countries" [Online: web] Accessed 9 February 2009 URL: http://www.hiebs.hku.hk/working_paper_updates/ wp.1052.pdf.

Fukao, *et al.* (2003), "Vertical Intra-Industry Trade and origin of Direct Investment in East Asia." The Institute of Economic Research, Hitotsubashi University, Tokyo, Discussion Paper Series *A* No. 434 January, [Online: web] Accessed 31 October 2008, URL: http:// ideas.repec.org/p/hit/hituec/a434.html.

Galtung, Johan (1979), "The Politics of Self-Reliance" Paper Presented during March 21-24 1979 at the 20th Annual Convention of the International Studies Association: Toronto.

Garnaut, R., and Huang, Y. (1995b), "China and the Future International Trading System", *Pacific Economic Papers*, No. 250, Australian-Japan Policy Centre, Australian National University: Canberra.

Gasiorowski, M. and Solomon W. Polachek (1982), "Conflict and Interdependence: East-West Trade and Linkages in the Era of Détente", *The Journal of Conflict Resolution*, 26 (4): 709-729.

Gelb, Bernard A. (2001), *Textile and Apparel Trade Issues*, CRS Reports for Congress, [Online: web] Accessed 21 March 2008, URL: http://ncseonline.org/nle/crsreports/economics/ econ-134.cfm.

Gereffi, Gary and Olga Memedovic (2003), *The Global Apparel Value Chain: What Prospects for upgrading by Developing Countries*, Vienna: United Nations Industrial Development Organization (UNIDO).

Gelpi, C. and J.M. Grieco (2001), "Economic Interdependence, the Democratic State, and the Liberal Peace", Department of Political Science, Duke University: Durham.

Gertler, Jeffrey L. (2003), "China's WTO Accession-The final Countdown" in Deborah Z. Cass *et al. (eds.)*, *China and the World Trading System-Entering the New Millennium*, London: Cambridge University Press.

Goodwin, R.M. and L. Punzo (1987), *The Dynamics of A Capitalistic Economy: A Multisectoral Approach,* Cambridge, UK: Basil Blackwell.

Goldstein, Morris (2003), "China's Exchange Rate Regime," Testimony before the Subcommittee on Domestic and International Monetary Policy, Trade, and Technology Committee on Financial Services, U.S. House of Representatives, Washington, DC. October 1, [Online:web] Accessed 21 May, 2009, URL: http://www.iie.com/publications/papers/ goldstein 1003.htm.

Goldstein, Morris, and Nicholas Lardy (2003), "A Modest Proposal for China's Renminbi," *Financial Times,* 26 August 2003, [Online: web] Accessed 22 May 2009 URL: http:// www.iie.com/publications/papers/goldstein0803.htm.

Gourevitch, P. (1978), "The Second Image Reversed: The International Sources of Domestic Politics", *International Organization*, 32 (4): 881-912.

Grabowski, R. (1994), "Import Substitution, Export Promotion, and the State in Economic Development", *The Journal of Developing Areas*, 28(4), pp. 535-554.

Gray, J. and G.W. Smith (1991), *JS Mill on Liberty in Focus*, New York: Routledge.

Graziani, G. (2001), "International Subcontracting in the Textile and Clothing Industry" in Sven W. Arndt and Henryk Kierzkoski (eds.) *Fragmentation: New Production Patterns in the World economy*, Oxford: Oxford University Press.

"Great Potential for China-EU Ties" (2000) *Beijing Review,* 43(14): 7.

Greenway, D. *et al.* (1995), "Vertical and Horizontal Intra-Industry Trade: A Cross Industry Analysis for the United Kingdom" *The Economic Journal*, 105 (433): 1505-1518.

Grubel, Herbert G. and Peter Lloyd (1975), *Intra-Industry Trade: The Theory and Measurement of International Trade in Differentiated Products*, London: MacMillan.

Guoxing Wang (2009), Personal Interview, Pudong Institute for the US Economy, Shanghai, 9 April 2009.

Hamrin, Carol Lee (1979), "Domestic Components and China's Evolving Three World Theory" in King C. Chen (eds.), *China and the Three Worlds*, London: McMillan Press Limited.

Hardy, A.P. (1980), "The Role of the Telephone in Economic Development", *Telecommunications Policy*, 4(4): 668-680.

Harney, Alexandra (2005), "The Challenger from China: Why Huawei is making the Telecom World Take Notice", *Financial Times*, UK, 11 January 2005.

Harwit, Eric (1998), "China's Telecommunications Industry: Development Patterns and Policies", *Pacific Affairs*, (2): 175-193.

Harwit, Eric (2008), *China's Telecommunications Revolution*, Oxford: Oxford University Press

Hathcote and Nam (1999), "Advantages of Sourcing Apparel from China, Taiwan, South Korea and Mexico", *The International Trade Journal*, 13(2): 157-185.

Ho Lok Sang (2009), Personal Interview, Centre for Public Studies, Lingnan University, Hong Kong 2 April 2009.

Holzman, F.D. and R. Legvoid (1975), "The Economics and Politics of East-West Relations", in C. Fred Bergsten and Lawrence B. Krause (eds.) *World Politics and International Economics*, Washington: Brookings.

Huang, Xiaoming (2000), "Managing fluctuations in US-China Relations: World Politics, National Priorities, and Policy Leadership" *Asian Survey*, 40(2): 269-295.

Huanguang, Qiu *et al.* (2007), "Impact of China—ASEAN Free Trade Area on China's International Agricultural Trade and Its Regional Development", *China & World Economy,* 15(4): 77-90.

Huawei Technologies (2005), *Annual Report 2004, Shenzhen*, China.

Hudson, Heather E. (1984), *When Telephones Reach the Village*, Norwood, New Jersy: Ablex Publishing.

Ianchovichina Elena and W. Martin (2001), "Trade Liberalization in China's Accession to the World Trade Organization", *Policy Research Working Paper* No. 2623, Washington DC: The World Bank.

Industry shakeup creates 3 telecom giants", [Online: web] Accessed 25 May 2008, URL: http://www.chinadaily.cn/china/2008-05/25/content_6709799. htm.

International Labour Organization (2005), "Promoting Fair Globalization in Textiles and Clothing in a Post-MFA Environment", [Online: web] Accessed 18 June 2009, URL: http://www.ilo.org/public/english/dialogue/sector/techmeet/tmtc-pmfa05/tmtc-pmfa-r.pdf.

Intven, H., Oliver J., *et al.* (2000), *Telecommunications Regulations Handbook*, Washington, DC: World Bank.

Irwin, Douglas A. (1996), *Against the Tide: An Intellectual History of Free Trade*, Princeton: Princeton University Press.

Jacobson, Harold K. (1979), Networks *of Interdependence: International Organizations and the Global Political System*, USA: Alfred A Knopf Inc.

Jain, R. *et al.* (2000), "A Study of Telecom Growth and Reform in China", [Online: web] Accessed 12 June 2007, URL: www.iimahd.ernet.in.

Janda, R. (1999), "Benchmarking A Chinese Offer on Telecommunications: Context and Comparisons" *International Journal of Communications Law and Policy* Issue, (3): 1-27.

JETRO (2001), "Current and Future Prospects of Foreign Direct Investment by Japanese Companies in 21st Century", JETRO: Tokyo.

Joan, E. (1981), *The Politics of International Economic Relations*, New York: St. Martin's Press.

Jones, R.W. and H. Kierzkowski (1990), "The Role of Services in Production and International Trade: A Theoretical Framework," in R.W. Jones and A.O. Krueger (eds.), *The Political Economy of International Trade*, Oxford: Blackwell.

Kan, K.L. (1999), "Where to go for Chinese Telecommunications Industry?", *Posts and Telecommunications Economic Management*, (10): 8-12.

Kanungo, Anil K. (2007), "FTAs Have Their Uses", *The Times of India*, New Delhi, 16 October 2007.

Kanungo, Anil K. (2005) "Service Sector in China after Its Accession to the WTO", *International Studies*, 42 (3&4): 329-345.

Kanungo, Anil K. (2007), "Setting Up of Special Economic Zones in China: Reforms and Policy Recommendations" *Foreign Trade Review*, 42(2): 3-26.

Kanungo, Anil K. (2001), "Fractured Verdict from Doha", *The Hindu BusinessLine*, Chennai 25 December 2001.

Kanungo, Anil K. (2006), "New Shopping Experience" *The Times of India*, New Delhi, 5 December 2006.

Keohane, Robert O. and Josef S. Nye (1977), *Power and Interdependence*, Boston: Little Brown.

Keohane, Robert, O. (1984), *After Hegemony: Cooperation and Discord in the World Political Economy*, Princeton, NJ: Princeton University Press.

Keohane, R.O. and Nye, J.S. (1989), *Power and interdependence* (2nd ed.), New York: HarperCollins.

Klintworth, Gary (1995), "China's Evolving Relationship with APEC", *International Journal*, 50 (3): 488-515.

Knappe, M. (2003), "Textiles and Clothing: What Happens after 2005?" *International Trade Forum*, (2): 16-20.

Kobayashi, Yoka (2007), The Impact of World Trade Organization on China's Trade Policy: A Case Study of Telecommunications Sector in Ka Zeng (eds.) *China's Foreign Trade Policy* UK: Routledge

Krugman, P. (1979), "Increasing Returns, Monopolistic Competition, and International Trade", *Journal of International Economics* 9(4): 469-480.

Krugman, P. (1993), "Regionalism versus Multilateralism: Analytical Notes" in Jaime de Melo and Arvind. Panagariya, (eds.) *New Dimensions in Regional Integration*, Cambridge, UK: Cambridge University Press.

Kuhn, Robert L. (2010), *How China's Leaders Think*, Singapore: John Wiley & Sons (Asia) Pvt. Ltd.

Lall, S. and M. Albaladejo (2002), "The Competitive Impact of China on Manufactured Exports by Emerging Economies in Asia" in Carlos A. Magarinos, Long Yongtu and Francisco C. Sercovich (eds.), *China in the WTO: the Birth of A New Catching Up Strategy*, New York: Palgrave.

Lall, S. and M. Albaladejo (2004), "China's Competitive Performance: A Threat to East Asian Manufactured Exports", *World Development*, 32 (9): 1441-1466.

Lampton, David M. (2001), *Same Bed, Different Dreams: Managing US-China Relations: 1989-2000*, Berkeley: University of California Press.

Lancaster K. (1980), "Intra-Industry Trade under Perfect Monopolistic Competition", *Journal of International Economics*, 10(1): 151-175.

Laperrouza, M. (2006), "*China's Telecom Policy making in the context of Trade and Economic Reforms*", Ph.D. Thesis, UK: London School of Economics.

Lardy, N.R. (1994), *China in the World Economy*, Washington DC: Institute for International Economics.

Lardy, N. (2001), "Issues in China's WTO Accession" [Online: web] Accessed 14 September 2009, URL: http://www.brookings.edu/testimony/2001/0509foreignpolicy_lardy.aspx.

Lawrence, R.Z. (1999), "Regionalism, Multilateralism and Deeper Integration: Changing Paradigms for Developing Countries" in M. Rodríguez Mendoza, B. Kotschwar and P. Low (eds.) *Trade Rules in the Making*, Organization of American States, Washington DC: Brookings Institution Press.

Lee Branstetter and Nicholas Lardy, (2006) "China's Embrace of Globalization", Working Paper 12373, [Online: web] Accessed 9 February 2009, URL: http://www.nber.org/papers/w12373.

Lei, Xue (2009), Personal Interview, Shanghai Institutes for International Studies, Shanghai 8 April 2009.

Lemonie F. (2000), "*FDI and the Opening up of China's Economy*", Centre D'etudes rospectives Et D'informations Internationalles CEPII No. 00-11, [Online: web] Accessed 24 October 2008, URL: http://www.cepii.fr/anglaisgraph/workpap/summaries/2000/wp00-11.htm.

Li, F. and J. Li (1999), *Foreign Investment in China*, UK: Palgrave.

Li, Cheng (2006), "China's Telecom Industry on the Move: Domestic Competition, Global ambition and Leadership Transition", [Online: web] Accessed 8 June, 2007 URL: http://media.hoover.org/documents/clm19_cl.pdf.

Madelyn, Ross C. (1995), "China's International Economic Behaviour", in Thomas W. Robinson and David Shambaugh (eds.), *Chinese Foreign Policy: Theory and Practice*, Oxford: Clarendon Press.

Mallampally, Padma and Zbigniew Zimny (2000), "Foreign Direct Investment in Services: Trends and Patterns", in Yair Aharoni and Lilac Nachum (eds.) *Globalization of Services: Some Implications for Theory and Practice*, UK: Routledge.

Mansfield E. and Brian M. Pollins (2001), *Economic Interdependence and International Conflict*, USA: The University of Michigan Press.

Mansfield E. and Reinhardt (2003), "Multilateral Determinants of Regionalism: The Effects of GATT/WTO on the Formation of Preferential Trading Arrangements", *International Organization*, 57(4): 829-862.

Martin, W. and Manole, V. (2008), "China's Emergence as the Workshop of the World', in B.M. Fleisher, N.C. Hope, A.L. Pena and D. Tao Yang (eds.) *Policy Reform and Chinese Markets: Progress and Challenges*, USA: Edward Elgar Publishing.

Martin, W. and Ianchovichina, E. (2001), "Implications of China's Accession to the World Trade Organization for China and the WTO", *World Economy*, 29(9): 1205-1219.

Martinelli, A. (2005), "From World System to World Society?", *Journal of World-Systems Research*, 11(2): 241-260.

Mattoo, A. (2002), "China's Accession to the WTO: The Services Dimension", *Policy Research Working Paper* No. 2932, Washington DC: The World Bank.

Mattoo, A. (2003), "China's Accession to the WTO: The Services Dimension", *Journal of International Economic Law*, 6(2): 299-339.

McMillan, Charles J. (1996), *The Japanese Industrial System*, Germany: Walter de Gruyter.

Messerlin, P. (2004), "China in the WTO: Antidumping and safeguards", in D. Bhattasali, Shantong Li and W. Martin (eds.), *China and the WTO: WTO Accession, Policy Reform and Poverty Reduction Strategies*, Washington DC: Oxford University Press and the World Bank.

_______ "Ministry of Information Industry (1999) Annual Report on China's Information Industry, Beijing, China: Ministry of Information Industry, 2000.

_______ "China-EU Relations" (2001), Ministry of Foreign Affairs of the People's Republic of China, [Online: web] Accessed 16 August 2009, URL:http://www.fmprc.gov.cn/eng/gjhdq/dqzzywt/2633/2634/t15542.htm

Mody, Bella *et al.* (1995), *Telecommunications Politics: Ownership and Control of the Information Highway in Developing Countries*, USA: Lawrence Erlbaum Associates.

Moore, Thomas G. (2002), *China in the World Market: Chinese Industry and International Source of Reform in Post-Mao Era*, USA: Cambridge University Press.

Morrison, Charles and Whiting, Allen S. (1992), "China's Role in the Asia-Pacific Region" in Mark Borthwich (ed.) *Pacific Century: The Emergence of Modern Pacific Asia*, USA: Westview Press.

Morrow, James D. (1999), "How Could Trade Affect Conflict?" *Journal of Peace Research* 36(4): 481-489.

Motwani, J. and S. Ahuja (2000), "International Purchasing Practices of US and Indian Managers: A Comparative Analysis", *Industrial Management and Data Systems,* 100(4): 172-179.

Moules, J. (2005), "China to Lead Export by 2010, Says OECD", *The Financial Times,* London, 17 September 2005.

Narlikar, A. and D. Tussie (2003), "The G 20 at the Cancun Ministerial: Developing Countries and their Evolving Coalitions in the WTO", *World Economy*, 27(7): 947-966.

Naughton, Barry (2007), *The Chinese Economy: Transitions and Growth*, Cambridge, MA: The MIT Press.

Nayyar, Deepak (1983), "International Relocation of Production and Industrialization in LDCs", *Economic and Political Weekly*, 18: 13-26.

NCTO (2008), "China's Share of Apparel Imports Surge Phenomenally" [Online: web] Accessed 4 June 2009, URL: http://www.fibre2fashion.com/news/fashion-news/newsdetails.aspx?news_id=67080&page=1

Nordås, Hildegunn Kyvik (2004), "The Global Textile and Clothing Industry post the Agreement on Textiles and Clothing," *Discussion Paper* No. 5, World Trade Organization [Online:web] Accessed on October 24, 2008, URL: http://www.wto.org/english/res_e/booksp_e/discussion_papers5_e.pdf.

Qimao, Chen (1987), "The Taiwan Issue and the Sino-US Relation: A PRC View" *Asian Survey*, 27(11): 1161-1175.

Organization for Economic Co-operation and Development (2000), *A New Economy? The Changing Role of Innovation and Information Technology in Growth*, Paris: OECD.

Oneal, John R. and Lee Ray James (1997), "New Tests of the Democratic Peace: Controlling for economic interdependence", *Political Research Quarterly*, 150(4): 751-775.

Organization for Economic Co-operation and Development (2005c) *Policy Brief: Economic Survey of China* Published 16 September, [Online: web] Accessed 28 January 2008, URL:http://www.oecd.org/dataoecd/10/25/35294862.pdf.

Panagariya, A. (1996), "The Free Trade Area of the Americas: Good for Latin America?", *World Economy*, 19(5): 485-515.

Panagariya, A. (2003), "Alternative Approaches to Reciprocal Tariff Liberalization", [Online: web) Accessed 9 April 2010, URL: http://econpapers.repec.org/paper/wpawuwpit/0309006.htm.

Panagariya, A. (2008), *India: The Emerging Giant*, New York: Oxford University Press.

_______ "China Mobile Communication Industry Growth Rate Ranks First in the World", *People's Daily* 23 June 2000, [online: web] Accessed 28 June 2008, URL: http://english.peopledaily.com.cn.

_______ "New Company Ends Shanghai Telecom Monopoly", *People's Daily* 3 July 2000 [Online: web] Accessed 29 June 2008, URL: http://english.peopledaily.com.cn.

_______ "Market Share of Domestic Mobile Phones Up", *People's Daily*, 7 August 2000, [Online: web] Accessed 1 July 2008, URL: http://english.peopledaily.com.cn.

_______ "Siemens Launches 1.5 billion Dollar Investment Programme in Asia", *People's Daily*, 26 June 2000 [Online: web] accessed 4 July 2008, URL: http://english.peopledaily.com.cn.

_______ "China's Mobile Phone Export Value Doubled in January-August 31", *People's* Daily, 31 August 2004 [Online: web] Accessed 3 July 2009, URL: http://english.peopledaily.com.cn/200408/31/eng20040831_ 155384.html

_______ "Ministry: No Surge Expected in China's Textile Exports" *People's Daily*, 22 January 2009 [Online: web] Accessed 3 July 2009, URL: http://english.people.com.cn/90001/90776/90884/6579775.html

Pevehouse, Jon C. (2004), "Interdependence Theory and Measurement of International Conflict", *The Journal of Politics*, 66 (1): 247-266.

Pitt D. C., Levine N. & Xu Y. (1996), "Touching Stones to Cross the River: Evolving Telecommunications Policy Priorities in Contemporary China", *Journal of Contemporary China*, 5 (13): 347-365.

_______ "Practice" (2000), *Beijing Review*, 43(12): 4.

Prebisch, R. (1959), "Commercial Policy in the Underdeveloped Countries", *American Economic Review*, 49: 251-273

Preeg, Ernest H. (2002), "Exchange Rate Manipulation to Gain an Unfair Competitive Advantage: The Case Against Japan and China," Presented at the Conference at the Institute for International Economics: Washington DC, [Online: web] Accessed 23 May 2009, URL: http://www.mapi.net/filepost/ExchangeRateManipulations.pdf.

_______ "Premier Stresses Opening-Up" (2001) *Beijing Review*, 44 (40): 5.

Rae, Allan N. *et al*. (2001), "The Sectoral Approach to Trade Liberalization: Should We Try to Do Better?" *International Trade Journal*, 15 (3): 293-322.

Reinert, K.A. (2000), "Give Us Virtue, but Not Yet: Safeguard Actions under the Agreement on Textiles and Clothing", *World Economy* 23 (1): 25-55.

Rosecrance, R. (1986), "Supplying with a Long Spoon: Dependence and Interdependence in Sino-American Relations", *The China Journal*, 43: 55-81.

Saunders, Robert J., *et al*. (1994), *Telecommunications and Economic Development*, USA: The John Hopkins University Press.

Selvarajah, K, Sidak and J. Gregory (1997), *Foreign Investment in American telecommunications*, Chicago, USA: University of Chicago Press.

Sharma, Shalendra D. (2009), "Dealing with the Contagion: China and India in the Aftermath of Sub-prime Meltdown", *China and the World economy*, 17 (2):1-14.

Shaked, A. and J. Sutton ((1984), "Natural Oligopolies and International Trade": in H. Kierzkowski, (ed.), *Monopolistic Competition and International Trade,* Oxford: Oxford University Press.

Shi Zhiyu and Chih-yu Shih (1993), *China's Just World*, USA: Lynne Rienner Publishers.

_______ "Sino-Australian Relations to Be Enhanced" (1999), *Beijing Review,* 42 (39): 7.

_______ "Sino-US WTO Agreement leads to pressure for Industrial Reform" (1999), *Xinhua* 21 November 1999.

SIIA-Swedish Institute of International Affairs (2005) *Landguiden,* [Online: web]: Accessed 24 October 2008, URL:http://www.landguiden.se.bibl. proxy.hj.se/

Song, Hong (2000), *China's Entry into the WTO: the Analysis of the China's Industries*, Social Sciences Documentation Publishing House, Beijing,

Song, Hong (2009), Personal Interview Institute of World Economics and Politics (IWEP), Chinese Academy of Social Sciences, Beijing,16 April, 2009.

Steinbock, Dan (2006), "As China's Mobile Revolution Takes off Foreign Operators" *Beijing Review*, 49 (8): 36-37.

Steinbock, Dan (2005), "Nokia's China Ambition" *Beijing Review*, 48 (39): 26-28.

Tao, Ma (2009), Personal Interview, Institute of World Economics and Politics (IWEP), Chinese Academy of Social Sciences, Beijing, 16 April, 2009.

Tewari, M. (2008), "Deepening Intraregional Trade and Investment in South Asia: The Case of Textiles and clothing Industry", *ICRIER Working Paper* No. 213, [Online: web] Accessed 22 May 2009, URL: http://www.icrier.org/publication/working_papers_213.html.

"The Law of the People's Republic of China on Joint Ventures Using China and Foreign Investment" (1979), *Beijing Review* 22 (4): 8.

Trade Policy Review, Report by the Government of People's Republic of China" (2006) [Online web] Accessed 20 January 2009, URL: http://www.wto.org/english/tratop_e/tpr_e/g161_e.doc.

Tsou T. (1986), *The Cultural Revolution and Post Mao Reforms*, Chicago, USA, Chicago University Press.

Tung, Chen Yuan (2004), "Economic Relations between Taiwan and China" *UNISCI Discussion Paper*, 4: 1-7.

World Investment Report (1995), *Transnational Corporations and Competitiveness*, New York: UNCTAD: 56.

United States International Trade Commission (2004), "*Textiles and apparel: Assessment of the Competitiveness of Certain Foreign Suppliers to the US Market Investigation*" *No. 332-448*. (Publication 3671). Washington DC: United States International Trade Commission.

"US Ambassador Supports China's WTO Entry" (2000), *Beijing Review,* 43 (11): 5.
Ure, John (1997), *Telecommunications in Asia: Policy, Planning and Development*, Hong Kong: Hong Kong University Press.
Ure, John (2007) "Study on the Future Opportunities and Challenges of EU-China Trade and Investment Relations", [Online: web] Accessed 29 June 2008, URL: http://trade.ec.europa.eu/doclib/docs/2007/february/tradoc_133312.pdf.
Wenli, Ding (2005) "Wireless Intel", *Beijing Review*, 48 (23): 38-39.
Xiangshuo, Yin (2009), Personal Interview, School of Economics, Fudan University, Shanghai, China 9 April, 2009.
Xin, An (2005) "3G Spring is in the Air", *Beijing Review*, 48(9): 36-39.
Xu, Y. (2002), "China's Accession to the WTO and Its Implications for Foreign Direct Investment in Chinese Telecommunications", *Communications Strategies*, 45(21).
Yan, Xu and Douglas, Pitt (2002), *Chinese Telecommunications Policy*, Boston, USA: Artech House.
Yanjun, Li (2005) "A New Chapter in foreign Investment" *Beijing Review*, 48(35): 30-32.
Yanrui, Wu (2005), "China: Growth and Reform in Telecommunications", in Allan Brown *et al.* (eds.) *Telecommunications Reform in the Asia-Pacific Region*, USA: Edward Elgar Publisher.
Yong Wang (2009), Personal Interview, School of International Studies Peking University, Beijing, China 13 April 2009.
Yu, Y. *et al.* (1999), *The Research Report on China's Entry into WTO: The Chinese Industries*, Beijing: Social Sciences Documentation Publishing House.
Viner, Jacob (1985), "Peace as an Economic Problem." in R. Art and R. Jervis (eds.) *International Politics*, Boston: little brown.
Viner, Jacob (l950), *The Customs Union Issue*, New York: Carnegie Endowment for International Peace.
Viner, Jacob (1951), *International Economics*, Illinois: Free Press.
Walsham, G. and Sahay, S. (2005), "Research on information systems in developing countries: current landscape and future prospects." *Information Technology for Development*, 12(1): 7-24.
"Wider Scope for Foreign Investment in Guangzhou", *Beijing Review*, 23(11): 6.
World Trade Organization (2005c) "*A summary of the Final Act of the Uruguay Round*", [Online: web] Accessed 11 June 2008: URL: http://www.wto.org/english/docs_e/legal_e/ursum_e.htm#cAgreement.
"WTO Entry to Help Expand Cross-Straits Ties" [Onlineweb] Accessed 5 July 2010 URL: http://english.peopledaily.com.cn/200203/12/eng20020312_91986.shtml
World Trade Organization (2008) *International Trade Statistics 2008* Geneva.
World Trade Organization (2001), *Market Access: Unfinished Business*, Special Studies No. 6 [Online: web] Accessed 22 May 2009 URL: http;//www.wto.org/English/res_e/booksp_e/special_study_6_e.pdf Accessed May 22 2009.
"WTO Agreement Signed between China and Australia" (1999), *Beijing Review,* 42 (31): 7.
"WTO Entry Gets Closer" (2001), *Beijing Review*, 44(39): 4.
World Trade Organization (2001), "WTO Ministerial Conference Approves China's Accession" [Online: web] Accessed 22 May 2008, URL: http://www.wto.org/english/news_e/pres01_e/pr252_e.htm
"WTO membership" (2001), *Beijing Review*, 44 (40): 5.
"WTO Membership Protocol Signed" (2001), *Beijing Review*, 44 (47): 4.
Wu Friedrich W.Y. (1981), "From Self-Reliance to Interdependence: Development Strategy and Foreign Economic Policy in Post-Mao China", *Modern China*, 7: 445-482.
Xiangshuo Yin (2009), Personal Interview, School of Economics, Fudan University, Shanghai, China 9 April, 2009
Yong, Wang (2000) "China's Domestic WTO Debate" *China Business Review* 27 (1): 1-9.

Yong, Wang (2002), "China's Stakes in WTO Accession-The Internal Decision-Making Process", in Heike Holbige and Robert Ash (eds.) *China's Accession to the World Trade Organization: National and International Perspectives*, UK: Rouledge Curzon Press.

Yong, Wang (2009), Personal Interview, Centre for International Political Economy, Peking University, Beijing, China 13 April, 2009

Yu, Liu (2005), "China Gets Connected", *Beijing Review*, 48(3): 30-34.

Yu, Yongding, Zheng, Bingwen and Song, Hong (eds.) (1999), *The Research Report on China's Entry into WTO: The Chinese Industries*, Social Sciences Documentation Publishing House, Beijing

Zhang, Ming (2009) Personal Interview, International Finance Division, Institute of World Economics and Politics, Chinese Academy of Social Science, Beijing 13 January 13 2009

Zhang, X.G. (2000), "China's Entry to the WTO: A general Equilibrium Analysis of the Recent Tariff Reductions", in Drysdale, P. and Song, L. (eds.) *China's Entry to the WTO: Strategic Issues and quantitative Assessments*, London: Routledge.

Zhao, Q. and Guoli Liu (2010), "Managing the Challenges of Complex Interdependence: China and the United States in the Era of Globalization", *Asian Politics & Polity*, 2 (1): 1-23.

Zhu Andong (2009), Personal Interview, Centre for Political Economy, Tsinghua University, Beijing, 14 April 2009.

Zhong, C. and Yang, Y. (2000), "China's Textile and Clothing exports in the Post Uruguay Round", in Drysdale, P. and Song, L. (eds.) *China's Entry to the WTO: Strategic Issues and quantitative Assessments*, London: Routledge.

Zurn, Michael (2002), "From Interdependence to Globalization" in (eds.) Carlsnaes, Walter *et al.*, *Handbook of International Relations*, London: Sage.

Index